Computer Viruses and Malware

T0181752

Advances in Information Security

Sushil Jajodia

Consulting Editor
Center for Secure Information Systems
George Mason University
Fairfax, VA 22030-4444
email: jajodia@gmu.edu

The goals of the Springer International Series on ADVANCES IN INFORMATION SECURITY are, one, to establish the state of the art of, and set the course for future research in information security and, two, to serve as a central reference source for advanced and timely topics in information security research and development. The scope of this series includes all aspects of computer and network security and related areas such as fault tolerance and software assurance.

ADVANCES IN INFORMATION SECURITY aims to publish thorough and cohesive overviews of specific topics in information security, as well as works that are larger in scope or that contain more detailed background information than can be accommodated in shorter survey articles. The series also serves as a forum for topics that may not have reached a level of maturity to warrant a comprehensive textbook treatment.

Researchers, as well as developers, are encouraged to contact Professor Sushil Jajodia with ideas for books under this series.

Additional titles in the series:

Additional information about this series can be obtained from
http://www.springeronline.com

Computer Viruses and Malware

by

John Aycock
University of Calgary
Canada

 Springer

John Aycock
University of Calgary
Dept. Computer Science
2500 University Drive N.W.
CALGARY AB T2N 1N4
CANADA

Computer Viruses and Malware
by John Aycock, University of Calgary, AB, Canada

ISBN-13: 978-1-4419-4016-2   e-ISBN-13: 978-0-387-34188-0

Printed on acid-free paper.

To all the two-legged critters
in my house

Contents

List of Figures

Preface

It seemed like a good idea at the time. In 2003, I started teaching a course on computer viruses and malicious software to senior undergraduate and graduate students at the University of Calgary. It's been an interesting few years. Computer viruses are a controversial and taboo topic, despite having such a huge impact on our society; needless to say, there was some backlash about this course from outside the University.

One of my initial practical concerns was whether or not I could find enough detailed material to teach a 13-week course at this level. There were some books on the topic, but (with all due respect to the authors of those books) there were none that were suitable for use as a textbook.

I was more surprised to find out that there was a lot of information about viruses and doing "bad" things, but there was very little information about anti-virus software. A few quality minutes with your favorite web search engine will yield virus writing tutorials, virus source code, and virus creation toolkits. In contrast, although it's comprised of some extremely nice people, the anti-virus community tends to be very industry-driven and insular, and isn't in the habit of giving out its secrets. Unless you know where to look.

Several years, a shelf full of books, and a foot-high stack of printouts later, I've ferreted out a lot of detailed material which I've assembled in this book. It's a strange type of research for a computer scientist, and I'm sure that my academic colleagues would cringe at some of the sources that I've had to use. Virus writers don't tend to publish in peer-reviewed academic journals, and anti-virus companies don't want to tip their hand. I would tend to characterize this detective work more like historical research than standard computer science research: your sources are limited, so you try and authenticate them; you piece a sentence in one document together with a sentence in another document, and you're able to make a useful connection. It's painstaking and often frustrating.

Technical information goes out of date very quickly, and in writing this book I've tried to focus on the concepts more than details. My hope is that the concepts will still be useful years from now, long after the minute details of operating systems and programming languages have changed. Having said that, I've included detail where it's absolutely necessary to explain what's going on, and used specific examples of viruses and malicious software where it's useful to establish precedents for certain techniques. Depending on why you're reading this, a book with more concrete details might be a good complement to this material.

Similarly, if you're using this as a textbook, I would suggest supplementing it with details of the latest and greatest malicious software that's making the rounds. Unfortunately there will be plenty of examples to choose from. In my virus course, I also have a large segment devoted to the law and ethics surrounding malicious software, which I haven't incorporated here – law is constantly changing and being reinterpreted, and there are already many excellent sources on ethics. Law and ethics are very important topics for any computer professional, but they are especially critical for creating a secure environment in which to work with malicious software.

I should point out that I've only used information from public sources to write this book. I've deliberately excluded any information that's been told to me in private conversations, and I'm not revealing anyone's trade secrets that they haven't already given away themselves.

I'd like to thank the students I've taught in my virus course, who pushed me with their excellent questions, and showed much patience as I was organizing all this material into some semi-coherent form. Thanks too to those in the anti-virus community who kept an open mind. I'd also like to thank the people who read drafts of this book: Jörg Denzinger, Richard Ford, Sarah Gordon, Shannon Jaeger, Cliff Marcellus, Jim Uhl, James Wolfe, and Mike Zastre. Their suggestions and comments helped improve the book as well as encourage me. Finally, Alan Aycock suggested some references for Chapter 10, Stefania Bertazzon answered my questions about rational economics, Moustafa Hammad provided an Arabic translation, and Maryam Mehri Dehnavi translated some Persian text for me. Of course, any errors that remain are my own.

JOHN AYCOCK

Chapter 1

WE'VE GOT PROBLEMS

In ancient times, people's needs were simple: food, water, shelter, and the occasional chance to propagate the species. Our basic needs haven't changed, but the way we fulfill them has. Food is bought in stores which are fed by supply chains with computerized inventory systems; water is dispensed through computer-controlled water systems; parts for new shelters come from suppliers with computer-ridden supply chains, and old shelters are bought and sold by computer-wielding realtors. The production and transmission of energy to run all of these systems is controlled by computer, and computers manage financial transactions to pay for it all.

It's no secret that our society's infrastructure relies on computers now. Unfortunately, this means that a threat to computers *is* a threat to society. But how do we protect our critical infrastructure? What are the problems it faces?

1.1 Dramatis Personae

There are four key threats to consider. These are the four horsemen of the electronic apocalypse: spam, bugs, denials of service, and malicious software.

Spam The term commonly used to describe the abundance of unsolicited bulk email which plagues the mailboxes of Internet users worldwide. The statistics vary over time, but suggest that over 70% of email traffic currently falls into this category.[1]

Bugs These are software errors which, when they crop up, can kill off your software immediately, if you're lucky. They can also result in data corruption, security weaknesses, and spurious, hard-to-find problems.

Denials of service Denial-of-service attacks, or DoS attacks,[2] starve legitimate usage of resources or services. For example, a DoS attack could use up all available disk space on a system, so that other users couldn't make use of it; generating reams of network traffic so that real traffic can't get through would also be a denial of service. Simple DoS attacks are relatively easy to mount by simply overwhelming a machine with requests, as a toddler might overwhelm their parents with questions. Sophisticated DoS attacks can involve more finesse, and may trick a machine into shutting a service down instead of flooding it.

Malicious software The real war is waged with malicious software, or malware. This is software whose intent is malicious, or whose effect is malicious. The spectrum of malware covers a wide variety of specific threats, including viruses, worms, Trojan horses, and spyware.

The focus of this book is malware, and the techniques which can be used to detect, detain, and destroy it. This is not accidental. Of the four threats listed above, malware has the deepest connection to the other three. Malware may be propagated using spam, and may also be used to send spam; malware may take advantage of bugs; malware may be used to mount DoS attacks. Addressing the problem of malware is vital for improving computer security. Computer security is vital to our society's critical infrastructure.

1.2   The Myth of Absolute Security

Obviously we want our computers to be secure against threats. Unfortunately, there is no such thing as absolute security, where a computer is either secure or it's not. You may take a great deal of technical precautions to safeguard your computers, but your protection is unlikely to be effective against a determined attacker with sufficient resources. A government-funded spy agency could likely penetrate your security, should they be motivated to do so. Someone could drive a truck through the wall of your building and steal your computers. Old-fashioned ways are effective, too: there are many ways of coercing people into divulging information.[3]

Even though there is no absolute computer security, relative computer security can be considered based on six factors:

- What is the importance of the information or resource being protected?

- What is the potential impact, if the security is breached?

- Who is the attacker likely to be?

- What are the skills and resources available to an attacker?

- What constraints are imposed by legitimate usage?

- What resources are available to implement security?

Breaking down security in this way changes the problem. Security is no longer a binary matter of secure or not-secure; it becomes a problem of risk management,[4] and implementing security can be seen as making tradeoffs between the level of protection, the usability of the resulting system, and the cost of implementation.

When you assess risks for risk management, you must consider the risks posed to you by others, *and* consider the risks posed to others by you. Everybody is your neighbor on the Internet, and it isn't farfetched to think that you could be found negligent if you had insufficient computer security, and your computers were used to attack another site.[100]

1.3 The Cost of Malware

Malware unquestionably has a negative financial impact, but how big an impact does it really have?[101] It's important to know, because if computer security is to be treated as risk management, then you have to accurately assess how much damage a lapse in security could cause.

At first glance, gauging the cost of malware incidents would seem to be easy. After all, there are any number of figures reported on this, figures attributed to experts. They can vary from one another by an order of magnitude, so if you disagree with one number, you can locate another more to your liking. I use the gross domestic product of Austria, myself – it's a fairly large number, and it's as accurate an estimate as any other.

In all fairness, estimating malware cost is a very hard problem. There are two types of costs to consider: real costs and hidden costs.

Real costs These are costs which are apparent, and which are relatively easy to calculate. If a computer virus reduced your computer to a bubbling puddle of molten slag,[5] the cost to replace it would be straightforward to assess. Similarly, if an employee can't work because their computer is having malware removed from it, then the employee's lost productivity can be computed. The time that technical support staff spend tracking down and fixing affected computers can also be computed. Not all costs are so obvious, however.

Hidden costs Hidden costs are costs whose impact can't be measured accurately, and may not even be known. Some businesses, like banks and computer security companies, could suffer damage to their reputation from a publicized malware incident. Regardless of the business, a leak of proprietary information or customer data caused by malware could result in enormous damage to a company, no different than industrial espionage. Any downtime could drive existing customers to a competitor, or turn away new, potential customers.

This has been cast in terms of business, but malware presents a cost to individuals, too. Personal information stolen by malware from a computer, such as passwords, credit card numbers, and banking information, can give thieves enough for that tropical vacation they've always dreamed of, or provide a good foundation for identity theft.

1.4   The Number of Threats

Even the exact number of threats is open to debate. A quick survey of competing anti-virus products shows that the number of threats they claim to detect can vary by as much as a factor of two. Curiously, the level of protection each affords is about the same, meaning that more is not necessarily better.

Why? There is no industry-wide agreement on what constitutes a "threat," to begin with. It's not surprising, given that fact alone, that different anti-virus products would have different numbers – they aren't all counting the same thing. For example, there is some dispute as to whether or not automatically-generated viruses produced by the same tool should be treated as individual threats, or as only one threat. This came to the fore in 1998, when approximately 15,000 new automatically-generated viruses appeared overnight.[102] It is also difficult to amass and correctly maintain a malware collection,[103] and inadvertent duplication or misclassification of malware samples is always a possibility. There is no single clearinghouse for malware.

Another consideration is that the reported numbers are only for threats that are known about. Ideally, computers should be protected from both known *and* unknown threats. It's impossible to know about unknown threats, of course, which means that it's impossible to precisely assess how well-protected your computers are against threats.

Different anti-virus products may employ different detection techniques, too. Not all methods of detection rely on exhaustive compilations of known threats, and generic detection techniques routinely find both known and unknown threats without knowing the exact nature of what they're detecting.

Even for known threats, not all may endanger your computers. The majority of malware is targeted to some specific combination of computer architecture and operating system, and sometimes even to a particular application. Effectively these act as preconditions for a piece of malware to run; if any of these conditions aren't true – for instance, you use a different operating system – then that malware poses no direct threat to you. It is inert with respect to your computers.

Even if it can't run, malware may carry an indirect liability risk if it passes through your computers from one target to another. For example, one unaffected computer could provide a shared directory; someone else's compromised computer could deposit malware in that shared directory for later propagation. It is prudent to look for threats to all computers, not just to your own.

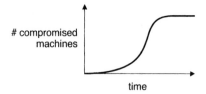

Figure 1.1. Worm propagation curve

1.5 Speed of Propagation

Once upon a time, the speed of malware propagation was measured in terms of weeks or even months. This is no longer the case.

A typical worm propagation curve is shown in Figure 1.1. (For simplicity, the effects on the curve from defensive measures aren't shown.) At first, the worm spreads slowly to vulnerable machines, but eventually begins a period of exponential growth when it spreads extremely rapidly. Finally, once the majority of vulnerable machines have been compromised, the worm reaches a saturation point; any further growth beyond this point is minimal.

For a worm to spread more quickly, the propagation curve needs to be moved to the left. In other words, the worm author wants the period of exponential growth to occur earlier, preferably before any defenses have been deployed. This is shown in Figure 1.2a.

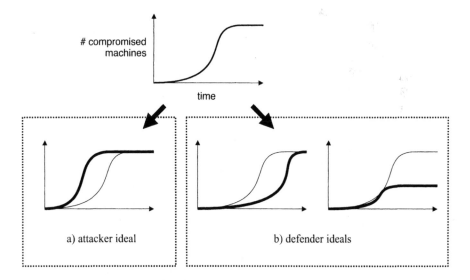

Figure 1.2. Ideal propagation curves for attackers and defenders

On the other hand, a defender wants to do one of two things. First, the propagation curve could be pushed to the right, buying time to construct a defense before the worm's exponential growth period. Second, the curve could be compressed downwards, meaning that not all vulnerable machines become compromised by the worm. These scenarios are shown in Figure 1.2b.

The time axis on these figures has been deliberately left unlabeled, because the exact propagation rate will depend on the techniques that a particular worm uses. However, the theoretical maximum speed of a carefully-designed worm from initial release until saturation is startling: 510 milliseconds to 1.3 seconds.[6] In less than two seconds, it's over. No defense that relies on any form of human intervention will be fast enough to cope with threats like this.

1.6   People

Humans are the weak link on several other fronts too, all of which are taken advantage of by malware.

By their nature, humans are trusting, social creatures. These are excellent qualities for your friends to have, and also for your victims to possess: an entire class of attacks, called social engineering attacks, are quick to exploit these desirable human qualities.

Social engineering aside, many people simply aren't aware of the security consequences of their actions. For example, several informal surveys of people on the street have found them more than willing to provide enough information for identity theft (even offering up their passwords) in exchange for chocolate, theater tickets, and coffee vouchers.[104]

Another problem is that humans – users – don't demand enough of software vendors in terms of secure software. Even for security-savvy users who want secure software, the security of any given piece of software is nearly impossible to assess.

Secure software is software which can't be exploited by an attacker. Just because some software hasn't been compromised is no indication that it's secure – like the stock market, past performance is no guarantee of future results. Unfortunately, that's really the only guideline users have to judge security: the absence of an attack. Software security is thus an anti-feature for vendors, because it's intangible. It's no wonder that vendors opt to add features rather than improve security. Features are easier to sell.

Features are also easier to buy. Humans are naturally wooed by new features, which forms a vicious cycle that gives software vendors little incentive to improve software security.

1.7 About this Book

Malware poses an enormous problem in the context of faulty humans and faulty software security. It could be that malware is the natural consequence of the presence of these faults, like vermin slipping through building cracks in the real world. Indeed, names like "computer virus" and "computer worm" bring to mind their biological real-world counterparts.

Whatever the root cause, malware is a problem that needs to be solved. This book looks at malware, primarily viruses and worms, and its countermeasures. The next chapter lays the groundwork with some basic definitions and a timeline of malware. Then, on to viruses: Chapters 3, 4, and 5 cover viruses, anti-virus techniques, and anti-anti-virus techniques, in that order. Chapter 6 explains the weaknesses that are exploited by malware, both technical and social – this is necessary background for the worms in Chapter 7. Defenses against worms are considered in Chapter 8. Some of the possible manifestations of malware are looked at in Chapter 9, followed by a look at the people who create malware and defend against it in Chapter 10. Some final thoughts on defense are in Chapter 11.

The convention used for chapter endnotes is somewhat unusual. The notes tend to fall into two categories. First, there are notes with additional content related to the text. These have endnote numbers from 1–99 within a chapter. Second, there are endnotes that provide citations and pointers to related material. This kind of endnote is numbered 100 or above. The intent is to make the two categories of endnote easily distinguishable in the text.

A lot of statements in this book are qualified with "can" and "could" and "may" and "might." Software is infinitely malleable and can be made to do almost anything; it is hubris to make bold statements about what malware can and can't do.

Finally, this is not a programming book, and some knowledge of programming (in both high- and low-level languages) is assumed, although pseudocode is used where possible. A reasonable understanding of operating systems and networks is also beneficial.

1.8 Some Words of Warning

Self-replicating software like viruses and worms has proven itself to be very difficult to control, even from the very earliest experiments.[7] While self-replicating code may not intentionally be malicious, it can have similar effects regardless. Of course, the risks of overtly malicious software should be obvious. Any experiments with malware, or analysis of malware, should be done in a secure environment designed specifically for that purpose. While it's outside the scope of this book to describe such a secure environment – the details would be quickly out of date anyway – there are a number of sources of information available.[105]

Another thing to consider is that creation and/or distribution of malware may violate local laws. Many countries have computer crime legislation now,[8] and even if the law was violated in a different jurisdiction from where the perpetrator is physically located, extradition agreements may apply.[106] Civil remedies for victims of malware are possible as well.

Ironically, some dangers lurk in defensive techniques too. Some of the material in this book is derived from patent documents; the intent is to provide a wide range of information, and is not in any way meant to suggest that these patents should be infringed. While every effort has been made to cite relevant patents, it is possible that some have been inadvertently overlooked. Furthermore, patents may be interpreted very broadly, and the applicability of a patent may depend greatly on the skill and financial resources of the patent holder's legal team. Seek legal advice before rushing off to implement any of the techniques described in this book.

Notes for Chapter 1

1 Based on MessageLabs' sample size of 12.6 billion email messages [203]. This has a higher statistical significance than 99% of statistics you would normally find.

2 Note the capitalization – "DOS" is an operating system, "DoS" is an attack.

3 In cryptography, this has been referred to as "rubber-hose" cryptanalysis [279].

4 Schneier has argued this point of view, and that computer security is an untapped market for insurance companies, who are in the business of managing risk anyway [280].

5 Before any urban legends are started, computer viruses can't do this.

6 These numbers (510 ms for UDP-based worms, 1.3 s for TCP-based worms) are the time it takes to achieve 95% saturation of a million vulnerable machines [303].

7 For example, Cohen's first viruses progressed surprisingly quickly [74], as did Duff's shell script virus [95], and an early worm at Xerox ran amok [287].

8 Computer crime laws are not strictly necessary for prosecuting computer crimes that are just electronic versions of "traditional" crimes like fraud [56], but the trend is definitely to enact computer-specific laws.

100 Owens [237] discusses liability potential in great detail.

101 This section is based on Garfink and Landesman [117], and Ducklin [94] touches on some of the same issues too.

102 Morley [213]. Ducklin [94] has a discussion of this issue, and of other ways to measure the extent of the virus problem.

103 Bontchev [39] talks about the care and feeding of a "clean" virus library.

104 The informal surveys were reported in [30] (chocolate), [31, 274] (theater tickets), and [184] (coffee vouchers). Less amusing, but more rigorous, surveys have been done which show similar problems [270, 305].

105 There are a wide range of opinions on working with malware, ranging from the inadequate to the paranoid. As a starting point, see [21, 75, 187, 282, 288, 312].

106 Although U.S.-centric, Soma et al. [295] give a good overview of the general features of extradition treaties.

Chapter 2

DEFINITIONS AND TIMELINE

It would be nice to present a clever taxonomy of malicious software, one that clearly shows how each type of malware relates to every other type. However, a taxonomy would give the quaint and totally incorrect impression that there is a scientific basis for the classification of malware.

In fact, there is no universally-accepted definition of terms like "virus" and "worm," much less an agreed-upon taxonomy, even though there have been occasional attempts to impose mathematical formalisms onto malware.[100] Instead of trying to pin down these terms precisely, the common characteristics each type of malware typically has are listed.

2.1 Malware Types

Malware can be roughly broken down into types according to the malware's method of operation. Anti-"virus" software, despite its name, is able to detect all of these types of malware.

There are three characteristics associated with these malware types.

1 *Self-replicating* malware actively attempts to propagate by creating new copies, or *instances*, of itself. Malware may also be propagated passively, by a user copying it accidentally, for example, but this isn't self-replication.

2 The *population growth* of malware describes the overall change in the number of malware instances due to self-replication. Malware that doesn't self-replicate will always have a zero population growth, but malware with a zero population growth may self-replicate.

3 *Parasitic* malware requires some other executable code in order to exist. "Executable" in this context should be taken very broadly to include anything that can be executed, such as boot block code on a disk, binary code

in applications, and interpreted code. It also includes source code, like application scripting languages, and code that may require compilation before being executed.

2.1.1   Logic Bomb

Self-replicating: no
Population growth: zero
Parasitic: possibly

A *logic bomb* is code which consists of two parts:

1 A *payload*, which is an action to perform. The payload can be anything, but has the connotation of having a malicious effect.

2 A *trigger*, a boolean condition that is evaluated and controls when the payload is executed. The exact trigger condition is limited only by the imagination, and could be based on local conditions like the date, the user logged in, or the operating system version. Triggers could also be designed to be set off remotely, or – like the "dead man's switch" on a train – be set off by the absence of an event.

Logic bombs can be inserted into existing code, or could be standalone. A simple parasitic example is shown below, with a payload that crashes the computer using a particular date as a trigger.

```
legitimate code
if date is Friday the 13th:
    crash_computer()
legitimate code
```

Logic bombs can be concise and unobtrusive, especially in millions of lines of source code, and the mere threat of a logic bomb could easily be used to extort money from a company. In one case, a disgruntled employee rigged a logic bomb on his employer's file server to trigger on a date after he was fired from his job, causing files to be deleted with no possibility of recovery. He was later sentenced to 41 months in prison.[101] Another case alleges that an employee installed a logic bomb on 1000 company computers, date-triggered to remove all the files on those machines; the person allegedly tried to profit from the downturn in the company's stock prices that occurred as a result of the damage.[1]

2.1.2   Trojan Horse

Self-replicating: no
Population growth: zero
Parasitic: yes

There was no love lost between the Greeks and the Trojans. The Greeks had besieged the Trojans, holed up in the city of Troy, for ten years. They finally took the city by using a clever ploy: the Greeks built an enormous wooden horse, concealing soldiers inside, and tricked the Trojans into bringing the horse into Troy. When night fell, the soldiers exited the horse and much unpleasantness ensued.[102]

In computing, a *Trojan horse* is a program which purports to do some benign task, but secretly performs some additional malicious task. A classic example is a password-grabbing login program which prints authentic-looking "username" and "password" prompts, and waits for a user to type in the information. When this happens, the password grabber stashes the information away for its creator, then prints out an "invalid password" message before running the *real* login program. The unsuspecting user thinks they made a typing mistake and re-enters the information, none the wiser.

Trojan horses have been known about since at least 1972, when they were mentioned in a well-known report by Anderson, who credited the idea to D. J. Edwards.[103]

2.1.3 Back Door

Self-replicating: no
Population growth: zero
Parasitic: possibly

A *back door* is any mechanism which bypasses a normal security check. Programmers sometimes create back doors for legitimate reasons, such as skipping a time-consuming authentication process when debugging a network server.

As with logic bombs, back doors can be placed into legitimate code or be standalone programs. The example back door below, shown in gray, circumvents a login authentication process.

```
username = read_username()
password = read_password()
if username is "l33t h4ck0r":
    return ALLOW_LOGIN
if username and password are valid:
    return ALLOW_LOGIN
else:
    return DENY_LOGIN
```

One special kind of back door is a *RAT*, which stands for Remote Administration Tool or Remote Access Trojan, depending on who's asked. These programs allow a computer to be monitored and controlled remotely; users may deliberately install these to access a work computer from home, or to allow help desk staff to diagnose and fix a computer problem from afar. However, if malware surreptitiously installs a RAT on a computer, then it opens up a back door into that machine.

2.1.4   Virus

Self-replicating: yes
Population growth: positive
Parasitic: yes

A *virus* is malware that, when executed, tries to replicate itself into other executable code; when it succeeds, the code is said to be *infected*.[2] The infected code, when run, can infect new code in turn. This self-replication into existing executable code is the key defining characteristic of a virus.

When faced with more than one virus to describe, a rather silly problem arises. There's no agreement on the plural form of "virus." The two leading contenders are "viruses" and "virii;" the latter form is often used by virus writers themselves, but it's rare to see this used in the security community, who prefer "viruses."[104]

If viruses sound like something straight out of science fiction, there's a reason for that. They are. The early history of viruses is admittedly fairly murky, but the first mention of a computer virus is in science fiction in the early 1970s, with Gregory Benford's *The Scarred Man* in 1970, and David Gerrold's *When Harlie Was One* in 1972.[105] Both stories also mention a program which acts to counter the virus, so this is the first mention of anti-virus software as well.

The earliest real academic research on viruses was done by Fred Cohen in 1983, with the "virus" name coined by Len Adleman.[106] Cohen is sometimes called the "father of computer viruses," but it turns out that there were viruses written prior to his work. Rich Skrenta's Elk Cloner was circulating in 1982, and Joe Dellinger's viruses were developed between 1981–1983; all of these were for the Apple II platform.[107] Some sources mention a 1980 glitch in Arpanet as the first virus, but this was just a case of legitimate code acting badly; the only thing being propagated was data in network packets.[108] Gregory Benford's viruses were not limited to his science fiction stories; he wrote and released non-malicious viruses in 1969 at what is now the Lawrence Livermore National Laboratory, as well as in the early Arpanet.

Some computer games have featured self-replicating programs attacking one another in a controlled environment. Core War appeared in 1984, where programs written in a simple assembly language called Redcode fought another; a combatant was assumed to be destroyed if its program counter pointed to an invalid Redcode instruction. Programs in Core War existed only in a virtual machine, but this was not the case for an earlier game, Darwin. Darwin was played in 1961, where a program could hunt and destroy another combatant in a non-virtual environment using a well-defined interface.[109] In terms of strategy, successful combatants in these games were hard-to-find, innovative, and adaptive, qualities that can be used by computer viruses too.[3]

Traditionally, viruses can propagate within a single computer, or may travel from one computer to another using human-transported media, like a floppy disk, CD-ROM, DVD-ROM, or USB flash drive. In other words, viruses don't propagate via computer networks; networks are the domain of worms instead. However, the label "virus" has been applied to malware that would traditionally be considered a worm, and the term has been diluted in common usage to refer to any sort of self-replicating malware.

Viruses can be caught in various stages of self-replication. A *germ* is the original form of a virus, prior to any replication. A virus which fails to replicate is called an *intended*. This may occur as a result of bugs in the virus, or encountering an unexpected version of an operating system. A virus can be *dormant*, where it is present but not yet infecting anything – for example, a Windows virus can reside on a Unix-based file server and have no effect there, but can be exported to Windows machines.[4]

2.1.5 Worm

Self-replicating: yes
Population growth: positive
Parasitic: no

A *worm* shares several characteristics with a virus. The most important characteristic is that worms are self-replicating too, but self-replication of a worm is distinct in two ways. First, worms are standalone,[5] and do not rely on other executable code. Second, worms spread from machine to machine across networks.

Like viruses, the first worms were fictional. The term "worm" was first used in 1975 by John Brunner in his science fiction novel *The Shockwave Rider*. (Interestingly, he used the term "virus" in the book too.)[6] Experiments with worms performing (non-malicious) distributed computations were done at Xerox PARC around 1980, but there were earlier examples. A worm called Creeper crawled around the Arpanet in the 1970s, pursued by another called Reaper which hunted and killed off Creepers.[7]

A watershed event for the Internet happened on November 2, 1988, when a worm incapacitated the fledgling Internet. This worm is now called the Internet worm, or the Morris worm after its creator, Robert Morris, Jr. At the time, Morris had just started a Ph.D. at Cornell University. He had been intending for his worm to propagate slowly and unobtrusively, but what happened was just the opposite. Morris was later convicted for his worm's unauthorized computer access and the costs incurred to clean up from it. He was fined, and sentenced to probation and community service.[8] Chapter 7 looks at this worm in detail.

2.1.6 Rabbit

Self-replicating: yes
Population growth: zero
Parasitic: no

Rabbit is the term used to describe malware that multiplies rapidly. Rabbits may also be called *bacteria*, for largely the same reason.

There are actually two kinds of rabbit.[110] The first is a program which tries to consume all of some system resource, like disk space. A "fork bomb," a program which creates new processes in an infinite loop, is a classic example of this kind of rabbit. These tend to leave painfully obvious trails pointing to the perpetrator, and are not of particular interest.

The second kind of rabbit, which the characteristics above describe, is a special case of a worm. This kind of rabbit is a standalone program which replicates itself across a network from machine to machine, *but* deletes the original copy of itself after replication. In other words, there is only one copy of a given rabbit on a network; it just hops from one computer to another.[9] Rabbits are rarely seen in practice.

2.1.7 Spyware

Self-replicating: no
Population growth: zero
Parasitic: no

Spyware is software which collects information from a computer and transmits it to someone else. Prior to its emergence in recent years as a threat, the term "spyware" was used in 1995 as part of a joke, and in a 1994 Usenet posting looking for "spy-ware" information.[111]

The exact information spyware gathers may vary, but can include anything which potentially has value:

1 Usernames and passwords. These might be harvested from files on the machine, or by recording what the user types using a *keylogger*. A keylogger differs from a Trojan horse in that a keylogger passively captures keystrokes only; no active deception is involved.

2 Email addresses, which would have value to a spammer.

3 Bank account and credit card numbers.

4 Software license keys, to facilitate software pirating.

Viruses and worms may collect similar information, but are not considered spyware, because spyware doesn't self-replicate.[112] Spyware may arrive on a machine in a variety of ways, such as bundled with other software that the user installs, or exploiting technical flaws in web browsers. The latter method causes the spyware to be installed simply by visiting a web page, and is sometimes called a *drive-by download*.

2.1.8 Adware

Self-replicating: no
Population growth: zero
Parasitic: no

Adware has similarities to spyware in that both are gathering information about the user and their habits. Adware is more marketing-focused, and may pop up advertisements or redirect a user's web browser to certain web sites in the hopes of making a sale. Some adware will attempt to target the advertisement to fit the context of what the user is doing. For example, a search for "Calgary" may result in an unsolicited pop-up advertisement for "books about Calgary."

Adware may also gather and transmit information about users which can be used for marketing purposes. As with spyware, adware does not self-replicate.

2.1.9 Hybrids, Droppers, and Blended Threats

The exact type of malware encountered in practice is not necessarily easy to determine, even given these loose definitions of malware types. The nature of software makes it easy to create hybrid malware which has characteristics belonging to several different types.[10]

A classic hybrid example was presented by Ken Thompson in his ACM Turing award lecture.[11] He prepared a special C compiler executable which, besides compiling C code, had two additional features:

1 When compiling the login source code, his compiler would insert a back door to bypass password authentication.

2 When compiling the compiler's source code, it would produce a special compiler executable with these same two features.

His special compiler was thus a Trojan horse, which replicated like a virus, and created back doors. This also demonstrated the vulnerability of the compiler tool chain: since the original source code for the compiler and login programs wasn't changed, none of this nefarious activity was apparent.

Another hybrid example was a game called Animal, which played twenty questions with a user. John Walker modified it in 1975, so that it would copy the most up-to-date version of itself into all user-accessible directories whenever it was run. Eventually, Animals could be found roaming in every directory in the system.[113] The copying behavior was unknown to the game's user, so it would be considered a Trojan horse. The copying could also be seen as self-replication, and although it didn't infect other code, it didn't use a network either – not really a worm, not really a virus, but certainly exhibiting viral behavior.

There are other combinations of malware too. For example, a *dropper* is malware which leaves behind, or *drops*, other malware.[12] A worm can propagate itself, depositing a Trojan horse on all computers it compromises; a virus can leave a back door in its wake.

A *blended threat* is a virus that exploits a technical vulnerability to propagate itself, in addition to exhibiting "traditional" characteristics. This has considerable overlap with the definition of a worm, especially since many worms exploit technical vulnerabilities. These technical vulnerabilities have historically required precautions and defenses distinct from those that anti-virus vendors provided, and this rift may account for the duplication in terms.[114] The Internet worm was a blended threat, according to this definition.

2.1.10   Zombies

Computers that have been compromised can be used by an attacker for a variety of tasks, unbeknownst to the legitimate owner; computers used in this way are called *zombies*. The most common tasks for zombies are sending spam and participating in coordinated, large-scale denial-of-service attacks.

Sending spam violates the acceptable use policy of many Internet service providers, not to mention violating laws in some jurisdictions. Sites known to send spam are also blacklisted, marking sites that engage in spam-related activity so that incoming email from them can be summarily rejected. It is therefore ill-advised for spammers to send spam directly, in such a way that it can be traced back to them and their machines. Zombies provide a windfall for spammers, because they are a free, throwaway resource: spam can be relayed through zombies, which obscures the spammer's trail, and a blacklisted zombie machine presents no hardship to the spammer.[13]

As for denials of service, one type of denial-of-service attack involves either flooding a victim's network with traffic, or overwhelming a legitimate service on the victim's network with requests. Launching this kind of attack from a single machine would be pointless, since one machine's onslaught is unlikely to generate enough traffic to take out a large target site, and traffic from one machine can be easily blocked by the intended victim. On the other hand, a large number of zombies all targeting a site at the same time can cause grief. A coordinated, network-based denial-of-service attack that is mounted from a large number of machines is called a *distributed denial-of-service* attack, or *DDoS* attack.

Networks of zombies need not be amassed by the person that uses them; the use of zombie networks can be bought for a price.[14] Another issue is how to control zombie networks. One method involves zombies listening for commands on Internet Relay Chat (IRC) channels, which provides a relatively anonymous, scalable means of control. When this is used, the zombie networks are referred to as *botnets*, named after automated IRC client programs called *bots*.[15]

2.2 Naming

When a new piece of malware is spreading, the top priority of anti-virus companies is to provide an effective defense, quickly. Coming up with a catchy name for the malware is a secondary concern.

Typically the primary, human-readable name of a piece of malware is decided by the anti-virus researcher[16] who first analyzes the malware.[115] Names are often based on unique characteristics that malware has, either some feature of its code or some effect that it has. For example, a virus' name may be derived from some distinctive string that is found inside it, like "Your PC is now Stoned!"[17] Virus writers, knowing this, may leave such clues deliberately in the hopes that their creation is given a particular name. Anti-virus researchers, knowing *this*, will ignore obvious naming clues so as not to play into the virus writer's hand.[18]

There is no central naming authority for malware, and the result is that a piece of malware will often have several different names. Needless to say, this is confusing for users of anti-virus software, trying to reconcile names heard in alerts and media reports with the names used by their own anti-virus software. To compound the problem, some sites use anti-virus software from multiple different vendors, each of whom may have different names for the same piece of malware.[19] Common naming would benefit anti-virus researchers talking to one another too.[20]

Unfortunately, there isn't likely to be any central naming authority in the near future, for two reasons.[21] First, the current speed of malware propagation precludes checking with a central authority in a timely manner.[22] Second, it isn't always clear what would need to be checked, since one distinct piece of malware may manifest itself in a practically infinite number of ways.

Recommendations for malware naming do exist, but in practice are not usually followed,[23] and anti-virus vendors maintain their own separately-named databases of malware that they have detected. It would, in theory, be possible to manually map malware names between vendors using the information in these databases, but this would be a tedious and error-prone task.

A tool called VGrep automates this process of mapping names.[116] First, a machine is populated with the malware of interest. Then, as shown in Figure 2.1, each anti-virus product examines each file on the machine, and outputs what (if any) malware it detects. VGrep gathers all this anti-virus output and collates

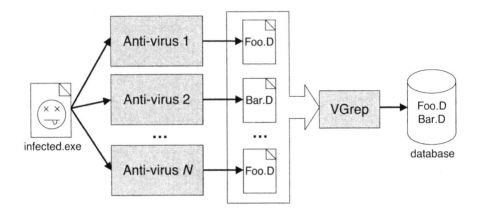

Figure 2.1.   VGrep operation

it for later searching. The real technical challenge is not collating the data, but simply getting usable, consistent output from a wide range of anti-virus products.

The naming problem and the need for tools like VGrep can be demonstrated using an example. Using VGrep and cross-referencing vendor's virus databases, the partial list of names below for the same worm can be found.[24]

    Bagle.C
    Email-worm.Win32.Bagle.c
    W32/Bagle.c@MM
    W32.Beagle.C@mm
    WORM_BAGLE.C
    Worm.Bagle.A3

These results highlight some of the key identifiers used for naming malware:[117]

Malware type. This is the type of the threat which, for this example, is a worm.

Platform specifier. The environment in which the malware runs; this worm needs the Windows 32-bit operating system API ("W32" and "Win32").[25] More generally, the platform specifier could be any execution environment, such as an application's programming language (e.g., "VBS" for "Visual Basic Script"), or may even need to specify a combination of hardware and software platform.

Family name. The family name is the "human-readable" name of the malware that is usually chosen by the anti-virus researcher performing the analysis. This example shows several different, but obviously related, names. The relationship is not always obvious: "Nachi" and "Welchia" are the same worm, for instance.

Variant. Not unlike legitimate software, a piece of malware tends to be released multiple times with minor changes.[26] This change is referred to as the malware's *variant* or, following the biological analogy, the *strain* of the malware.

Variants are usually assigned letters in increasing order of discovery, so this "C" variant is the third B[e]agle found. Particularly persistent families with many variants will have multiple letters, as "Z" gives way to "AA." Unfortunately, this is not unusual – some malware has dozens of variants.[27]

Modifiers. Modifiers supply additional information about the malware, such as its primary means of propagation. For example, "mm" stands for "mass mailing."

The results also highlight the fact that not all vendors supply all these identifiers for every piece of malware, that there is no common agreement on the specific identifiers used, and that there is no common syntax used for names.

Besides VGrep, there are online services where a suspect file can be uploaded and examined by multiple anti-virus products. Output from a service like this also illustrates the variety in malware naming:[28]

Worm/Mydoom.BC	Win32:Mytob-D	I-Worm/Mydoom
Win32.Worm.Mytob.C	Worm.Mytob.C	Win32.HLLM.MyDoom.22
W32/Mytob.D@mm	W32/Mytob.C-mm	Net-Worm.Win32.Mytob.c
Win32/Mytob.D	Mytob.D	

Ultimately, however, the biggest concern is that the malware is detected and eliminated, not what it's called.

2.3 Authorship

People whose computers are affected by malware typically have a variety of colorful terms to describe the person who created the malware. This book will use the comparatively bland terms *malware author* and *malware writer* to describe people who create malware; when appropriate, more specific terms like *virus writer* may be used too.

There's a distinction to be made between the malware author and the malware distributor. Writing malware doesn't imply distributing malware, and vice versa, and there have been cases where the two roles are known to have been played by different people.[29] Having said that, the malware author and distributor will be assumed to be the same person throughout this book, for simplicity.

Is a malware author a "hacker?" Yes and no. The term *hacker* has been distorted by the media and popular usage to refer to a person who breaks into computers, especially when some kind of malicious intent is involved. Strictly speaking, a person who breaks into computers is a *cracker*, not a hacker,[118] and there may be a variety of motivations for doing so. In geek parlance, being called a hacker actually has a positive connotation, and means a person who is skilled at computer programming; hacking has nothing to do with computer intrusion or malware.

Hacking (in the popular sense of the word) also implies a manual component, whereas the study of malware is the study of large-scale, automated forms of attack. Because of this distinction and the general confusion over the term, this book will not use it in relation to malware.

2.4   Timeline

Figure 2.2 puts some important events in context. With the exception of adware and spyware, which appeared in the late 1990s, all of the different types of malware were known about in the early 1970s. The prevalence of virus, worms, and other malware has been gradually building steam since the mid-1980s, leaving us with lots of threats – no matter how they're counted.

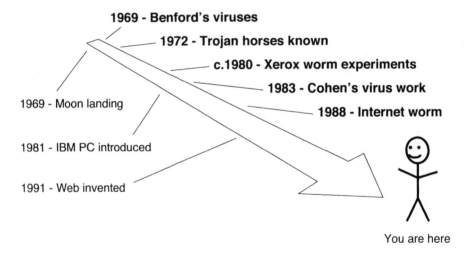

Figure 2.2.   Timeline of events

Notes for Chapter 2

1 This case doesn't appear to have gone to trial yet, so the person may yet be found not guilty. Regardless, the charges in the indictment [327] serve as an example of how a logic bomb can be used maliciously.

2 The term "computer virus" is preferable if there's any possibility of confusion with biological viruses.

3 Bassham and Polk [28] note that innovation is important for the longevity of computer viruses, especially if the result is something that hasn't yet been seen by anti-virus software. They also point out that non-destructive viruses have an increased chance of survival, by not drawing attention to themselves.

4 These three definitions are based on Harley et al. [137]; Radatti [258] talks about viruses passing through unaffected platforms, which he calls 'Typhoid Mary Syndrome.'

5 Insofar as a worm can be said to stand.

6 This farsighted book also included ideas about an internet and laser printers [50].

7 The Xerox work is described in Shoch and Hupp [287], and both they and Dewdney [91] mention Creeper and Reaper. There were two versions of Creeper, of which the first would be better called a rabbit, the second a worm.

8 This version of the event is from [329]. An interesting historical twist: Morris, Jr.'s father was one of the people playing Darwin in the early 1960s at Bell Labs, and created 'The species which eventually wiped out all opposition...' [9, page 95].

9 Nazario [229] calls this second kind of rabbit a "jumping executable worm."

10 "Hybrid" is used in a generic sense here; Harley et al. [137] use the term "hybrid viruses" to describe viruses that execute concurrently with the infected code.

11 From Thompson [322]; he simply calls it a Trojan horse.

12 This differs from Harley et al. [137], who define a dropper to be a program that installs malware. However, this term is so often applied to malware that this narrower definition is used here.

13 There are many other spamming techniques besides this; Spammer-X [300, Chapter 3] has more information. Back-door functionality left behind by worms has been used for sending spam in this manner [188].

14 Acohido and Swartz [2] mention a \$2000–\$3000 rental fee for 20,000 zombies, but prices have been dropping [300].

15 Cooke et al. [79] looks at botnet evolution, and takes the more general view that botnets are just zombie armies, and need a controlling communication channel, but that channel doesn't have to be IRC. There are also a wide variety of additional uses for botnets beyond those listed here [319].

16 In the anti-virus industry, people who analyze malware for anti-virus companies are referred to as "researchers." This is different from the academic use of the term.

17 This was one suggested way to find the Stoned virus [290].

18 Lyman [189], but this is common knowledge in the anti-virus community.

19 Diversity is usually a good thing when it comes to defense, and large sites will often use different anti-virus software on desktop machines than they use on their gateway machines. In a panel discussion at the 2003 *Virus Bulletin* conference, one company revealed that they used *eleven* different anti-virus products.

20 While the vast majority of interested parties want common naming, their motivations for wanting this may be different, and they may treat different parts of the name as being significant [182].

21 Having said this, an effort has been announced recently to provide uniform names for malware. The "Common Malware Enumeration" will issue a unique identifier for malware causing major outbreaks, so users can refer to highly mneumonic names like "CME-42," which intuitively may have been issued before "CME-40" and "CME-41" [176].

22 Of course, this begs the question of why such a central authority wasn't established in the early days of malware prevalence, when there was less malware and the propagation speeds tended to be much, much slower.

23 CARO, the Computer Antivirus Research Organization, produced virus-naming guidelines in 1991 [53], which have since been updated [109].

24 Vendor names have been removed from the results.

25 "API" stands for "application programming interface."

26 Not all variants necessarily come from the same source. For example, the "B" variant of the Blaster worm was released by someone who had acquired a copy of the "A" variant and modified it [330].

27 A few, like Gaobot, have hundreds of variants, and require three letters to describe their variant!

28 This example is from [47], again with vendor information removed.

29 Dellinger's "Virus 2" spread courtesy of the virus writer's friends [87], and secondhand stories indicate that Stoned was spread by someone besides its author [119, 137, 290]. Malware writers are rarely caught or come forward, so discovering these details is unusual.

100 For example, Adleman [3] and Cohen [75].

101 The details of the case may be found in [328]; [326] has sentencing information.

102 Paraphrased liberally from Virgil's Aeneid, Book II [336].

103 Anderson [12].

104 A sidebar in Harley et al. [137, page 60] has an amusing collection of suggested plural forms that didn't make the cut.

105 Benford [33] and Gerrold [118], respectively. Benford talks about his real computer viruses in this collection of reprinted stories.

106 As told in Cohen [74].

107 Skrenta [289] and Dellinger [87].

108 The whole sordid tale is in Rosen [267].

109 The original Core War article is Dewdney [91]; Darwin is described in [9, 201].

110 Bontchev [46].

111 Vossen [338] and van het Groenewoud [331], respectively.

112 This definition of spyware and adware follows Gordon [124].

113 Walker wrote a letter to Dewdney [340], correcting Dewdney's explanation of Animal in his column [92] (this column also mentions Skrenta's virus).

114 Chien and Ször [70] explain blended threats and the historical context of the anti-virus industry with respect to them.

115 Bontchev [44] and Lyman [189] describe the process by which a name is assigned.

116 VGrep was originally by Ian Whalley; this discussion of its operation is based on its online documentation [333].

117 This description is based on the CARO identifiers and terminology [109].

118 The Jargon File lists the many nuances of "hacker," along with a hitchhiker's guide to the hacker subculture [260].

Chapter 3

VIRUSES

A computer virus has three parts:[100]

Infection mechanism How a virus spreads, by modifying other code to contain a (possibly altered) copy of the virus. The exact means through which a virus spreads is referred to as its *infection vector*. This doesn't have to be unique – a virus that infects in multiple ways is called *multipartite*.

Trigger The means of deciding whether to deliver the payload or not.

Payload What the virus does, besides spread. The payload *may* involve damage, either intentional or accidental. Accidental damage may result from bugs in the virus, encountering an unknown type of system, or perhaps unanticipated multiple viral infections.

Except for the infection mechanism, the other two parts are optional, because infection is one of the key defining characteristics of a virus. In the absence of infection, only the trigger and payload remain, which is a logic bomb.

In pseudocode, a virus would have the structure below. The `trigger` function would return a boolean, whose value would indicate whether or not the trigger conditions were met. The `payload` could be anything, of course.

```
def virus():
    infect()
    if trigger() is true:
        payload()
```

Infection is done by selecting some target code and infecting it, as shown below. The target code is locally accessible to the machine where the virus runs, applying the definition of viruses from the last chapter. Locally accessible targets may include code in shared network directories, though, as these directories are made to appear locally accessible.

Generally, *k* targets may be infected each time the infection code below is run. The exact method used to select targets varies, and may be trivial, as in the case of the boot-sector infectors in Section 3.1.1. The tricky part of `select_target` is that the virus doesn't want to repeatedly re-infect the same code; that would be a waste of effort, and may reveal the presence of the virus. `Select_target` has to have some way to detect whether or not some potential target code is already infected, which is a double-edged sword. If the virus can detect itself, then so can anti-virus software. The `infect_code` routine performs the actual infection by placing some version of the virus' code in the target.

```
def infect():
    repeat k times:
        target = select_target()
        if no target:
            return
        infect_code(target)
```

Viruses can be classified in a variety of ways. The next two sections classify them along orthogonal axes: the type of target the virus tries to infect, and the method the virus uses to conceal itself from detection by users and anti-virus software. Virus creation need not be difficult, either; the virus classification is followed by a look at do-it-yourself virus kits for the programming-challenged.

3.1   Classification by Target

One way of classifying viruses is by what they try to infect. This section looks at three: boot-sector infectors, executable file infectors, and data file infectors (a.k.a. macro viruses).

3.1.1   Boot-Sector Infectors

Although the exact details vary, the basic boot sequence on most machines goes through these steps:

1 Power on.

2 ROM-based instructions run, performing a self-test, device detection, and initialization. The boot device is identified, and the boot block is read from it; typically the boot block consists of the initial block(s) on the device.[1] Once the boot block is read, control is transferred to the loaded code. This step is referred to as the *primary boot*.

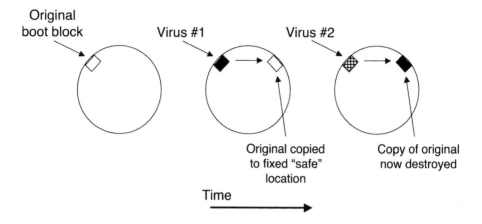

Figure 3.1. Multiple boot sector infections

3 The code loaded during the primary boot step loads a larger, more sophisti- cated program that understands the boot device's filesystem structure, and transfers control to it. This is the *secondary boot*.

4 The secondary boot code loads and runs the operating system kernel.

A *boot-sector infector*, or BSI, is a virus that infects by copying itself to the boot block. It may copy the contents of the former boot block elsewhere on the disk first,[2] so that the virus can transfer control to it later to complete the booting process.

One potential problem with preserving the boot block contents is that block allocation on disk is filesystem-specific. Properly allocating space to save the boot block requires a lot of code, a luxury not available to BSIs. An alternate method is to always copy the original boot block to some fixed, "safe" location on disk. This alternate method can cause problems when a machine is infected multiple times by different viruses that happen to use that same safe location, as shown in Figure 3.1. This is an example of unintentional damage being done by a virus, and has actually occurred: Stoned and Michelangelo were BSIs that both picked the same disk block as their safe location.[101]

In general, infecting the boot sector is strategically sound: the virus may be in a known location, but it establishes itself before any anti-virus software starts or operating system security is enabled. But BSIs are rare now. Machines are rebooted less often, and there is very little use of bootable media like floppy disks.[3] From a defensive point of view, most operating systems prevent writing to the disk's boot block without proper authorization, and many a BIOS[4] has boot block protection that can be enabled.

3.1.2   File Infectors

Operating systems have a notion of files that are executable. In a broader sense, executable files may also include files that can be run by a command-line user "shell." A *file infector* is a virus that infects files which the operating system or shell consider to be executable; this could include batch files and shell scripts, but binary executables are the most common target.

There are two main issues for file infectors:

1 Where is the virus placed?

2 How is the virus executed when the infected file is run?

For BSIs, the answer to these questions was apparent. A BSI places itself in the boot block and gets executed through a machine's normal boot sequence. File infectors have a few more options at their disposal, though, and often the answers to these questions are interdependent. The remainder of this section is organized around the answer to the first question: where is the virus placed?

3.1.2.1   Beginning of File

Older, very simple executable file formats like the .COM MS-DOS format would treat the entire file as a combination of code and data. When executed, the entire file would be loaded into memory, and execution would start by jumping to the beginning of the loaded file.[102]

In this case, a virus that places itself at the start of the file gets control first when the infected file is run, as illustrated in Figure 3.2. This is called a *prepending* virus. Inserting itself at the start of a file involves some copying, which isn't difficult, but isn't the absolute easiest way to infect a file.

3.1.2.2   End of File

In contrast, appending code onto the end of a file is extremely easy. A virus that places itself at the end of a file is called an *appending* virus.

How does the virus get control? There are two basic possibilities:

- The original instruction(s) in the code can be saved, and replaced by a jump to the viral code. Later, the virus will transfer control back to the code it infected. The virus may try to run the original instructions directly in their saved location, or the virus may restore the infected code back to its original state and run it.

- Many executable file formats specify the start location in a file header. The virus can change this start location to point to its own code, then jump to the original start location when done.

Figure 3.3 shows an appending virus using the latter scheme.

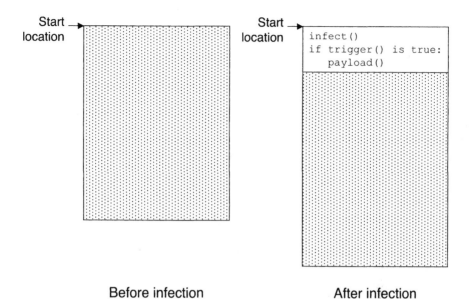

Figure 3.2. Prepending virus

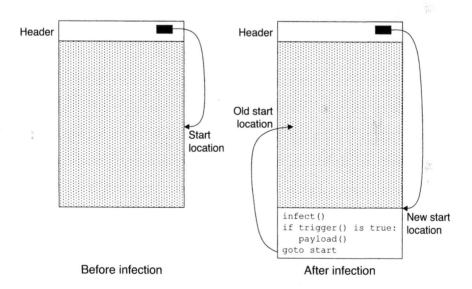

Figure 3.3. Appending virus

3.1.2.3 Overwritten into File

An *overwriting* virus places itself *atop* part of the original code.[5] This avoids an obvious change in file size that would occur with a prepending or appending virus, and the virus' code can be placed in a location where it will get control.

Obviously, overwriting code blindly is almost certain to break the original code and lead to rapid discovery of the virus. There are several options, with varying degrees of complexity and risk.

- The virus can look for, and overwrite, sections of repeated values in the hopes of avoiding damage to the original code.[6] Such values would tend to appear in a program's data rather than in the code, so a mechanism for gaining control during execution would have to be used as well. Ideally, the virus could restore the repeated value once it has finished running.

- The virus can overwrite an arbitrary part of a file if it can somehow preserve the original contents elsewhere, similar to the BSI approach. An innocent-looking data file of some kind, like a JPEG file, could be used to stash the original contents. A less-portable approach might take low-level details into account: many filesystems overallocate space for files, and an overwriting virus could quietly use this extra disk space without it showing up in normal filesystem operations.

- Space may be overallocated inside a file too. Parts of an executable file may be padded so that they are aligned to a page boundary, so that the operating system kernel can efficiently map the executables into memory. The net result is unused space inside executable files where a virus may be located.[7]

- Conceivably, a virus could compress a part of the original code to make space for itself, and decompress the original code when the virus has completed execution. However, room would have to be made for both the virus and the decompression code.

None of these options is likely to yield a large amount of space, so overwriting viruses must be small.

3.1.2.4   Inserted into File

Another possibility is that a virus can insert itself into the target code, moving the target code out of the way, and even interspersing small pieces of virus code with target code. This is no easy feat: branch targets in the code have to be changed, data locations must be updated, and linker relocation information needs modification. Needless to say, this file infection technique is rarely seen.[8]

3.1.2.5   Not in File

A *companion* virus is one which installs itself in such a way that it is naturally executed before the original code. The virus never modifies the infected code, and gains control by taking advantage of the process by which the operating system or shell searches for executable files. Although this bears the hallmarks of a Trojan horse, a companion virus is a "real" virus by virtue of self-replication.

The easiest way to explain companion viruses is by example.[103]

- The companion virus can place itself earlier in the search path, with the same name as the target file, so that the virus will be executed first when an attempt is made to execute the target file.

- MS-DOS searches for an executable named `foo` by looking for `foo.com`, `foo.exe`, and `foo.bat`, in that order. If the target file is a .EXE file, then the companion virus can be a .COM file with the same name.

- The target file can be renamed, and the companion virus can be given the target file's original name.

- Windows associates file types (as determined by the filename's extension) with applications in the Registry. With strategic Registry changes, the association for .EXE files can be made to run the companion virus instead of the original executable. Effectively, all executable files are infected at once.

- The ELF file format commonly used on recent Unix systems has an "interpreter" specified in each executable's file header – this invariably points to the system's run-time linker.[104] A companion virus can replace the run-time linker, again causing all executables to be infected at once.

- Companion viruses are possible even in GUI-based environments. A target application's icon can be overlaid with the icon for the companion virus. When a user clicks on what they *think* is the application's icon, the companion virus runs instead.

3.1.3 Macro Viruses

Some applications allow data files, like word processor documents, to have "macros" embedded in them. Macros are short snippets of code written in a language which is typically interpreted by the application, a language which provides enough functionality to write a virus. Thus, *macro viruses* are better thought of as data file infectors, but since their predominant form has been macros, the name has stuck.

When a macro-containing document is loaded by the application, the macros can be caused to run automatically, which gives control to the macro virus. Some applications warn the user about the presence of macros in a document, but these warnings may be easily ignored.

A proof-of-concept of macro viruses was published in 1989,[105] in response to rumors of their existence. Macro viruses didn't hit the mainstream until 1995, when the Concept virus was distributed, targeting Microsoft Word documents across multiple platforms.[9]

Concept's operation is shown in Figure 3.4. Word has a persistent, global set of macros which apply to all edited documents, and this is Concept's target:

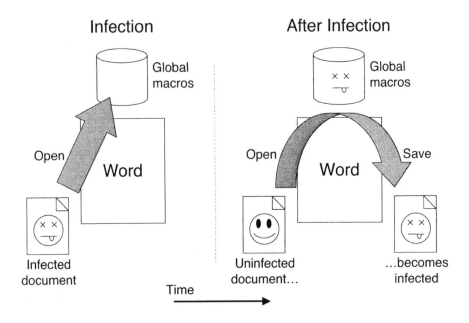

Figure 3.4. Concept in action

once installed in the global macros, it can infect all documents edited in the
future. A document infected by Concept includes two macros that have special
properties in Word.

AutoOpen Any code in the AutoOpen macro is run automatically when the
file is opened. This is how an infected document gains control.

FileSaveAs The code in the FileSaveAs macro is run when its namesake menu
item (File... Save As...) is selected. In other words, this code can be used
to infect any as-yet-uninfected document that is being saved by the user.

From a technical standpoint, macro languages are easier to use than lower-
level programming languages, so macro viruses drastically lower the barrier to
virus creation.

3.2   Classification by Concealment Strategy

Another way of classifying viruses is by how they try to conceal themselves,
both from users and from anti-virus software.

3.2.1   No Concealment

Not hiding at all is one concealment strategy which is remarkably easy to
implement in a computer virus. It goes without saying, however, that it's not

Before Decryption

After Decryption

```
for i in 0…length(body):
    decrypt body_i
goto decrypted_body
```

```
for i in 0…length(body):
    decrypt body_i
goto decrypted_body
```
```
decrypted_body:
    infect()
    if trigger() is true:
        payload()
```

Figure 3.5. Encrypted virus pseudocode

very effective – once the presence of a virus is known, it's trivial to detect and analyze.

3.2.2   Encryption

With an *encrypted* virus, the idea is that the virus *body* (infection, trigger, and payload) is encrypted in some way to make it harder to detect. This "encryption" is not what cryptographers call encryption; virus encryption is better thought of as obfuscation. (Where it's necessary to distinguish between the two meanings of the word, I'll use the term "strong encryption" to mean encryption in the cryptographic sense.)

When the virus body is in encrypted form, it's not runnable until decrypted. What executes first in the virus, then, is a *decryptor loop*, which decrypts the virus body and transfers control to it. The general principle is that the decryptor loop is small compared to the virus body, and provides a smaller profile for anti-virus software to detect.

Figure 3.5 shows pseudocode for an encrypted virus. A decryptor loop can decrypt the virus body in place, or to another location; this choice may be dictated by external constraints, like the writability of the infected program's code. This example shows an in-place decryption.

How is virus encryption done? Here are six ways:[106]

Simple encryption. No key is used for simple encryption, just basic parameterless operations, like incrementing and decrementing, bitwise rotation, arithmetic negation, and logical NOT:[10]

Encryption	Decryption
inc $body_i$	dec $body_i$
rol $body_i$	ror $body_i$
neg $body_i$	neg $body_i$

Static encryption key. A static, constant key is used for encryption which
doesn't change from one infection to the next. The operations used would
include arithmetic operations like addition, and logical operations like XOR.
Notice that the use of reversible operations is a common feature of simpler
types of virus encryption. In pseudocode:

Encryption	Decryption
$body_i$ + 123	$body_i$ - 123
$body_i$ xor 42	$body_i$ xor 42

Variable encryption key. The key begins as a constant value, but changes as
the decryption proceeds. For example:

```
key = 123
for i in 0...length(body):
    body_i = body_i xor key
    key = key + body_i
```

Substitution cipher. A more general encryption could employ lookup tables
which map byte value between their encrypted and decrypted forms. Here,
encrypt and decrypt are 256-byte arrays, initialized so that if encrypt[j]
= k, then decrypt[k] = j:

Encryption	Decryption
$body_i$ = encrypt[$body_i$]	$body_i$ = decrypt[$body_i$]

This substitution cipher is a 1:1 mapping, but in actual fact, the virus body
may not contain all 256 possible byte values. A homophonic substitution
cipher allows a 1:n mapping, increasing complexity by permitting multiple
encrypted values to correspond to one decrypted value.

Strong encryption. There is no reason why viruses cannot use strong encryption. Previously, code size might have been a factor, if the virus would
have to carry strong decryption code with it, but this is no longer a problem:

most systems now contain strong encryption libraries which can be used by viruses.[107]

The major weakness in the encryption schemes above is that the encrypted virus body is the same from one infection to the next. That constancy makes a virus as easy to detect as one using no concealment at all! With *random encryption* keys,[108] this error is avoided: the key used for encryption changes randomly with each new infection. This idea can be applied to any of the encryption types described here. Obviously, the virus' decryptor loop must be updated for each infection to incorporate the new key.

3.2.3 Stealth

A *stealth* virus is a virus that actively takes steps to conceal the infection itself, not just the virus body. Furthermore, a stealth virus tries to hide from everything, not just anti-virus software. Some examples of stealth techniques are below.[109]

- An infected file's original timestamp can be restored after infection, so that the file doesn't look freshly-changed.

- The virus can store (or be capable of regenerating) all pre-infection information about a file, including its timestamp, file size, and the file's contents. Then, system I/O calls can be intercepted, and the virus would play back the original information in response to any I/O operations on the infected file, making it appear uninfected. This technique is applicable to boot block I/O too.

  The exact method of intercepting I/O calls depends on the operating system. Under MS-DOS, for instance, I/O requests are made with interrupt calls, whose handlers are located via user-accessible interrupt vectors; the virus need only modify the interrupt vector to insert itself into the chain of interrupt handlers. On other systems, I/O is performed using shared libraries, so a virus can impose itself into key shared library routines to intercept I/O calls for most applications.

- Some systems store the secondary boot loader as consecutive disk blocks, to make the primary boot loader's task simpler. On these systems, there are two views of the secondary boot loader, as a sequence of blocks, and as a file in the filesystem. A virus can insert itself into the secondary boot loader's blocks, relocating the original blocks elsewhere in the filesystem. The end result is that the usual, filesystem view shows no obvious changes, but the virus is hidden and gets run courtesy of the real primary boot loader.[110]

A variation is a *reverse stealth* virus, which makes everything look infected – the damage is done by anti-virus software frantically (and erroneously) trying to disinfect.[111]

Stealth techniques overlap with techniques used by *rootkits*. Rootkits were originally toolkits for people who had broken into computers; they used these toolkits to hide their tracks and avoid detection.[112] Malware now uses rootkits too: for example, the Ryknos Trojan horse tried to hide itself using a rootkit intended for digital-rights management.[113]

3.2.4   Oligomorphism

Assuming an encrypted virus' key is randomly changed with each new infection, the only unchanging part of the virus is the code in the decryptor loop. Anti-virus software will exploit this fact for detection, so the next logical development is to change the decryptor loop's code with each infection.

An *oligomorphic* virus, or *semi-polymorphic* virus, is an encrypted virus which has a small, finite number of different decryptor loops at its disposal. The virus selects a new decryptor loop from this pool for each new infection. For example, Whale had 30 different decryptor variants, and Memorial had 96 decryptors.[114]

In terms of detection, oligomorphism only makes a virus marginally harder to spot. Instead of looking for one decryptor loop for the virus, anti-virus software can simply have all of the virus' possible decryptor loops enumerated, and look for them all.

3.2.5   Polymorphism

A *polymorphic* virus is superficially the same as an oligomorphic virus. Both are encrypted viruses, both change their decryptor loop on each infection.[115] However, a polymorphic virus has, for all practical purposes, an infinite number of decryptor loop variations. Tremor, for example, has almost six *billion* possible decryptor loops![116] Polymorphic viruses clearly can't be detected by listing all the possible combinations.

There are two questions that arise with respect to polymorphic viruses. First, how can a virus detect that it has previously infected a file, if its presence is hidden sufficiently well? Second, how does the virus change its decryptor loop from infection to infection?

3.2.5.1   Self-Detection

At first glance, it might seem easy for a polymorphic virus to detect if it has previously infected some code – when the virus morphs for a new infection, it can also change whatever aspect of itself that it looks for. This doesn't work, though, because a virus must be able to recognize infection by *any* of its practically-infinite forms. This means that the infection detection mechanism must be independent of the exact code used by the virus:

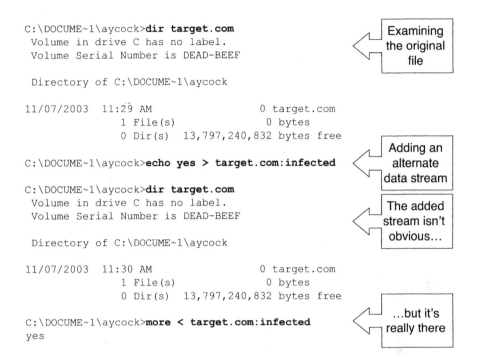

Figure 3.6. Fun with NTFS alternate data streams

File timestamp. A virus could change the timestamp of an infected file, so that the sum of its time and date is some constant value K for all infections.[117] A lot of software only displays the last two digits of the year, so an infected file's year could be increased by 100 without attracting attention.[118]

File size. An infected file could have its size padded out to some meaningful size, such as a multiple of 1234.[11]

Data hiding. In complex executable file formats, like ELF, not all parts of the file's information may be used by a system. A virus can hide a flag in unused areas, or look for an unusual combination of attributes that it has set in the file. For example, Zperm looks for the character "Z" as the minor linker version in an executable's file header on Windows.[119]

Filesystem features. Some filesystems allow files to be tagged with arbitrary attributes, whose existence is not always made obvious. These can be used by a virus to store code, data, or flags which indicate that a file has been infected. Figure 3.6 shows such "alternate data streams" being used in an NTFS filesystem to attach a flag to a file; the presence of this flag doesn't show up in directory listings, the file size, or in the graphical filesystem browser.[12]

External storage. The indication that a file is infected need not be directly associated with the file itself. For example, a virus could use a hash function to map an infected file's name into an obfuscated string, and use that string to create a key in the Windows Registry. The virus could then use the existence of that key as an infection indicator. Even if the Registry key was discovered, it wouldn't immediately reveal the name of the infected file (especially if a strong cryptographic hash function was used).

Note that none of these mechanisms need to work perfectly, because a false positive only means that the virus won't infect some code that it might have otherwise. Also, since all these infection-detection methods work for polymorphic viruses, they also work for the more specific case of non-polymorphic viruses too. Viruses which retain some constancy can just look for one or two bytes of their own code,[120] rather than resorting to more elaborate methods.

It was once suggested that systems could be *inoculated* against specific viruses by faking the virus' self-detection indicator on an uninfected system.[121] Unfortunately, there are too many viruses now to make this feasible.

3.2.5.2   Changing the Decryptor Loop

The code in a polymorphic virus is transformed for each fresh infection using a *mutation engine*.[122] The mutation engine has a grab-bag of code transformation tricks which take as input one sequence of code and output another, equivalent, sequence of code. Choosing which technique to apply and where to apply it can be selected by the engine using a pseudo-random number generator.[123] The result is an engine which is extensible and which can permute code in a large number of ways. Some sample transformations are shown below.[124]

Instruction equivalence. Especially on CISC architectures like the Intel x86, there are often many single instructions which have the same effect. All these instructions would set register r1 to zero:

```
clear r1
xor r1,r1
and 0,r1
move 0,r1
```

Instruction sequence equivalence. Instruction equivalence can be generalized to sequences of instructions. While single-instruction equivalence is at the mercy of the CPU's instruction set, instruction sequence equivalence is more portable, and applies to both high-level and low-level languages:

$$x = 1 \quad \Leftrightarrow \quad \begin{aligned} y &= 21 \\ x &= y - 20 \end{aligned}$$

Instruction reordering. Instructions may have their order changed, so long as constraints imposed by inter-instruction dependencies are observed.

```
r1 = 12                 r2 = r3 + r2
r2 = r3 + r2   ⇔        r1 = 12
r4 = r1 + r2            r4 = r1 + r2
```

Here, the calculation of r4 depends on the values of r1 and r2, but the assignments to r1 and r2 are independent of one another and may be done in any order.

Instruction reordering is well-studied, because it is an application of the instruction scheduling done by optimizing compilers to increase instruction-level parallelism.

Register renaming. A minor, but significant, change can be introduced simply by changing the registers that instructions use. While this makes no difference from a high-level perspective, such as a human reading the code, renaming changes the bit patterns that encode the instructions; this complicates matters for anti-virus software looking for the virus' instructions. For example:

```
r1 = 12                 r3 = 12
r2 = 34        ⇔        r1 = 34
r3 = r1 + r2            r2 = r3 + r1
```

The concept of register renaming naturally extends to variable renaming in higher-level languages, such as those a macro virus might employ.

Reordering data. Changing the locations of data in memory will have a similar effect in terms of altering instruction encoding as register renaming. This would not necessarily have a corresponding transformation in a high-level language, as the variable names themselves would not be changed, just their order.

Making spaghetti. Although some programmers are naturally gifted when it comes to producing "spaghetti code," others are not as fortunate. Happily, code can be automatically transformed so that formerly-consecutive instructions are scattered, and linked together by unconditional jumps:

```
       start:                     L1:
           r1 = 12                     r2 = 34
           r2 = 34          ⇒          goto L2
           r3 = r1 + r2            start:
                                       r1 = 12
                                       goto L1
                                  L2:
                                       r3 = r1 + r2
```

The instructions executed, and their execution order, is the same in both pieces of code.

Inserting junk code. "Junk" computations can be inserted which are inert with respect to the original code – in other words, running the junk code doesn't affect what the original code does. Two examples of adding junk code are below:

```
    r1 = 12               r1 = 12                  r5 = 42
    inc r1          ⇐     r2 = 34          ⇒       r1 = 12
    inc r1                r3 = r1 + r2        X:
    r1 = r1 - 2                                    r2 = 34
    r2 = 34                                        dec r5
    r3 = r1 + r2                                   bne X
                                                   r3 = r1 + r2
```

The code on the left shows the difference between inserting junk code and using instruction sequence equivalence: with junk code, the original code isn't changed. The one on the right inserts a loop as junk code.

Run-time code generation. One way to transform the code is to not have all of it present until it runs. Either fresh code can be generated at run time, or existing code can be modified.

```
        r1 = 12               r1 = 12
        r2 = 34          ⇒    r2 = 34
        r3 = r1 + r2          generate r3 = r1 + r2
                              call generated_code
```

Interpretive dance. The way code is executed can be changed, from being directly executed to being interpreted by some application-specific virtual machine.[125] A "classical" interpreter for such virtual machine code mimics the operation of a real CPU as it fetches, decodes, and executes instructions. In the example below, two of the real instructions are assigned different virtual machine opcodes. Another opcode forces the interpreter loop to exit, demonstrating the mixing of interpreted and real code. In the interpreter, the variable ipc is the interpreter's program counter, and controls the instruction fetched and executed from the CODE array.

```
r1 = 12                 ipc = 0
r2 = 34          ⇒   loop:
r3 = r1 + r2            switch CODE[ipc]:
                           case 0:
                              exit loop
                           case 1:
                              r2 = 34
                           case 2:
                              r1 = 12
                           inc ipc
                        r3 = r1 + r2
                        ...
                        CODE:
                           2
                           1
                           0
```

This transformation can be repeated multiple times, giving multiple levels of interpreters.

Concurrency. The original code can be separated into multiple threads of execution, which not only transforms the code, but can greatly complicate automatic analysis:[13]

```
r1 = 12                 start thread T
r2 = 34          ⇒   r1 = 12
r3 = r1 + r2            wait for signal
                        r3 = r1 + r2
                        ...
                        T:
                           r2 = 34
                           send signal
                           exit thread T
```

Inlining and outlining. Code *inlining* is a technique normally employed to avoid subroutine call overhead,[14] that replaces a subroutine call with the subroutine's code:

```
     ...                          ...
  call S1                     r1 = 12
  call S2                     r2 = r3 + r2
     ...                 ⇒    r4 = r1 + r2
S1:
     r1 = 12                  r1 = 12
     r2 = r3 + r2             r2 = 34
     r4 = r1 + r2             r3 = r1 + r2
     return                      ...
S2:
     r1 = 12
     r2 = 34
     r3 = r1 + r2
     return
```

Outlining is the reverse operation; it need not preserve any logical code grouping, however:

```
     ...                          ...
  r1 = 12                     r1 = 12
  r2 = r3 + r2                r2 = r3 + r2
  r4 = r1 + r2                call S12
                        ⇒     r3 = r1 + r2
  r1 = 12                        ...
  r2 = 34                     S12:
  r3 = r1 + r2                   r4 = r1 + r2
     ...                         r1 = 12
                                 r2 = 34
                                 return
```

Another option is to convert the code into *threaded code*, which has nothing to do with threads used for concurrent programming, despite the name. Threaded code is normally used as an alternative way to implement programming language interpreters.[126] Subroutines in threaded code don't return to the place from which they were invoked, but instead directly jump to the next subroutine; the threaded code itself is simply an array of code addresses:

```
        ...                         ...
   r1 = 12                     next = &CODE
   r2 = r3 + r2                goto [next]
   r4 = r1 + r2                CODE:
                        ⇒         &I1
   r1 = 12                          &I2
   r2 = 34                          &X
   r3 = r1 + r2                X:
        ...                         r1 = 12
                                    r2 = 34
                                    r3 = r1 + r2
                                    ...
                               I1:
                                    r1 = 12
                                    inc next
                                    goto [next]
                               I2:
                                    r2 = r3 + r2
                                    r4 = r1 + r2
                                    inc next
                                    goto [next]
```

Subroutine interleaving. Inlining and outlining transformations maintain the original code, but rebundle it in different ways. Code can also be transformed by combining independent subroutines together, as in the following example.

```
        ...                         ...
   call S1                     call S12
   call S2                          ...
        ...                ⇒   S12:
   S1:                             r5 = 12
       r1 = 12                     r1 = 12
       r2 = r3 + r2                r6 = r3 + r2
       r4 = r1 + r2                r2 = 34
       return                      r4 = r5 + r6
   S2:                             r3 = r1 + r2
       r1 = 12                     return
       r2 = 34
       r3 = r1 + r2
       return
```

The code from S1 has had some registers renamed to avoid collisions with registers used by S2. The overall effect in the interleaved subroutine is the same as the original code in terms of the values computed.

A number of these transformations are also used in the (legitimate) field of code obfuscation; code obfuscation research is used to try and prevent reverse engineering. There are also many, many elaborate code transformations performed by optimizing compilers. Not all compiler techniques and code obfuscation techniques have yet been used by virus writers.

Instead of supplying transformations for the mutation engine to pick from, a virus writer may create a mutation engine that will *automatically* produce a distinct, equivalent decryptor loop. In compilers, automatically searching for a code sequence is referred to as *superoptimization*, and the search may be implemented in a variety of ways: brute-force, automated theorem proving, or any technique for searching a large search space.[127] Zellome, for example, uses a genetic algorithm in its mutation engine.[128] Enormous computational demands are required by such a search, although a clever algorithm may avoid generating too much illegal code and thus improve search time.[15] For now, this mutation method is a curiosity only.

3.2.6   Metamorphism

'Viruses aim to keep their size as small as possible and it is impractical to make the main virus body polymorphic.'   – Tarkan Yetiser[129]

Metamorphic viruses are viruses that are polymorphic in the virus body.[130] They aren't encrypted, and thus need no decryptor loop, but avoid detection by changing: a new version of the virus body is produced for each new infection.

The code-modifying techniques used by polymorphic viruses all apply to metamorphic viruses. Both employ a mutation engine, except a polymorphic virus need not change its engine on each infection, because it can reside in the encrypted part of the virus. In contrast, a metamorphic virus' mutation engine has to morph itself anew for each infection.

Some metamorphic viruses are very elaborate. Simile's mutation engine, about 12,000 lines of assembly code, translates Simile from machine code to a machine-independent intermediate code. Operating on the intermediate code, the mutation engine undoes old obfuscations, applies new transformations, and generates fresh machine code.[131] Metamorphic mutation engines whose input and output are machine code must be able to disassemble and reassemble machine code.[16]

Metamorphism is relatively straightforward to implement in viruses that spread in source code form, such as macro viruses. A virus may rely on system tools for metamorphism, too. Apparition, for instance, is written in Pascal[17] and carries its own source code; if a compiler is found on an infected system, the virus inserts junk code into its source and recompiles itself.

While polymorphic and metamorphic viruses are decidedly nontrivial to detect by anti-virus software, they are also hard for a virus writer to implement correctly – the numbers of these viruses are small in comparison to other types.

3.2.7 Strong Encryption

The encryption methods discussed so far result in viruses that, once captured, are susceptible to analysis. The major problem is not the encryption method, because that can always be strengthened; the major problem is that viruses carry their decryption keys with them.[132]

This might seem a necessary weakness, because if a virus doesn't have its key, it can't decrypt and run its code. There are, however, two other possibilities.

1 The key comes from outside an infected system:

  ■ A virus can retrieve the key from a web site, but that would mean that the virus would then have to carry the web site's address with it, which could be blocked as a countermeasure. To avoid knowing a specific web site's name, a virus could use a web search engine to get the key instead.

  Generally, any electronic data stream that a virus can monitor would be usable for key delivery, especially ones with high volumes of traffic that are unlikely to be blocked: email messages, Usenet postings, instant messaging, IRC, file-sharing networks.

  ■ A *binary virus* is one where the virus is in two parts, and doesn't become virulent until both pieces are present on a system.[133] There have only been a few binary viruses, such as Dichotomy and RMNS.[18]

  One manifestation of binary viruses would be where virus V_1 has strongly-encrypted code, and virus V_2 has its key. But this scheme is unlikely to work well in practice. If V_1 and V_2 travel together, then both will bear the same risk of capture and analysis, defeating the purpose of separating the encryption key. If V_1 and V_2 spread separately (e.g., V_2 is released a month after V_1, and uses a different infection vector) then their spread would be independent.

  Now, say that P_1 is the probability of V_1 reaching a given machine, and P_2 is that probability for V_2. With an independent spread, the probability of them both finding the same machine and becoming virulent is $P_1 \times P_2$, i.e., smaller.[19]

2 The key comes from *inside* an infected system. Using *environmental key generation*, the decryption key is constructed of elements already present in the target's environment, like:

- the machine's domain name;
- the time or date;
- some data in the system (e.g., file contents);
- the current user name;
- the interface's language setting (e.g., Chinese, Hebrew).

This makes it very easy to target viruses to particular individuals or groups. A target doesn't even know that they possess the key!

Combined with strong encryption, environmental key generation would render a virus unanalyzable even if captured. To fully analyze an encrypted virus, it has to be decrypted, and while the elements comprising the key may be discovered, the exact value of the key will not.[20] In this case, the only real hope of decryption lies in a poor choice of key. A poorly-chosen key with a relatively small range of possible values (e.g., the language setting) would be susceptible to a brute-force attack.

How can the virus know that its decryption was successful? It doesn't. While the virus could carry a checksum with it to verify that the decryption worked,[21] that might give away information to an analyst. An alternative method is to catch exceptions that invalid code may cause, then try to run the decrypted "code" and see if it works.

3.3   Virus Kits

Humans love their tools, and it's not surprising that a variety of tools exists for writing viruses. A *virus kit* is a program which automatically produces all or part of a virus' code.[134] They have different interfaces, from command-line tools to menu-based tools to full-blown graphical user interfaces. Figures 3.7 and 3.8 show two versions of a GUI-based virus kit.[22]

Programming libraries are available, too, such as add-on mutation engines which will turn any virus into a polymorphic virus. In an Orwellian twist, though, success is failure. The more popular a virus kit or library, the greater the chance that anti-virus researchers have devoted time to detecting all of its progeny.

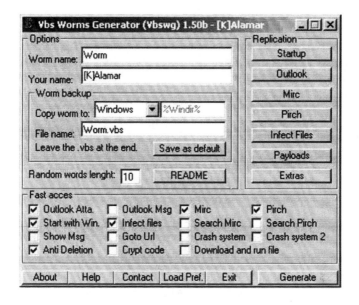

Figure 3.7. Virus kit

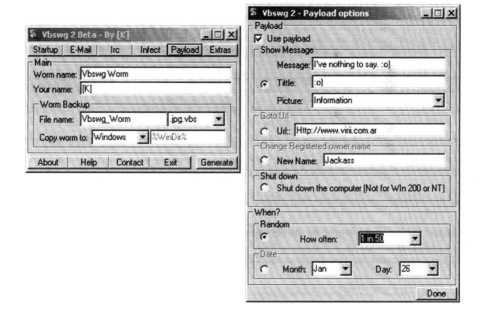

Figure 3.8. Virus kit, the next generation

Notes for Chapter 3

1   Even though there may be several initial blocks/sectors involved, I'll refer to this as the boot block (singular) for convenience.

2   Disks are used for concreteness, but really this could be any bootable media.

3   Although media is used which can potentially be bootable, like CD-ROMs, they are not often booted from.

4   "BIOS" stands for "Basic Input/Output System;" this refers to in-ROM code on PCs.

5   This section was originally based on Harley et al. [137]. Some sources would classify viruses using some of these techniques as "cavity infectors" [77], but as cavity infection involves overwriting, this distinction seems unnecessary.

6   The ZeroHunt virus looked for sequences of bytes with the value 0, for instance [198].

7   This technique was employed for viruses back in 1987 [95], and is still in use [27, 58].

8   Having said that, Zmist does it [106].

9   Ironically, it was shipped out by Microsoft on some CD-ROMs [17]. The Concept source code is still easily obtainable, and an analysis can be found in many sources [122, 137, 187].

10 For the pedantic, there's an implied key of 1 for these operations.

11 Executable files infected by the CTX virus, for example, will have their size adjusted to be a multiple of 101 bytes [195].

12 The Stream virus uses NTFS' alternate data streams, but not to detect infection. Stream is an overwriting virus that saves the original code as a separate data stream called "STR" that is associated with the infected file [313].

13 This example is only for illustration; threads do not typically share register contents.

14 The term "subroutine" will be used generically to describe either a procedure, function, or method.

15 Joshi et al. [155] note their speedup compared to a brute-force algorithm. Agapow [4] examines clustering of functional code in the space of all possible programs, arguing that mutation from one piece of functional code to another is possible.

16 The Mental Driller [320]; Lakhotia et al. [178] also discuss the mutation engine, and argue that metamorphic viruses are ultimately constrained in their complexity, because of their need to disassemble and de-obfuscate their own code.

17 Borland's Object Pascal for Windows, to be precise [162].

18 Kaspersky [159, 160]. Interestingly, the 1961 Darwin players tried an experiment with such multi-part programs, and declared the experiment a 'flop' [201].

19 Recall that probabilities fall in the range [0, 1], so their product can't be greater than either one.
20 Even if the exact key isn't discovered, general information about the virus' intent may be revealed by the elements used for the key.
21 Bontchev [46]. The *random decryption algorithm* (RDA) works along these lines: the virus doesn't carry its key, but doesn't get its key from the environment, either. An RDA virus decrypts itself by brute force, trying different decryption keys until it locates a known value in the decrypted code [208].
22 Okay, it depends on how "virus" is defined – this is really a worm generator, but it has one of the best GUIs. These are both by [K]alamar.

100 These parts are from Harley et al. [137]. The phrase "infection mechanism" is also used extensively in biology.
101 As reported in [14].
102 Levine [183].
103 The first is from Bontchev [38]; *everyone* mentions the second [38, 137, 187]; the third and final ones are from Harley et al. [137]. The fourth is mentioned in [77].
104 Levine [183].
105 Highland [141].
106 The first three are from [13], the fourth from [248].
107 As pointed out by one of my students.
108 Wells [13].
109 The first two are from Harley et al. [137].
110 Bontchev [38].
111 Bontchev [46].
112 Hoglund and Butler [144].
113 Florio [112] analyzes Ryknos; the infamous rootkit in question was outed by Russinovich [271].
114 [161] and [309], respectively.
115 Definition based on [217, 351].
116 Fischer [108].
117 Ludwig [187].
118 Ludwig again, and Ferbrache [103].
119 Szor [311].
120 Ferbrache [103].
121 Ferbrache [103].

122 Nachenberg [217].

123 Yetiser [351].

124 These are from Cohen [75] (upon whom this organization was originally based) and Collberg et al. [76]; additional sources are noted below.

125 Klint [166].

126 Bell [32]. There are other variations, like indirect threaded code [90].

127 The seminal superoptimization paper was Massalin [196], who used a brute-force search; Joshi et al. [155] use automated theorem proving, and Michalewicz and Fogel [206] cover a wide variety of heuristic search methods.

128 Ferrie and Shannon [105].

129 Yetiser [351].

130 This section is based on Ször and Ferrie [314].

131 Perriot et al. [249].

132 Unless stated otherwise, this section is based on Filiol [107] and Riordan and Schneier [265].

133 Skulason [291] first described the idea, for the more general case of a multi-part virus; the term "binary virus" is from Bontchev [46].

134 This section is based on Tarala [316].

Chapter 4

ANTI-VIRUS TECHNIQUES

'... it is trivial to write a program that identifies all infected programs with 100% accuracy.'
                                                                    – Eugene Spafford[1]

Anti-virus software does up to three major tasks:[100]

Detection Detecting whether or not some code is a virus or not which, in the purest form of detection, results in a Boolean value: yes, this code is infected, or no, this code is not infected. Ultimately, detection is a losing game. Precisely detecting viruses by their appearance or behavior is provably undecidable[101] – a virus writer can always construct a virus which is undetectable by some anti-virus software. (Then the anti-virus software can be updated to detect the new virus, at which point the virus writer can build another new virus, and so on.)

Should a virus always be detected, even if it can't run? Yes. Even if a virus is dormant on one system, it is still useful to detect it so that the virus doesn't affect another system. Anti-virus software is regularly applied to incoming email, for instance, where the email recipient's machine is different from the machine running the mail server and anti-virus software. The other case is where a virus won't run on *any* system. Finding an intended virus may point to some underlying security flaw, and thus it can be useful to detect those viruses too.

Identification Once a virus is detected, which virus is it? The identification process may be distinct from detection, or identification may occur as a side effect of the detection method being used.

Disinfection Disinfection is the process of removing detected viruses; this is sometimes called *cleaning*. Normally a virus would need to be precisely identified in order to perform disinfection.

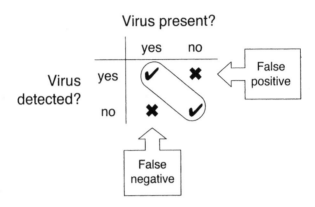

Figure 4.1. Virus detection outcomes

Detection and disinfection can be performed using *generic* methods that try to work with known and unknown viruses, or using *virus-specific* methods which only work with known viruses. (Virus-specific methods may catch unknown variants of known viruses, however.)

The majority of this chapter is devoted to detection. It is arguably the most important of the three tasks above, because identification and disinfection both require detection as a prerequisite. In addition, early detection (i.e., before an infection has occurred) completely alleviates the need for the other tasks.

There are five possible outcomes for detection. Figure 4.1 shows four of them. Perfect virus detection would always have the outcomes circled on the diagonal, where a virus is detected if one is really present, and no virus is detected if none is there. Detection isn't perfect, though. A *false positive* is when the anti-virus software reports a virus even though a virus isn't really there, which can waste time and resources on wild goose chases. A *false negative*, or a *miss*, is when anti-virus software doesn't detect a virus that's present. Either type of false reading serves to undermine user confidence in the anti-virus software. The fifth outcome is *ghost positives*, where a virus is detected that is no longer there, but a previous attempt at disinfection was incomplete and left enough virus remnants to still be detected.[102]

Detection methods can be classified as static or dynamic, depending on whether or not the virus' code is running when the detection occurs. This chapter first looks at detection methods using this classification, then disinfection and related issues, virus databases and virus description languages, and some miscellaneous short topics.

4.1 Detection: Static Methods

Static anti-virus techniques attempt virus detection without actually running any code. This section examines three static techniques: scanners, heuristics, and integrity checkers.

4.1.1 Scanners

The term "scanner" in the context of anti-virus software is another term which has been diluted through common usage, like "virus" itself. It is often applied generically to refer to anti-virus software, regardless of what technique the anti-virus software is using.

Scanners can be classified based on when they are invoked:[103]

On-demand On-demand scanners run when explicitly started by the user. Many anti-virus techniques draw upon a database of information about current threats, and forcing an on-demand scan is useful when a new virus database is installed. An on-demand scan may also be desirable when an infection is suspected, or when a questionable file is downloaded.

On-access An on-access scanner runs continuously, scanning every file when it's accessed. As might be expected, the extra I/O overhead and resources consumed by the scanner impose a performance penalty.

Some on-access scanners permit tuning, so that scans are only performed for read accesses or write accesses; normally scanning would be done for both. A machine where all files arrive via the network may only want scanning on write accesses, for example, because that would provide complete anti-virus coverage while minimizing the performance hit.[2]

In this section, a more restricted view is taken of scanners. Each virus is represented by one or more patterns, or *signatures*, sequences of bytes which (hopefully) uniquely characterize the virus. Signatures are sometimes called *scan strings*, and need not be constant strings. Some anti-virus software may support "don't care" symbols called *wildcards* that match an arbitrary byte, a part of a byte, or zero or more bytes.[104]

The process of searching for viruses by looking through a file for signatures is called *scanning*, and the code that does the search is called a *scanner*. More generally, the search is done through a stream of bytes, which would include the contents of a boot block, a whole file, part of a file being written or read, or network packets.

With hundreds of thousands of signatures to look for, searching for them one at a time is infeasible. The biggest technical challenge in scanning is finding algorithms which are able to look for multiple patterns efficiently, and which scale well. The next sections examine three such algorithms, which illustrate

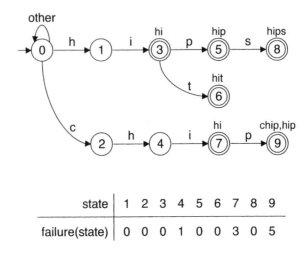

state	1	2	3	4	5	6	7	8	9
failure(state)	0	0	0	1	0	0	3	0	5

Figure 4.2. Aho-Corasick finite automaton and failure function

the general principles behind multiple-pattern search, and which have been used in both anti-virus software and the intrusion-detection systems of Chapter 8.

4.1.1.1   Algorithm: Aho-Corasick

The Aho-Corasick algorithm dates back to 1975 and was originally intended for bibliographic search.[105] The algorithm is best illustrated with an example. A scanner would be looking for signatures which could be composed of any byte values, but for simplicity, English words will be used in the example instead of signatures: hi, hips, hip, hit, chip.

Aho-Corasick needs two things for searching, both of which are shown in Figure 4.2:

1 A *finite automaton* is used to keep track of the state of the search. Conceptually, this is represented as a graph, where the circles represent search states and the edges are possible transitions that can be made from one state to another; the label on an edge indicates the character that causes that transition to be made. (The "other" label is a catch-all which matches any character for which there is no explicit transition.) A doubly-circled state is a final state, where output (i.e., a signature match) occurs, and the associated output is printed above its final state. The start state is denoted by an edge which doesn't originate at a state. The states are numbered for reference purposes.

2 A *failure function* tells the search algorithm which state to go to if no suitable transition is found in the finite automaton. Intuitively, this is the earliest place that the search can possibly resume matching.

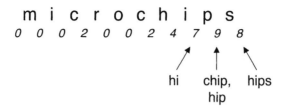

Figure 4.3. Aho-Corasick in operation

The computation of the finite automaton and failure function will be shown later, but for now, here is the search code that uses them:

```
state = START_STATE
while not end of input:
    ch = next input character
                    ch
    while no edge state→ t exists:
        state = failure(state)
    state = t
    if state is final:
        output matches
```

(The notation state$\overset{ch}{\rightarrow}$ t means an edge labeled ch from state state to some state t.)

Figure 4.3 gives the result of running the search code on the input string "microchips," showing the finite automaton's state numbers underneath. From the start state 0, the first two input characters just cause a transition back to state 0. The third character, c, causes a transition into state 2, but there is no transition from state 2 for the following r, so the failure function is used to locate a state from which to resume the search: state 0 again. Skipping ahead, the transition from state 4 on i leads to state 7, a final state where the signature "hi" is matched. Two signatures are matched next, in state 9. There are no transitions at all from state 9, so the failure function is used again, causing the search to resume at state 5, where there is a transition on s to final state 8. The Aho-Corasick algorithm thus searches in parallel for multiple signatures, even detecting overlapping ones.

How are the finite automaton and failure function constructed? There are three steps:

1 Build a trie from the signatures.[3] A *trie* is a tree structure used for searching, where the tree's edges are labeled. A signature has a unique path in the trie from the root to some leaf; signatures with common prefixes share trie paths as long as possible, then diverge.

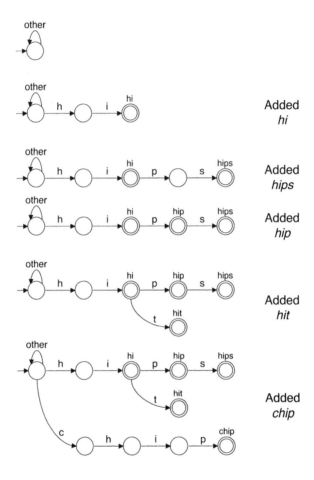

Figure 4.4. Trie building

Figure 4.4 shows the trie being built incrementally for the running example. The trie's root is the start state of the finite automaton, and a self-edge is added to it. A signature is added by starting at the root, tracing along existing paths until a necessary edge is absent, then adding the remaining edges and states. The end of a path becomes a final state.

2 Label the states in the trie. The trie states are assigned numbers such that states closer to the root have lower numbers. This corresponds to a breadth-first ordering of the states. (If the trie states are laid out as in previous figures, then numbering is a simple matter of stepping through the columns of states.) The breadth-first ordering and labels appear in Figure 4.5.

3 Compute the failure function and finish the automaton. The failure function is undefined for the start state, but must be computed for all other states.

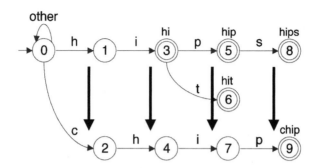

Figure 4.5. Trie labeling

Any state directly connected to the start state (in other words, at a depth of 1 in the trie) can only resume searching at the start state. For other states, the partially-computed failure function is used to trace back through the automaton to find the earliest place the search can resume. Processing states in breadth-first order ensures that needed failure function values are always present.

The computation algorithm is below. Notice that it not only fills in the failure function, but also updates the finite automaton. (The notation $r \xrightarrow{a} s$ means an edge from some state r with some label a to state s, and $\mathtt{state} \xrightarrow{a} t$ is an edge labeled a from state $\mathtt{state}$ to some state t.)

```
foreach state s where depth(s) = 1:
    failure(s) = START_STATE

foreach state s where depth(s) > 1, in breadth order:
    find the edge  r →s
                     a
    state = failure(r)
    while no edge state→ t exists:
                       a
        state = failure(state)
    failure(s) = t
    output(s)  ∪= output(t)
```

Returning to the example, the algorithm starts by initializing *failure*(1) = 0 and *failure*(2) = 0. Then, tracing through the rest of the algorithm:

s	$r \xrightarrow{a} s$	$state \xrightarrow{a} t$	$failure(s)$
3	$1 \xrightarrow{i} 3$	$0 \xrightarrow{i} 0$	0
4	$2 \xrightarrow{h} 4$	$0 \xrightarrow{h} 1$	1
5	$3 \xrightarrow{p} 5$	$0 \xrightarrow{p} 0$	0
6	$3 \xrightarrow{t} 6$	$0 \xrightarrow{t} 0$	0
7	$4 \xrightarrow{i} 7$	$1 \xrightarrow{i} 3$	3
8	$5 \xrightarrow{s} 8$	$0 \xrightarrow{s} 0$	0
9	$7 \xrightarrow{p} 9$	$3 \xrightarrow{p} 5$	5

Computing state 7's failure function value causes its output to change in the finite automaton, and makes it a final state. State 9's output is changed too. The final result is identical to Figure 4.2.

An alternative form of Aho-Corasick combines the finite automaton with the failure function. The result is a new finite automaton for searching that only makes one transition for every input character read, ensuring linear worst-case performance. In practice, Aho-Corasick implementations must solve the challenging problem of how best to represent the finite automaton in a time- and space-efficient manner.[106]

4.1.1.2   Algorithm: Veldman

The Aho-Corasick algorithm is not the only way to search for signatures. One insight leads to a new family of search algorithms: it may be good enough to perform a linear search on a reduced set of signatures. The search doesn't have to be done in parallel.

This insight underlies Veldman's signature search algorithm.[107] The set of signatures being looked for at any one time is filtered down to a manageable level, then a sequential search is done. The key is limiting the sequential search as much as possible.

Four adjacent, non-wildcard bytes are chosen from each signature. These four-byte pattern substrings are then used to construct two hash tables which are used for filtering during the search. Ideally, each pattern substring is chosen so that many signatures are represented by the substring. For example, Figure 4.6 shows that three pattern substrings are sufficient to express five signatures: blar?g, foo, greep, green, agreed. Two-byte pattern substrings are supported as a special case for signatures which are short or contain frequent wildcards, and the substrings don't have to be selected from the beginning of a signature.

After the pattern substrings are chosen, the hash tables are built. The first hash table is used for the first two bytes of a substring, the second hash table

Figure 4.6. Pattern substring selection for Veldman's algorithm

for the last two bytes of a substring, if present. At search time, the hash tables are indexed by adjacent pairs of input bytes. A single bit in the hash table entry indicates whether or not the pair of input bytes might be part of a pattern substring (and possibly part of a signature). A signature table is constructed along with the hash tables, too – this is an array of lists, where each list contains all the signatures that might match a pattern substring. The final hash table entry for a pattern substring is set to point to the appropriate signature list. Figure 4.7 illustrates the hash tables and signature table for the example above.

The search algorithm is given below. The match subroutine walks through a list of signatures and attempts to match each signature against the input. Matching also compensates for the inexact filtering done by the hash tables: for example, a byte sequence like "grar" or "blee" would pass through the hash tables, but would be winnowed out by match.

```
foreach byte sequence b₁b₂b₃b₄ in input:
    if HT1[b₁b₂] is "√":
        if two-byte pattern:
            signatures = HT1[b₁b₂]->st
            match(signatures)
        else:
            if HT2[b₃b₄] is "√":
                signatures = HT2[b₃b₄]->st
                match(signatures)
```

Veldman's algorithm easily supports wildcards of arbitrary complexity in signatures, something the stock Aho-Corasick algorithm doesn't handle.[108] However, the sequential search overhead of Veldman's algorithm must be carefully monitored, and both Veldman and Aho-Corasick look at every byte in the input. Is it possible to do better?

4.1.1.3   Algorithm: Wu-Manber

The Wu-Manber algorithm relies on the same insight as Veldman's algorithm, limiting the set of signatures that must be linearly searched.[109] The difference is that Wu-Manber is able to skip input bytes that can't possibly correspond to a match, resulting in improved performance. The same example signatures will be used to demonstrate the algorithm: blar?g, foo, greep, green, agreed.

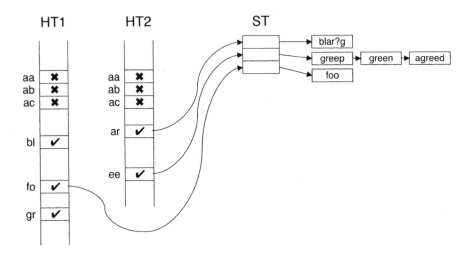

Figure 4.7. Data structures for Veldman's algorithm

The Wu-Manber search code is below:

```
i = MINLEN
while i < n:
    shift = SHIFT[b_{i-1}b_i]
    if shift = 0:
        signatures = HASH[b_{i-1}b_i]
        match(signatures)
        shift = 1
    i = i + shift
```

The bytes of the input are denoted b_1 to b_n, and MINLEN is the minimum length of any pattern substring; its calculation will be explained below. Two hash tables are used, as shown in Figure 4.8. SHIFT holds the number of input bytes that may safely be skipped, and HASH stores the sets of signatures to attempt matching against. The hash functions used to index into the hash tables have not been shown, and in practice, different hash functions may be used for the different hash tables. The match subroutine attempts to match the input text starting at $b_{i-MINLEN+1}$ against a list of signatures.

A trace of the algorithm for the running example is in Figure 4.9. MINLEN is three, and for this short input, only four hash table lookups in SHIFT occur, with one (successful) matching attempt finding "foo" starting at b_6.

This leaves the question of how the hash tables are constructed. It is a four-step process:

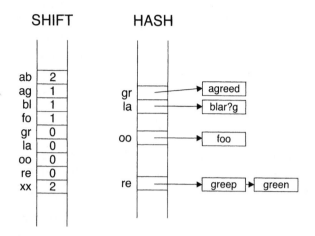

Figure 4.8. Wu-Manber hash tables

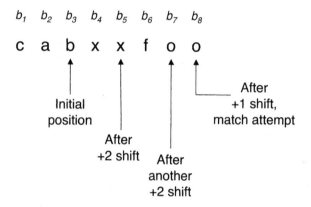

Figure 4.9. Wu-Manber searching

1 Calculating MINLEN. This is the minimum number of adjacent, non-wildcard bytes in any signature. For the example, MINLEN is 3 because of the signature "foo:"

Signature	Length
blar?g	4
foo	3
greep	5
green	5
agreed	6

2 Initializing the SHIFT table. Now, take one pattern substring for each signature containing MINLEN bytes: bla, foo, gre, agr. The Wu-Manber search code above examines adjacent pairs of input bytes, so consider every two-byte pair in the pattern substrings:

ag　fo　la　re
bl　gr　oo

If the pair of input bytes *isn't* one of these, then the search can safely skip MINLEN-1 input bytes. Because the SHIFT table holds the number of bytes to skip for any input byte pair, initialize each entry in it to MINLEN-1.

3 Filling in the SHIFT table. For each two-byte pattern substring pair xy, q_{xy} is the rightmost ending position of xy in *any* pattern substring. The SHIFT table is filled in by setting SHIFT[xy] = MINLEN-q_{xy}. For example:

xy	*Signature(s)*	q_{xy}
bl	bla	2
la	bla	3
gr	agr,gre	3

The bytes in the pattern substrings are numbered from 1, explaining why the ending position of "bl" in $b_1l_2a_3$ is 2, for instance.

4 Filling in the HASH table. If MINLEN-q_{xy} is zero for some xy above, then the search has found the rightmost end of a pattern substring. A match can be tried; HASH[xy] is set to the list of signatures whose pattern substring ends in xy.

The full Wu-Manber algorithm is much more general; only a simplified form of it has been presented here. It was designed to scale well and handle tens of thousands of signatures, even though its worst case is horrendous, requiring a sequential search through all signatures for every input byte. Tests have shown that it lives up to these design goals, outperforming advanced forms of Aho-Corasick except when the number of possible input values is very small.[4]

4.1.1.4 Testing

How can a user determine if their anti-virus scanner is working? Testing using live viruses may *seem* to be a good idea, and an endless supply of them is available on the Internet and in a typical mailbox.[110] Malware of any sort is potentially dangerous, though, and shouldn't be handled without special precautions, especially by users without any special training.

```
X5O!P%@AP[4\PZX54(P^)7CC)7)$EICAR-STANDARD-ANTIVIRUS-TEST-FILE!$H+H*
```

Figure 4.10. The EICAR test file

Testing can be done using non-viral code which the anti-virus software will recognize to be a test file. The EICAR test file is intended to fill the need for such a non-viral file. It is a legitimate MS-DOS program and, when run, prints the message:

```
EICAR-STANDARD-ANTIVIRUS-TEST-FILE!
```

All modern anti-virus software should detect this test file. The contents of the file were designed to be printable ASCII, and can be entered with any text editor. The only caveat is that the file's contents, in Figure 4.10, must be the first 68 bytes in the file. (The disassembly of this code is not particularly enlightening, and is omitted.) Some trailing whitespace is permitted, so long as the file doesn't exceed 128 bytes in length; nothing else may be in the file.

The drawback to the EICAR test file is that it *is* non-viral, and it hardly constitutes an exhaustive test of anti-virus software. Anti-virus software is unlikely to rely solely on a scanner anyway, and the EICAR test file does nothing to exercise other anti-virus techniques.

4.1.1.5 Improving Performance

Scanning an entire file for viruses is slow; it is referred to using the derogative term *grunt scanning*. There are four general approaches to improving scanner performance:

Reduce amount scanned. Scanning an entire file is not only slow, but increases the likelihood of false positives, as a signature may be erroneously found in the wrong place.[111] Instead, scanning can be targeted to specific locations based on assumptions about viral behavior.

- Assuming that viruses add themselves to the beginning or the end of an executable file, searches can be limited to those areas. This is called *top and tail* scanning.

- More complicated executable formats allow an executable's entry point to be specified. Scanning can be restricted to the program's entry point and instructions reachable from that entry point.

- If the exact positions of all virus signatures are known, then scanning can be specifically directed to those areas. The assumption here is that all viruses *are* known, along with their behavior in terms of file location. This is in contrast to the more generic assumptions about virus locations made above. In conjunction with the entry point scanning above, this is referred to as *fixed point scanning*.

■ Many viruses are small. The amount scanned in any location can be set according to the size of common viruses. For example, if most viruses are less than 8K in size, then the scanner may only examine 8K areas at the beginning and end of the executable.[112]

Use of scanning-reduction techniques implies that the scanner will no longer see the complete input. The input to a scanning algorithm doesn't have to be a faithful representation of a file's contents, however. The algorithms work equally well on an abridged view of the input.

Of the performance-enhancing approaches, reducing the amount scanned is the only approach that directly affects the potential correctness of the result.

Reduce amount of scans. Regardless of how much of a file is or isn't scanned, avoiding a scan completely is better.[5] This can be accomplished several ways:

■ Scanning can only be done for certain file types; only executable files may be scanned, for instance, and not data files. Viruses and other threats have been markedly versatile in choosing places to reside, making this scanning-avoidance option no longer viable.

■ Anti-virus software can compute and store state information for files that have been successfully scanned, and only re-scan files if they have changed.[113] While the technique is sound, a number of issues arise:[114]

   – What information about a file is stored? A file's state information must be sufficient to determine if the file has been changed or not. File state may include the file length and the date/time of the last file modification; these are easy to compare for changes, but also easy for a virus writer to fake.

     A stronger means of change detection would compute a checksum of the file, and store the checksum in the file's state information too. Note that the checksum is only used for avoiding scans, and isn't used for virus detection in this case, like integrity checkers (Section 4.1.3) do.

   – Where is state information stored? The possible locations include:

     1 In memory. An in-memory cache of file state information would not persist across machine reboots, or any other situation where the anti-virus software would be restarted. The size of a memory cache would necessarily be bounded to prevent too much memory from being consumed, and a cache replacement algorithm would be needed to select cache entries to evict when

the cache fills up. Removing file state from the cache doesn't change anti-virus accuracy, just performance – in the worst case, re-scanning would be required.

2 On disk, in a database. File state information can be stored in a database on disk. Persistence and size aren't problems, but the file state database becomes a target for attack. Also, if the database is keyed to filenames, then a file which is renamed or copied is a file which gets rescanned, because its new identity isn't present in the database.

3 On disk, tagged onto files. Extended filesystem attributes can be used to attach file state information onto the file itself. These attributes are carried along when a file is renamed or copied.

– What constitutes a change? Obviously, any differences between the stored file state and its current state would indicate a change. The comparison should be ordered so that cheaper operations, like fetching a file's length, are done before more expensive operations like checksumming.

Updates to the virus database, while not a change in file state *per se*, should appear as a change so that the file is re-scanned.[115] This is trivial to implement with an in-memory file state cache: a cache flush resets all stored file state information at once. For on-disk information, this can be implemented by adding the version of the virus database used for scanning into the file state information.

An alternative approach is to use *session keys*. A session key is a unique key which is changed each time the anti-virus software is run, and files have the current session key attached to them when they are scanned. The scanner checks for a file's session key before scanning it; a re-scan is done if the session key doesn't match or is absent.

– How are checksums computed efficiently?[116] Computing the checksum of an entire file can take longer than scanning it. This presents the same problem as grunt scanning had to begin with! Much the same solution is used: only checksum key areas of a file. The "key areas" of a file depend on the file type, though, which implies that checksumming code must be able to understand all the different types of file.

A more clever way to find the key areas of a file is to leverage the existing anti-virus software. The scanner is implicitly identifying key areas by virtue of where it looks for a signature. The anti-virus checksumming code can let the scanner proceed, recording the disk blocks accessed in the file – these are the key areas that should be checksummed.

– How is tampering avoided? On-disk information of any kind is subject to attack. File state information can be encrypted to make it slightly harder to forge. If session keys are used, the session key can be used as the encryption key to encrypt something that can be verified for correct decryption: a constant value, the filename, or the file state information.[6]

Lower resource requirements. Engineering tradeoffs may be made to improve on-access performance, such as lowering CPU and memory demands by using a smaller, less precise set of signatures. This doesn't have to impact overall accuracy, because additional verification can catch false positives, as Section 4.4 explains.

Signature selection is a difficult issue, and involves tradeoffs in precision as well as resource requirements. Short signatures can result in false positives and misidentification;[117] long signatures are more precise, but bloat the virus database. There is the additional danger of being *too* precise. Long signatures may be so specific as to not detect minor virus variants – ideally, signatures are chosen with possible variations in mind whenever possible, like changes to data strings. Compiler-generated code is not terribly distinctive for short signatures, either, and signatures may be better chosen from the data area for viruses written in high-level languages.[118]

Change the algorithm. There is an overwhelming amount of research done on efficient string-searching algorithms, and improving the basic searching algorithm is always a possibility.

One avenue that may be explored is the use of algorithms tailored to specific file types. There are many, many kinds of compressed, archived, encoded, and weakly encrypted files which may harbor viruses. Too many, in fact: typically, anti-virus scanners are preceded by a file type-specific decoder, which provides the scanner with a plaintext, logical view of the input. Scanning algorithms exist for directly searching specific file types, like compressed files, which would avoid the need for separate decoding.[119] This would only make good engineering sense for file types which are frequently-encountered and tend to have large file sizes.

Change the algorithm implementation. Tuning an algorithm's implementation is a touchy process, and the results may depend on the compiler, CPU, and memory as much as they depend on the code itself. For algorithms that are implemented using frequent lookups in tables whose data doesn't change, converting the algorithm and its data into directly-executable code has yielded performance dividends in the past.[120] Effectively, the tables are turned into code. Changing the underlying algorithm itself, rather than its implementation, is likely to have a bigger impact, though.[121]

These general approaches are not specific to scanners, and may be adapted to improve the performance of other anti-virus techniques.

4.1.2   Static Heuristics

Anti-virus software can employ *static heuristics* in an attempt to duplicate expert anti-virus analysis. Static heuristics can find known or unknown viruses by looking for pieces of code that are generally "virus-like," instead of scanning for specific virus signatures.[122] This is a static analysis technique, meaning that the code being analyzed is not running, and there is no guarantee that any suspicious code found would ever be executed.[123]

Static heuristic analysis is done is two steps:[124]

1 Data: the Gathering. Data can be collected using any number of static heuristics. Whether or not any one heuristic correctly classifies the input is not critical, because the results of many heuristics will be combined and analyzed later.

  A scanner can be used to locate short signatures which are generally indicative of suspicious code, called *boosters*.[125] The presence of a booster increases the likelihood that the code being analyzed is viral. For example:

  - Junk code.

  - Decryption loops.

  - Self-modifying code.

  - Use of undocumented API calls.

  - Manipulation of interrupt vectors.

  - Use of unusual instructions, especially ones that wouldn't be generated by a compiler.

  - Strings containing obscenities, or obvious cues like the word "virus."

  It is equally important to look for things that are present in "normal" code, things that viruses don't usually do. For example, viruses don't often create pop-up dialogue boxes for the user.[126] This would be considered a *negative heuristic*, or a *stopper*.

  Other heuristics can be computed which aren't based on scanning:

  - The difference between an executable's entry point and its end of file can be computed.[127] Too small a value, when compared to the same value for typical uninfected executables, may point to an appender.

- Spectral analysis of the code may be done, computing a histogram of the bytes or instructions used in the code. Encrypted code will have a different spectral signature from unencrypted code.[128]

2 Analysis. As hinted at by the terms "booster" and "stopper," analysis of static heuristic data may be as simple as weighting each heuristic's value and summing the results. If the sum passes some threshold, then the input is deemed to be infected.

   More elaborate methods of data analysis might use neural networks, expert systems, or data mining techniques.[129]

Signatures of suspicious code will most likely be chosen by expert anti-virus researchers. This process can be automated, however, at least for some restricted domains: IBM researchers automatically found static heuristic signatures for BSIs. They took two corpuses of boot blocks, one exclusively containing BSIs, one with no infections. A computer found trigrams – sequences of three bytes – which appeared frequently in the BSI corpus but not in the other corpus. Finally, they computed a 4-cover such that each BSI had at least four of the found BSI trigrams. After this process, they were left with a set of only fifty trigrams to look for. The presence or absence of these trigrams was used to classify a boot block as infected or not.[130]

Static heuristics may be viewed as a way to reduce the resource requirements of anti-virus scanners. Full virus signatures in a virus database can be distilled down to a set of short, generic, static heuristic signatures. (The distillation may even be done automatically, using the IBM technique just described.) An anti-virus scanner can look for these short signatures, loading in their associated set of full virus signatures only if a match is found. This alleviates the need to keep full signatures in memory.[131]

4.1.3   Integrity Checkers

With the exception of companion viruses, viruses operate by changing files. An *integrity checker* exploits this behavior to find viruses, by watching for unauthorized changes to files.[132]

Integrity checkers must start with a perfectly clean, 100% virus-free system; it is impossible to understate this. The integrity checker initially computes and stores a checksum for each file in the system it's watching. Later, a file's checksum is recomputed and compared against the original, stored checksum. If the checksums are different, then a change to the file occured.

There are three types of integrity checker:

1 Offline. Checksums are only verified periodically, e.g., once a week.

2 Self-checking. Executable files are modified to check themselves when run. Ironically, modifying executables to self-check their integrity involves

virus-like mechanisms. Self-checking can be done in a less-obtrusive way by adding the self-checking code into shared libraries.

In general, anti-virus software will perform integrity self-checking,[133] regardless of the anti-virus technique it uses. The allure of attacking anti-virus software is too great to ignore.

3 Integrity shells. An executable file's checksum is verified immediately prior to execution. This can be incorporated into the operating system kernel for binary executable files; the ideal positioning is less clear for other types of "executable" files, like batch files, shell scripts, and scripting language programs.

As Section 4.3 explains, integrity checkers have a long list of drawbacks, and are not suitable as the only means of anti-virus protection for a system.

4.2 Detection: Dynamic Methods

Dynamic anti-virus techniques decide whether or not code is infected by running the code and observing its behavior.

4.2.1 Behavior Monitors/Blockers

'Interestingly, viruses are detected now (and always have been) by behavioral recognition. Unfortunately, the customers are the ones who have been forced to perform this function.'   – Paul Schmehl[134]

A *behavior blocker* is anti-virus software which monitors a running program's behavior in real time, watching for suspicious activity. If such activity is seen, the behavior blocker can prevent the suspect operations from succeeding, can terminate the program, or can ask the user for the appropriate action to perform. Behavior blockers are sometimes called *behavior monitors*, but the latter term implies (rightly or wrongly) that no action is taken, and the burglars are only watched while they steal the silver.

What does a behavior blocker look for? Roughly speaking, a behavior blocker watches for a program to stray from what the blocker considers to be "normal" behavior. Normal behavior can be modeled in three ways, by describing:[135]

1 The actions that are permitted. This is called *positive detection*.

2 The actions that are not permitted, called *negative detection*.

3 Some combination of the two, in much the same way that static heuristics included boosters and stoppers.

An analogy can be drawn with natural immune systems, because behavior blockers are trying to discern *self* from *nonself*, or normal from anomalous

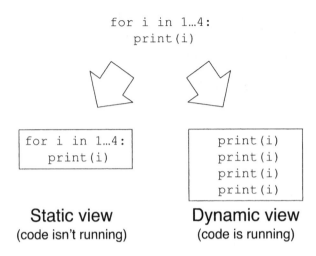

Figure 4.11. Static vs. dynamic

behavior. This is the same thing that immune systems need to do to distinguish normal cells from foreign invaders.[136] Care must be taken, however, because anomalous behavior does not automatically imply viral behavior.

The actions examined by behavior blockers do not need to include every instruction executed; they need only include actions of interest for virus detection. For example, most virus activity eventually needs to call some system functionality, like I/O operations – only these actions have to be considered. No matter how obfuscated the I/O calls are statically, the calls will appear clearly when the code runs.[137] This is a major benefit enjoyed by dynamic types of analysis like behavior blocking.

If each action that code performs is thought of as a symbol in a string, then behavior blockers can be seen to be looking for dynamic signatures instead of the static signatures used by static anti-virus techniques. (The same search algorithms can be used for dynamic signatures, but the "input string" is dynamically generated.) The difference is shown in Figure 4.11. Other ideas carry over from static techniques, too. Behavior blockers can look for short dynamic signatures which are generally indicative of virus-like behavior. Looking at I/O actions, for instance, an appending virus might exhibit a dynamic signature like:

1 Opening an executable, with both read and write permission.

2 Reading the portion of the file header containing the executable's start address.

3 Writing the same portion of the file header. (The start address can be checked separately for changes consistent with expected viral behavior.)

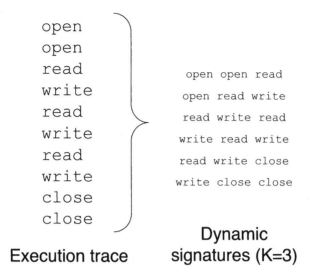

```
open
open
read
write
read
write
read
write
close
close
```

open open read
open read write
read write read
write read write
read write close
write close close

Execution trace

**Dynamic
signatures (K=3)**

Figure 4.12. From execution trace to dynamic signatures

4 Seeking to the end of the file.

5 Appending to the file.

Variations on this dynamic signature are obviously possible, and those variants can be enumerated and watched for too. Generic, dynamic signatures like these can be produced by human anti-virus experts.

Dynamic signatures specific to a given piece of code may be found automatically that characterize permitted actions for the code. The code is run and profiled before it becomes infected, watching the actions the code performs. To produce dynamic signatures of length K, the stream of actions is examined through a window of size K, saving all unique combinations of actions (Figure 4.12 is an example for $K = 3$); those are the code's dynamic signatures for normal behavior, which are recorded in a database. When the same code is run later, the same process is repeated, but this time the actions within the window are looked up in the database, to ensure that they were previously seen. Too many new action sequences indicate abnormal behavior. In practice, using system calls (without parameters) as actions, and a value of $K = 10$, this scheme was seen to work well for several Unix system programs.[138]

False positives from behavior blockers can be mitigated by taking context information into account. A notion of "ownership" is especially useful in this regard, because it gives applications a lot of leeway in terms of the behaviors they can exhibit when working with their files.[139] Web browsers maintain a cache of previously-downloaded data, for example. Web browsers also clear out their caches periodically, without warning, and a mass deletion of files looks more than a little bit like something that a virus would do. A behavior blocker that tracked the cache files' creation would know that they "belong" to the web browser, and so the file deletion is probably legitimate.

This file deletion example serves to illustrate a common criticism leveled at behavior blockers: the code whose behavior is being monitored is actually running. Any bad effects like file deletion that the behavior blocker doesn't prevent are allowed to proceed unchecked. A general, system-wide "undo" facility can alleviate some of these concerns by increasing the time window which the behavior blocker has to detect viral behavior without ill effect.[140] Not all operations can be undone, such as anything transmitting information outside the machine. A short-term undo ability for some asynchronous operations, like sending email, can be implemented by introducing a transmission delay in sending email to a remote machine.[141]

Finally, there is the question of how long a running program's behavior should be monitored. The duration of monitoring is a concern because monitoring adds run-time overhead. Assuming most viruses will reveal themselves early when an infected program runs, programs only need to be monitored when they start. However, this assumption is not always valid. In any case, behavior blockers can be enabled and disabled for a running program as needed.

4.2.2 Emulation

Behavior blocking allowed code to run on the real machine. In contrast, anti-virus techniques using *emulation* let the code being analyzed run in an emulated environment. The hope is that, under emulation, a virus will reveal itself. Because any virus found wouldn't be running on the real computer, no harm is done.

Emulation can be applied two ways, although the boundary between them is admittedly fuzzy:

Dynamic heuristics *Dynamic heuristics* are exactly the same as static heuristics. The only difference is in how the data is gathered: dynamic heuristic analysis gathers its data from the emulator about the code being analyzed. The analysis is done the same way as it is for static heuristics.

Dynamic heuristics can look for the same features as behavior blockers too, like system calls. The emulator is a safe virtual environment in which to monitor running code, however, and emulation doesn't run the code to completion. Dynamic heuristics can be used effectively to spot the dynamic signatures of metamorphic viruses.[142]

Generic decryption For polymorphic viruses, the decryptor loop can be very hard for anti-virus software to spot. *Generic decryption* skirts this issue by relying on the virus' own decryptor loop to decrypt the virus body. Once decrypted, the virus body can be detected using normal scanning methods.[143] This makes exact identification possible for known polymorphic viruses.

Generic decryption uses heuristics to determine when a virus has decrypted itself.[144] For example, the virus may try to execute an instruction which resides in a previously-modified (i.e., decrypted) memory location. Another indicator is the apparent size of the decryption, although this amount will vary with the architecture. On Intel x86 platforms, 24 bytes or more of modified/decrypted memory is a promising sign of decryption. A series of boosters followed by some stoppers is yet another indication that decryption is complete.

Besides heuristics, an emulator can scan memory for signatures periodically during emulation, and upon completion of the emulation.[145]

The rest of this section discusses the parts of an emulator, reasons to re-run the emulator, and ways to optimize emulation.

4.2.2.1 Emulator Anatomy

One way to execute code in a controlled way is to single-step through the code. Code could arguably be "emulated" this way.[146] However, single-stepping can be easily detected by a virus, and there is always the danger of a virus running in a non-virtual environment escaping. A more elaborate emulation mechanism is needed.

Conceptually, an emulator has five parts:[147]

1 CPU emulation.

2 Memory emulation. The full scope of the memory emulator's task is daunting: 32 bits of address means that potentially 4 G of address space must be emulated. Fortunately, the emulator does not run enough of the code's instructions for that much emulated memory to be chewed up.

   For generic decryption, as mentioned above, the memory emulator will need to keep track of how much memory has been modified, and where it is. This is not only useful for deciding if the decryptor loop has finished. Later scanner operation can be limited to the areas of memory which the suspected virus has modified.

3 Hardware and operating system emulation. Real operating system code isn't used in an emulator, but rather a stripped-down mock-up of it. Why? There are four reasons:[148]

   ▪ Copyright and licensing issues with the real operating system code.

   ▪ Size – the real operating system consumes a lot of memory and disk space.

- Startup time. The overhead is too great to boot an operating system in the emulator (or restore a snapshot) for *every* program being emulated.

- The emulator needs monitoring capability which isn't present in a real operating system.

Many operating system calls in an emulator will return faked, fixed values.

For hardware emulation, the parts typically used by viruses must be emulated, such as timers that a virus might use to generate random numbers. The low-level disk interface would have once been important to emulate, but any code now talking to that interface directly is probably up to no good.

4 Emulation controller. When does emulation stop? No attempt is made to run code being analyzed to completion (with the exception of running code in an anti-virus lab). There are two reasons for this. First, time spent emulating is time the user isn't getting any response from the program being analyzed. Second, some code never finishes; application programs run until the user tells them to quit, and network servers are meant to run indefinitely. This is related to the famous Halting Problem in computer science, which says that it is not possible in general for one program to decide if another program will ever stop running.

In practice, the emulation controller will use rules and heuristics to decide when to stop emulation. Some example rules are:

- The number of instructions emulated. The exact values are architecture-dependent, and the maximum thresholds will increase with increases in computer power. On an Intel x86, less than 1000 instructions usually need to be emulated; emulation times start becoming prohibitive at about the 30,000 instruction mark.[149]

- The amount of time spent emulating. One anti-virus' default setting is 45 seconds.

- The proportion of instructions that modify memory. Too low a proportion can mean non-viral code, or a virus which isn't encrypted.[150]

Heuristically, the emulation controller could watch for stoppers, things that viruses normally wouldn't do. For instance, most viruses won't perform output prior to decrypting.

5 Extra analyses. The emulator may gather additional data during emulation which can be used for additional, post-emulation analyses. For example, a histogram can be maintained of executed instructions which are typical of virus decryption. This can be used to find well-obscured polymorphic viruses. A histogram can also be used to detect metamorphic viruses by comparing the emulation histogram to histograms of known metamorphic viruses.[151]

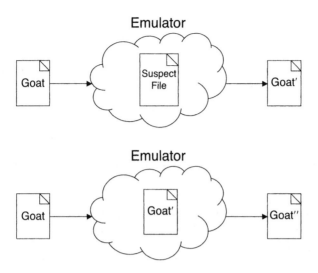

Figure 4.13. Herding goats

4.2.2.2   If at First You Don't Succeed

The emulation controller may re-invoke the emulator for a variety of reasons:

- Virus code may have results which are specific to a certain CPU and its properties. For example, self-modifying virus code may rely on how a particular CPU fetches its instructions, or instructions may be used which only work on a specific CPU. The emulator may need to be re-run with different CPU parameters.[152]

- If a virus is observed to install interrupt handlers, the emulator can be run on those handlers to test their behavior.[153]

- Some viruses do not take control at the usual entry point of an infected program, and instead have multiple entry points. The emulator can be run on each possible virus entry point.[154]

- The ability of a suspected virus to self-replicate can be confirmed using goat files.[155]

  A *goat* file is a "sacrificial" file that can be used as a decoy, where any modifications to the goat file indicate illicit activity. A goat file with known properties can also be used to deduce information about a virus.

  The goat file in Figure 4.13 is an executable which in this case simply exits without performing any I/O. The goat file is fed to a suspected virus inside the emulator. If the goat file is modified, then the emulator is re-run, feeding the original goat file to the modified goat file. An attempt to modify the original goat file must now indicate a virus, because self-replication has been demonstrated.

- One problem with emulation is that viral behavior may be (deliberately) sporadic, only manifesting itself under certain conditions, like a time-based trigger.

  The code for these viral behaviors is usually run or not run based on the result of a conditional branch in the virus' code. The emulator can watch for untaken branches that could signal this, and queue up the untaken branches along with an approximate machine state for each: register contents, program counter and stack pointer values, and some contents of the top of the stack. After the main emulation is done, the emulator can be re-run on the queued branches to try and flush out hidden behavior.[156]

- A related use of re-running the emulator is watching for unused memory areas in the virus which may be instructions. (The instructions could be executed through a mechanism which the emulator didn't discover.) The emulation controller can heuristically set a "virus region" of memory, and watch for parts of it that aren't executed during the main emulation. Later, a machine state can be guessed at, such as setting all the register contents to zero, and the emulator can try to run the unused memory areas.[157]

4.2.2.3   Emulator Optimizations

"Optimization" is a broad term. Emulator optimizations can address emulator size and complexity, as well as being used to improve emulator performance.

- Instead of emulating real filesystems, the emulator can *use* real filesystems.[158] Disk reads can be passed through to the real disk, and any disk writes can be stored in the emulator and not written through to the disk. Naturally, subsequent reads of changed information would return the copy stored in the emulator. This optimization reduces emulator size, complexity, and startup time.

- Data files may be emulated as though they contained code, because a virus may conceivably hide there. Code that makes extensive use of uninitialized registers is often an indication of a legitimate data file. This heuristic can be used to stop the emulator early.[159]

- A cache can be kept of previous emulator states, where a cached state record may include:[160]

  - the register contents;
  - the program counter's value;

- instructions around the memory location where the program counter points;
- the stack pointer;
- stack contents around where the stack pointer points;
- the size of the emulated file;
- the number of memory writes done by the emulated code;
- the number of memory bytes changed by the emulated code;
- a checksum of the data written to memory.

The emulator is run for some relatively small number of instructions: 400–1000 on an Intel x86. Normally the emulator would be paused here anyway, because if no decryption activity had been detected by this time, any virus would be assumed to be unencrypted, and the emulation controller could begin normal virus scanning.

A state record is constructed at this point, and the state cache is searched. A cache hit signifies that the code has been emulated previously and declared virus-free, so emulation may stop here. Otherwise, emulation resumes and continues to its normal termination. If the code is still deemed to be clean, the constructed state record is added to the state record cache for later. The net effect is a speed improvement, because emulation can be stopped early for previously-emulated code.

4.3 Comparison of Anti-Virus Detection Techniques

This chapter has presented a wide range of anti-virus techniques, each with relative strengths and weaknesses. No one technique is best for detecting every type of virus, and a combination of techniques is the most secure design.

Scanning

- Pro: Gives precise identification of any viruses that are found. This characteristic makes scanning useful by itself, as well as in conjunction with other anti-virus techniques.
- Con: Requires an up-to-date database of virus signatures for scanning to be effective. Even assuming that users update their virus databases right away, which isn't the case, there is a delay between the time when a new threat is discovered and when an anti-virus company has a signature update ready. This leaves open a window of opportunity in which systems can be compromised. Also, scanning only finds known viruses, and some minor variants of them.

Static heuristics

- Pro: Static heuristic analysis detects both known and unknown viruses.
- Con: False positives are a major problem, and a detected virus is neither identified, nor disinfectible except by using generic methods.

Integrity checkers

- Pro: Integrity checkers boast high operating speeds and low resource requirements. They detect known and unknown viruses.[161]
- Con: Detection only occurs *after* a virus has infected the computer, and the source of the infection can't necessarily be pinpointed. An integrity checker can't detect viruses in newly-created files, or ones modified legitimately, such as through a software update. Ultimately, the user will be called upon to assess whether a change to a file was made legitimately or not. Finally, found viruses can't be identified or disinfected.

Behavior blockers

- Pro: Known and unknown viruses are detected.[162]
- Con: While a behavior blocker knows which executable is the problem, unlike an integrity checker, it again cannot identify or disinfect the virus. Run-time overhead and false positives are a concern, as is the fact that the virus is already running on the system prior to being detected.

Emulation

- Pro: Any viruses found are running in a safe environment. Known and unknown viruses are detected, even new polymorphic viruses.[163]
- Con: Emulation is slow. The emulator may stop before the virus reveals itself, and even so, precise emulation is very hard to get correct. The usual concerns about identification and disinfection apply to emulation, too.

In general, dynamic methods impose a run-time overhead for monitoring that is not incurred by static methods. The tradeoff is that dynamic methods, by watching code run, effectively peel away a layer of obfuscation from viral code.

4.4   Verification, Quarantine, and Disinfection

Once a virus is detected, few people will want to have it remain on their computer. The tasks for anti-virus software that lie beyond detection are verification, quarantine, and disinfection. Compared to detection, these three tasks are performed rarely, and can be much slower and more resource-intensive if necessary.[164]

4.4.1 Verification

Virus detection usually doesn't provide the last word as to whether or not code is infected. Anti-virus software will often perform a secondary verification after the initial detection of a virus occurs.

Verification is performed for two reasons. First, it is used to reduce false positives that might happen by coincidence, or by the use of short or overly general signatures. Second, verification is used to positively identify the virus. Identification is normally necessary for disinfection, and to prevent being led astray; virus writers will sometimes deliberately make their virus look like another one. In the absence of verification, anti-virus software can misidentify the virus and do unintentional damage to the system when cleaning up after the wrong virus.

Verification may begin by transforming the virus so as to make more information available. One way to accomplish this, when an encrypted virus is suspected, is for the anti-virus software to try decrypting the virus body to reveal a larger signature. This process is called *X-raying*.[165] For emulation-based anti-virus software, X-raying is a natural side effect of operation.

X-raying may be automated in easier ways than emulation, if some simplifying assumptions are allowed. A virus using simple encryption or a static encryption key (with or without random encryption keys) does not hide the frequency with which encrypted bytes occur; these encryption algorithms preserve the frequency of values that was present in the unencrypted version. Cryptanalysts were taking advantage of frequency analysis to crack codes as early as the 9th century CE,[166] and the same principle applies to virus decryption.[167] Normal, uninfected executables (i.e., the plaintext) tend to have frequently-repeated values, like zeroes. Under the assumptions above, if the most frequently-occurring plaintext value is known, then the most frequently-occurring values in an encrypted version of code (ciphertext) should correspond to it. For example, say that 99 is the most frequent value in plaintext, and 27 is most frequent in the ciphertext. For XOR-based encryption, the key must be 120 (99 xor 27).

Back to verification, once all information is made available, verification may be done in a number of ways:[168]

- Comparing the found virus to a known copy of the virus. Shipping viruses with anti-virus software would be rather unwise, making this option only suitable for use in anti-virus labs.

- Using a virus-specific signature, for detection methods that aren't signature-based to begin with. If the initial detection was signature-based, then a longer signature can be used for verification.

- Checksumming all or part of the suspected virus, and comparing the computed checksum to the known checksum of that virus.

- Calling special-purpose code to do the verification, which can be written in a general-purpose or domain-specific programming language.

Except for special-purpose code, these are not viable solutions for metamorphic viruses, because they rely on the (unencrypted) virus body being the same for each infection.

4.4.2   Quarantine

When a virus is detected in a file, anti-virus software may need to *quarantine* the infected file, isolating it from the rest of the system.[169] Quarantine is only a temporary measure, and may only be done until the user decides how to handle the file (e.g., giving approval to disinfect it). In other cases, the anti-virus software may have generically detected a virus, but have no idea how to clean it. Here, quarantine may be done until an anti-virus update is available that can deal with the virus that was discovered.

Quarantine can simply be a matter of copying the infected file into a distinct "quarantine" directory, removing the original infected file, and disabling all permission to access the infected file. The problem is that the file permissions may be easily changed by a user, and files may be copied out of a quarantine directory in a virulent form. A good solution limits further spread by accident, or casual copying, but shouldn't be elaborate, as accessing the infected file for disinfection will still be necessary.

One solution is to encrypt quarantined files by some trivial means, like an XOR with a constant. The virus is thereby rendered inert, because an executable file encrypted this way will no longer be runnable, and copying the file does no harm. Also, an encrypted, quarantined file is readily accessible for disinfection.

Another solution is to render the files in the quarantine directory invisible – what can't be seen can't be copied. Anti-virus software can accomplish this feat using file-hiding techniques like stealth viruses and rootkits use. However, this may not be the best idea, as viruses may then try to hide in the quarantine directory, letting the anti-virus software cloak their presence. There could also be issues with false positives produced by virus-like behavior from anti-virus software.[170]

4.4.3   Disinfection

Disinfection does *not* mean that an infected system has been restored to its original state, even if the disinfection was successful.[171] In some cases, like overwriting viruses that don't preserve the original contents, disinfection is just not possible.

As with everything else anti-virus, there are different ways to do disinfection:

- Restore infected files from backups. Because everyone meticulously keeps backups of their files, the affected files can be restored to their backed-up state. Some files are meant to change, like data files, and consequently restoring these files may result in data loss. There are also viruses called *data diddlers*, which are viruses whose payload slowly changes files.[172] By the time a data diddler has been detected, it can have made many subtle changes, and those changed files – not the original ones – would have been caught on the backups.

- Virus-specific. Anti-virus software can encode in its database the information necessary to disinfect each known virus. Many viruses share characteristics, like relocating an executable's start address, so in many cases disinfection is a matter of invoking generic disinfection subroutines with the correct parameters.[173]

  Virus-specific information needed for disinfection can be derived automatically by anti-virus researchers, at least for relatively simple viruses. Goat files with different properties can be deliberately infected, and the resulting corpus of infected files can be compared to the originals. This comparison can reveal where a virus puts itself in an infected file, how the virus gets control, and where any relocated bytes from the original file may be found.[174] This can be likened to a chosen-plaintext attack in cryptography.[175]

- Virus-behavior-specific. Rather than customize disinfection to individual viruses, disinfection can be attempted based on assumptions about viral behavior. For prepending viruses, or appenders that gain control by modifying the program header, disinfection is a matter of: restoring the original program header; moving the original file contents back to their original location.

  Anti-virus software can store some information in advance for each executable file on an uninfected system which can be used later for disinfection.[176] The necessary information to store is the program header, the file length, and a checksum of the executable file's contents *sans* header. This disinfection technique integrates well with integrity checkers, since integrity checkers store roughly the same information anyway.

  For an infected file, the saved program header can be immediately restored. The tricky part is determining where the original file contents reside, because a prepending virus may have shifted them from their original location in the file. The disinfector knows the checksum of the original file contents, however – it can iterate over the infected file, checksumming the same number of bytes as were used for the original checksum (the uninfected file length minus the header length). If the new checksum matches the stored checksum, then the original file contents have been located and can be

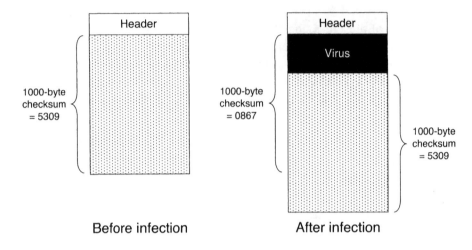

Figure 4.14. Disinfection using checksums

restored. This is shown in Figure 4.14. The number of checksum iterations needed in the worst case is equivalent to the added length of the virus, the difference between the lengths of the infected and uninfected files.

This method naturally enjoys several built-in safety checks which guard against situations where this disinfection method is inapplicable. The computed virus length can be checked for too-small, or even negative, values. Failure to match the stored checksum in the prescribed number of iterations also flags inapplicability.

- Using the virus' code:

    - Stealth viruses happily supply the uninfected contents of a file. Anti-virus software can exploit this to disinfect a stealth virus by simply asking the virus for the file's contents.[177]

    - *Generic disinfection* methods assume that the virus will eventually restore and jump to the code it infected. A generic disinfector executes the virus under controlled conditions, watching for the original code to be restored by the virus on the disinfector's behalf.[178]

        * One anti-virus system stepped through the viral code in a real, not emulated, environment. The system ran harmless-looking instructions, skipping potentially harmful ones until the virus jumped back to the original code. This turned out to be a dangerous approach, and virus writers eventually found ways to trick the disinfector.[179]

        * The infected code can be emulated until the virus jumps to the original code. The obvious way to do this is to have the emulator's controller heuristically watch for the jump.

A minor variant allows anti-virus disinfection code to run *inside* the emulator along with the infected code. The disinfection code can then be in native code and yet be portable (subject to the emulator's own portability). As needed, the virus' code can be called by the disinfection code, and the emulator can sport an interface by which the in-emulator disinfection code can export a clean version of the file.

Cruder disinfection can be done by zeroing out the virus, or simply deleting the infected file.[180] This will eradicate the virus, but won't restore the system at all.[7]

4.5 Virus Databases and Virus Description Languages

Up to now, the existence of a virus database for anti-virus software has been assumed but not discussed. Conceptually, a virus database is a database containing records, one for every known virus. When a virus is detected using a known-virus detection method, one side effect is to produce a virus identifier. This virus identifier may not be the virus' name, or even be human-readable, but can be used to index into the virus database and find the record corresponding to the found virus.[181]

A virus record will contain all the information that the anti-virus software requires to handle the virus. This may include:

- A printable name for the virus, to display for the user.

- Verification data for the virus. Again, a copy of the entire virus would not be present; the last section discussed other ways to perform verification.

- Disinfection instructions for the virus.

Any virus signatures stored in the database must be carefully handled. Why? Figure 4.15 illustrates a potential problem with virus databases, when more than one anti-virus program is present on a system. If virus signatures are stored in an unencrypted form, then one anti-virus program may declare another vendor's virus database to be infected, because it can find a wealth of virus signatures in the database file! The safest strategy is to encrypt stored virus signatures, and never to decrypt them. Instead, the input data being checked for a signature can be similarly encrypted, and the signature check can compare the encrypted forms.[182]

As new viruses are discovered, an anti-virus vendor will update their virus database, and all their users will require an updated copy of the virus database in order to be properly protected against the latest threats. This raises a number of questions:

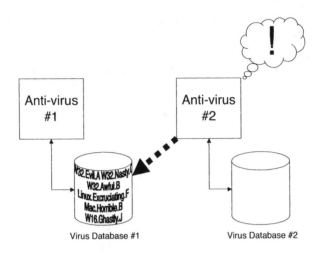

Figure 4.15. Problem with unencrypted virus databases

- How is a user informed of updates? The typical model is that users periodically poll the anti-virus vendor for updates. The polling is done automatically by the anti-virus software, although a user can manually force an update to occur. Another model is referred to as a *push model*, where the anti-virus vendor "pushes out" updates to users as soon as they are available. Many vendors use the polling model, but will email alerts about new threats to users upon request, permitting them to make an informed choice about updating.

- Should updates be manual or automatic? Automatic updates have the potential to provide current known-virus protection for users as soon as possible. Currency aside, some machines are not aggressively maintained by their users. Automatic updates are not always the best choice, however. Anti-virus software, like any software, can have bugs. It is rare, but possible, for a database update to cause substantial headaches for users because of this. In one case, a buggy update caused the networks of some Japanese railway, subway, and media organizations to be inaccessible for hours.[183]

- How often should updates be done? Frequency of updates is in part a reflection of the rate at which new threats appear. Once upon a time, monthly updates would have been sufficient; now, weekly and daily updates may not be often enough.

- How should updates be distributed? Electronic distribution of updates, especially via the Internet, is the only viable means to disseminate frequent updates. This means that anti-virus vendors must have infrastructures for distributing updates that are able to withstand heavy load – a highly-publicized threat may cause many users to update at the same time.

The update process is an attractive target for attackers. It is something that is done often by users, and compromising updates would create a huge pool of vulnerable machines. The compromise may occur in a number of ways:

- The vendor's machines that distribute the update may be attacked.

- An update may be compromised at the vendor *before* reaching the distribution machines. Anti-virus vendors are amply protected internally from malware, but an inside threat is always possible.

- A user machine may be spoofed, so that it connects to an attacker's machine instead of the vendor's machines.

- A "man-in-the-middle" attack may be mounted, where an attacker is able to intercept communications between the user and vendor. An attacker may modify the real update, or inject their own update into the communications channel.

There is also the practical matter of what form the update will take. Transmitting a fresh copy of the entire virus database is not feasible due to the bandwidth demands it would place on the vendor's update infrastructure, not to mention the comparatively limited bandwidth that many users have.

The virus database will have a relatively small number of changes between updates, so instead of sending the entire database, a vendor can just send the changes to the database. These changes are sometimes called *deltas*.[184] Furthermore, these deltas can be compressed to try and make them smaller still. Downloaded deltas should be verified to protect against attacks and transmission errors.

The update mechanism can also be used to update the anti-virus engine itself, not just the virus database.[185] This may be necessary to fix bugs, or add functionality required to detect new viruses. Known-virus scanners will need their data structures updated with the latest signatures as well.

Clearly, the information in the virus database and other updates from an anti-virus vendors must come from someplace. Anti-virus vendors often have an in-house *virus description language*, a domain-specific language designed to describe viruses, and how to detect, verify, and disinfect each one.[186] Two examples are given in Figure 4.16. Anti-virus researchers create descriptions such as these, and a compiler for the virus description language translates them into the virus database format.

Domain-specific languages tend to be very good at describing things in their domain, but not very good for general use. Virus description languages can have escape mechanisms to call code written in a general-purpose language,

VERV description

```
VIRUS example                          ; short alias for virus
NAME  An example virus                 ; full virus name
LOAD  S-EXE 0000 0500                  ; load bytes 0-500 from .EXE entry point
DEXOR1    0100 0500 0035 0000          ; XOR bytes 100-500 with key at byte 35
ZERO      0035 0001                    ; set key at byte 35 to zero
CODE      0000 0500 4a4f484e           ; is checksum of bytes 0-500 = 4a4f484e?
```

CVDL description

```
; looks for two words in virus' data
:example,"painfully" AND "contrived",#
```

Figure 4.16. Example virus descriptions

code which is compiled and either interpreted or run natively.[187] This allows special-purpose code to be written for detection, verification, or disinfection.

Special-purpose code can be used to direct the entire virus detection, instead of only being invoked when needed. For example, for viruses which have multiple entry points, special-purpose code can tell a scanner what locations it should scan.[188]

4.6   Short Subjects

To conclude this chapter, a veritable potpourri of short topics: anti-stealth techniques, macro virus detection, and the role of compiler optimization in anti-virus detection.

4.6.1   Anti-Stealth Techniques

One assumption made up to this point is that anti-virus software sees an accurate picture of the data being checked for viruses. But what if a virus is using stealth to hide?

Anti-stealth techniques are countermeasures used against stealth viruses. There are two options:

1 Detect and disable the stealth mechanism. For example, calls to the operating system can be examined to make sure they're going to the "right" place. Section 5.5 looks at this in more depth.

2 Bypass the usual mechanisms to call the operating system in favor of unsubvertible ones. For Unix, this would mean that anti-virus software only uses direct system calls (assuming, of course, that the operating system kernel is secure); for MS-DOS systems, this could mean making direct BIOS calls to get disk data.

4.6.2 Macro Virus Detection

Macro viruses present some interesting problems for anti-virus software.[189] Macros are in source form, and are easy to change and allow a lot of freedom with formatting. Macro language interpreters can be extremely robust in terms of bullishly continuing execution in the face of errors; a missing or damaged macro won't necessarily keep a macro virus from operating. Some specific problems with macro viruses:

- Accidental or deliberate changes to a macro virus, even to its formatting, may create a new macro virus. This may even happen automatically: Microsoft Word converts documents from one version of Word to another, and this conversion has created new macro viruses in the process.

- Bugs in macro virus propagation, or incomplete disinfection of a macro virus, can create new macro virus variants. Anti-virus software can accidentally create viruses if it's not careful!

- A macro virus can accidentally "snatch" macros from an environment it infects, becoming a new virus. In one case, a Word macro virus even swiped two macros from Microsoft's software that protects against macro viruses.[190]

Macro viruses, despite these problems, have one redeeming feature.[191] Macros operate in a restricted domain, so anti-virus detection can determine what constitutes "normal" behavior with a very high degree of confidence. This limits the number of false positives that might otherwise be incurred by detection.

All of the same ideas have been trotted out for macro viruses as have been used for other types of virus, including signature scanning, static heuristics, behavior blocking, and emulation.[192] Due to variability in formatting, methods looking for static signatures are facilitated by removing whitespace and comments, or translating it into some equivalent canonical form first.[8] A similar need for canonicalization arises from macro languages which aren't case sensitive, where foo, FOO, and Foo would all refer to the same variable.[193]

More systemic approaches to macro virus detection periodically examine documents on a system, and build a database of the documents and their properties.[194] In particular, macros in documents can be tracked; the sudden appearance of macros in a document, a change to known macros in a document, or a number of documents with the same changes to their macros are all signals that a macro virus may be active.

Macro viruses have not been parasitic, meaning they have not inserted viral code into legitimate code, but have acted more like companion viruses.[195] (Nothing prevents macro viruses from being parasitic; it's just slightly more effort to implement.) Disinfection strategies for macro viruses have consequently tended towards deletion-based approaches:

- Delete *all* macros in the infected document, including any unfortunate, legitimate user macros.

- Delete macros known to be associated with the virus found. This requires a known-macro-virus database.

- For macro viruses detected using heuristics, remove the macros found to contain the offending behavior.[196]

- Emulator-based detection can track the macros seen to be used by the macro virus and delete them.[197]

Applications supporting macros treat macros in a much more guarded fashion than they once did, and macro viruses are a much less prominent threat than they have been as a result.[198]

4.6.3   Compiler Optimization

Compiler techniques have natural overlaps with anti-virus detection. For example, some scanning algorithms are applied to match patterns in trees, for code generation;[199] scanning and parsing are needed for macro virus detection; work on efficient interpretation is applicable to emulation, and interpreting special-purpose code in the anti-virus engine.

One suggestion which rears its head occasionally is the possibility of using compiler optimizations for detection of viruses. Given that a number of compiler optimization techniques perform some sophisticated analyses, it isn't surprising to consider applying them to the problem of virus detection:

- *Constant propagation* replaces variables which are defined as constants with the constants themselves. This increases the information available about code being analyzed, and facilitates other optimizations. With the code below, constant propagation yields the name of the file being opened:

```
file = "c:\autoexec.bat"              file = "c:\autoexec.bat"
     ...                      ⇒           ...
f = open(file)                        f = open("c:\autoexec.bat")
```

  Constant propagation has been proposed to assist in the static analysis of macro viruses.[200]

- *Dead code* is code which is executed, but the results are never used. In the code below, for example, the first assignment to r1 is dead, because its value is not used before r1 is redefined:

```
r1 = 123
r1 = r2 + 7
```

Polymorphic viruses tend to exhibit a lot of dead code – more than 25% – especially when compared to non-viral code, so dead code analysis can make a useful heuristic to help with polymorphic virus detection.[201]

However, some problems loom. Compiler optimization algorithms are not known for efficiency, with the exception of algorithms designed specifically for use in dynamic, or just-in-time, compilers. Such algorithms tend to trade speed increases for decreases in accuracy, though. It is often possible to concoct programs which exercise the worst case performance of optimization algorithms, or programs which make the task of precise analysis undecidable. Virus writers will undoubtedly take advantage of this if anti-virus' use of compiler optimization becomes widespread.

Notes for Chapter 4

1   And the rest of the quote: 'Unfortunately, this program must identify *every* (or nearly so) program as infected, whether it is or not!' [299, page 258]
2   Until the anti-virus signatures are updated or files are accessed from a non-network source, at which point a full on-demand scan would be indicated.
3   Obligatory Knuth citation: [168]. He says that the pronunciation of "trie" is "try."
4   Navarro and Raffinot [227]. "Very small" means 4–8 values, whereas scanning inputs will have 256 possible values for each input byte.
5   Unless the scan would take less effort than deciding whether or not to scan in the first place!
6   Although if this is done incorrectly, it opens the door for a brute-force attack on the session key.
7   With the exception of simple companion viruses.
8   This is obvious to compiler writers, who've been handling whitespace (and lack thereof) since compiling Fortran in the 1950s, but seemingly not so for patent examiners: Kuo [175].

100   Harley et al. [137] was used for this introductory section.
101   Cohen [74]. Harrison et al. [138] make some interesting follow-on points regarding Cohen's proof and Turing-compatibility.
102   Muttik [214].
103   Harley et al. [137].
104   Mallén-Fullerton [192] considers the case of wildcards that match one byte; Bontchev [46] takes a more general view.
105   Not surprisingly, Aho and Corasick [5]. The version of the algorithm given here is a slight reformulation of the first version of the algorithm that Aho and Corasick give in their paper.
106   Tuck et al. [324] discuss many of these implementation choices for Aho-Corasick.
107   The version here is an much-abstracted form of Veldman's algorithm. The unadulterated version is in Bontchev [46].
108   Kumar and Spafford [174] adapted Aho-Corasick for wildcards.
109   The original algorithm is described in Wu and Manber [349], and is very general; the version here is a simplification along the lines of [227, 324].
110   This section is based on [96].
111   This item is based on Bontchev [46]. Top and tail scanning, entry point scanning, and size-based scanning assumptions are also in Nachenberg [217].
112   Nachenberg [217].

113 Carr [54].

114 Unless otherwise noted, this item is based on Flint and Hughes [111].

115 Carr [54].

116 This item is based on Nachenberg [215].

117 Mallén-Fullerton [192] talks about the signature length tradeoff.

118 Muttik [214].

119 For example, Navarro and Tarhio [228].

120 For example, Pennello [245].

121 Bentley [34].

122 Gryaznov [133], Symantec [307], and Zenkin [354].

123 Gryaznov [133].

124 Symantec [307], who apply this division to static *and* dynamic heuristics.

125 The "booster" and "stopper" terminology is from Nachenberg [221], who uses them in the context of emulation.

126 Gryaznov [133].

127 Nachenberg [221].

128 Ludwig [187]; detristan et al. [89] look at spectrum analysis in the context of intrusion detection systems. Muttik [214] talks about opcode frequency analysis too. Weber et al. [342] use instruction frequencies to try and spot hand-written assembly code, on the premise that more viruses are written in assembly code than high-level languages.

129 See [318, 307, 283], respectively.

130 Tesauro et al. [318].

131 Kephart et al. [163].

132 This section is based on Bontchev [38].

133 Bontchev [46].

134 Schmehl [278].

135 The first two are from Esponda et al. [101].

136 Like the Spanish Inquisition. No one ever expects them. Oh, right: Hofmeyr et al. [143].

137 Nachenberg [216].

138 Hofmeyr et al. [143].

139 Ford and Michalske [113], who also supply the browser story.

140 Ford and Thompson [114].

141 El Far et al. [98] look at a related idea: being able to recall unread messages from a remote machine soon after transmission.

142 Jordan [154] argues this for emulation with dynamic heuristics, but of the course the argument applies equally well to behavior blockers.

143 Nachenberg [217].

144 These first two heuristics are from Nachenberg [220], the third from [221].

145 Nachenberg [222].

146 Natvig [225] and Szor [308].

147 Based on Veldman [332], who had a four-part organization.

148 This item is based on Natvig [225].

149 Nachenberg [220].

150 Nachenberg [222].

151 Nachenberg [222].

152 Nachenberg [223].

153 Chambers [59].

154 Nachenberg [219].

155 Chambers [59] and Natvig [225].

156 Chambers [59] and Nachenberg [220].

157 Nachenberg [220].

158 Natvig [225].

159 Nachenberg [221].

160 This item is based on Nachenberg [223].

161 Pros and cons from [38, 354].

162 [Dis]advantages of behavior blockers are from Zenkin [354]. A mostly-overlapping set of disadvantages is in Nachenberg [216].

163 Veldman [332] mentions emulator advantages and disadvantages.

164 Chess [64] points this out for verification.

165 Nachenberg [217]; also Perriot and Ferrie [248], who argue the use of X-raying for virus detection.

166 Al-Kadi [7].

167 Itshak et al. [151].

168 All but the second are from Chess [64].

169 This section is based on Templeton [317].

170 This solution, and one of the attendant problems, was suggested by [306].

171 Harley et al. [137].

172 Bontchev [46].

173 Nachenberg [218].

174 Chess et al. [66].

175 Schneier [279].

176 This method is from Mann [193].

177 Bontchev [46].

178 Szor [308].

179 This, and the "minor variant" below, are from Nachenberg [218].

180 Templeton [317].

181 From Kouznetsov et al., along with the virus record contents below [170].

182 Bontchev [46]. Carr [54] mentions a virus database which is compressed and encrypted.

183 Japan Times [153].

184 This, and the bandwidth problem, are from Kouznetsov and Ushakov [170].

185 Pak et al. [238].

186 For examples, see [54, 64, 238, 251, 252, 259]. The examples in Figure 4.16 use the descriptions of VERV [64] and CVDL [251, 252, 259].

187 Nachenberg [219] and Pak et al. [238].

188 Nachenberg [219].

189 These problems are from Bontchev [43].

190 See [42, 200].

191 Zenkin [354].

192 See [61, 175] (signature scanning), [61, 169] (static heuristics), [341, 354] (behavior blocking), and [69] (emulation).

193 Bontchev [43].

194 Chess et al. [65].

195 Bontchev [43], who also gives the first three disinfection methods below.

196 Chen et al. [61], who also proposed cleaning within macros by replacing detected macro virus instructions with non-viral instructions.

197 Chi [69].

198 Bontchev [45] opines on this at length.

199 Aho et al. [6].

200 Ko [169].

201 Perriot [247], who also discusses lots of other optimizations and their application to polymorphic virus detection.

Chapter 5

ANTI-ANTI-VIRUS TECHNIQUES

All viruses self-replicate, but not all viruses act in an openly hostile way towards anti-virus software. Anti-anti-virus techniques are techniques used by viruses which do one of three things:

1 Aggressively attack anti-virus software.

2 Try to make analysis difficult for anti-virus researchers.

3 Try to avoid being detected by anti-virus software, using knowledge of how anti-virus software works.

The lack of clear definitions in this field comes into play again: arguably, any of the encryption methods described in Chapter 3 is an attempt to achieve the latter two goals.

To further confuse matters, "anti-anti-virus" is different from "anti-virus virus." Anti-virus virus has been used variously to describe: a virus that attacks other viruses; anti-virus software that propagates itself through viral means; software which drops viruses on a machine, then offers to sell "anti-virus" software to remove the viruses it put there.[100]

Back to the relatively well-defined anti-anti-virus, this includes seven techniques: retroviruses, entry point obfuscation, anti-emulation, armoring, tunneling, integrity checker attacks, and avoidance.

5.1   Retroviruses

A virus that actively tries to disable anti-virus software running on an infected machine is referred to as a *retrovirus*.[1] This is a generic term for a virus employing this type of active defense, and doesn't imply that any particular technique is used.

Having said that, a common retrovirus technique is for a virus to carry a list with it of process names used by anti-virus products. When it infects a machine, a retrovirus will enumerate the currently-running processes, and kill off any processes which match one of the names in the list. A partial list is shown below:[2]

Avgw.exe
F-Prot.exe
Navw32.exe
Regedit.exe
Scan32.exe
Zonealarm.exe

It's not unusual to see lists like this appear in malware analyses. This particular list not only includes anti-virus process names, but also other security products like firewalls, and system utilities like the Windows Registry editor.

A more aggressive retrovirus can target the antivirus software on disk as well as in memory, so that antivirus protection is disabled even after the infected system is rebooted. For example, Ganda kills processes that appear to be anti-virus software, using the above list-based method; it also examines the programs run at system startup, looking for anti-virus software using the same list of names. If Ganda finds anti-virus software during this examination, it locates the executable image on disk and replaces the first instruction with a "return" instruction. This causes the anti-virus software to exit immediately after starting.[101]

The above methods have one major drawback: by killing off the anti-virus software, they leave a telltale sign. An alert user might notice the absence of the anti-virus icon.[3] For the purposes of retroviruses, it's sufficient to render anti-virus software incapable of full operation, disabling it rather than killing it off completely.

How can this be done? One approach would be to try and starve anti-virus software of CPU time. A retrovirus with appropriate permission could reduce the priority of anti-virus software to the minimum value possible, to (ideally) keep it from running.[102] Most operating system schedulers have a mechanism to boost the priority of CPU-starved processes,[4] however, so attacking anti-virus software by reducing process priority is unlikely to be very effective. Another way to disable anti-virus software is to adjust the way a computer looks up hostname information on the network, to prevent anti-virus software from being able to connect to the anti-virus company's servers and update its database.

5.2 Entry Point Obfuscation

Modifying an executable's start address, or the code at the original start address, constitutes extremely suspicious behavior for anti-virus heuristics. A virus can try to get control elsewhere instead; this is called *entry point obfuscation* or EPO.

Picking a random location in an executable to gain control isn't a brilliant survival strategy, because a infrequently-executed error handler may be chosen as easily as a frequently-executed loop. A more controlled selection of a location is better. Simile and Ganda both use EPO, and look for calls to the ExitProcess API function; these calls are overwritten to point to the viral code instead.[103] Because ExitProcess is called when a program wants to quit, these viruses get control upon the infected code's exit.

Locations for EPO may also be chosen by looking for known code sequences in executables.[104] Compilers for high-level languages emit repetitive code, and a virus can search the executable for such repetitive instruction sequences to overwrite with a jump to the virus' code. As the sequence being replaced is known, the virus can always restore and run the original instructions later.

5.3 Anti-Emulation

Techniques to avoid anti-virus emulators can be divided into three categories, based on whether they try to outlast, outsmart, or overextend the emulator. The fix for the latter two categories is just to improve the emulator, although this tends to come at the cost of increased emulator complexity.

5.3.1 Outlast

Except in an anti-virus lab, the amount of time an emulator has to spend running a program is strictly limited by the user's patience.[105] How can a virus evade detection long enough for the emulator to give up?

- Code can be added to the virus which does nothing, wasting time until the emulator quits – then the real viral code can run.[106] The emulator may look for obvious junk code, so the code would need to be disguised as a valid operation, like computing the first n digits of π.

- A virus need not replicate every time it's run. It can act benign nine times out of every ten, for example, in a statistical ploy to appear harmless 90% of the time. If the anti-virus software is using the performance-improving tricks in Section 4.2.2.3, then the virus might get lucky and have an infected program be marked as clean when emulated; a later execution of that infected program would give the virus a free hand.

- Emulators operate under the assumption that viral code will intercept execution at or near the start of an infected program. Entry point obfuscation, besides an anti-heuristic measure, can also be considered an anti-emulation technique, because it can delay execution of viral code.

5.3.2   Outsmart

An alternative to waiting until emulator scrutiny is over is to restructure the viral code so that it doesn't look suspicious when it's emulated. The decryptor code could be spread all over, instead of appearing as one tight loop; multiple decryption passes could be used to decrypt the virus body.[107] Most techniques for avoiding dynamic heuristics would be candidates here.

5.3.3   Overextend

A virus can push the boundaries of an emulator in an effort to either crash the emulator – not likely for a mature anti-virus emulator – or detect that the virus is being run under emulation, so that the virus can take appropriate (in)action. Here are some ways to try and overextend an emulator:

- Some CPUs, especially CISC ones, have undocumented instructions.[108] A virus can use these instructions in the hopes that an emulator will not support them, and thus give itself away.

- The same idea can be applied to bugs that a CPU may exhibit, or differences between different processor implementations. The emulator may need to track results that are processor-dependent to correctly emulate such a virus.

- The emulator's memory system can be exercised by trying to access unusual locations that, on a real machine, might cause a memory fault or access some memory-mapped I/O.[109] A cruder attack may simply try to exhaust an emulator's memory by accessing lots of locations. Memory system attacks are not particularly effective, however.

- Assuming emulators return fixed values for calls to many operating system and other API functions, a virus can check for differences between two calls of the same function where a change *should* occur. For example, a virus could ask for the current time twice, assuming an emulated environment will return the same value both times.

- An emulator may be taxed by importing obscure, but standard, libraries in case the emulator doesn't handle all of them.[110]

- External resources are next to impossible to properly emulate. A virus could take advantage of this by looking for external things like web pages.[111]

- Finally, checks specific to certain emulators can be performed. An emulator may only support a well-known set of I/O devices, or may have an interface to the "outside world" which can be tested for.[5]

5.4 Armoring

A virus is said to be *armored* if it uses techniques which try to make analysis hard for anti-virus researchers. In particular, *anti-debugging* methods can be used against dynamic analysis, and *anti-disassembly* methods can be used to slow static analysis. Interestingly, these techniques have been in use since at least the 1980s to guard against software piracy.[112]

5.4.1 Anti-Debugging

Making dynamic analysis a painful process for humans is the realm of anti-debugging. These techniques target peculiarities of how debuggers work.[6] This is a last gasp, though – if the viral code is already being analyzed in a debugger, then its survival time is dwindling. If the goal is to annoy the human analyst, then the best bet in survival terms is to follow a false trail when a debugger is detected, and avoid any viral behavior.[113]

There are three weak points in a debugger that can be used to detect its presence: idiosyncrasies, breakpoints, and single-stepping.

Debugger-specific idiosyncrasies. As with emulators, debuggers won't present a program being debugged with an environment identical to its normal environment, and a virus can look for quirks of known debuggers.[114]

Debugger breakpoints. Debuggers implement breakpoints by modifying the program being debugged, inserting special breakpoint instructions at points where the debugger wants to regain control. Typical breakpoint instructions cause the CPU to trap to an interrupt service routine.[115]

A virus can look for signs of debugging by being introspective: it can examine its own code for breakpoint instructions. Since the virus may use external library code where debugger breakpoints can be set, breakpoint instructions can also be looked for at the entry points to library API functions.[116]

More generally, a virus can look for *any* changes to itself. From the virus' point of view, a change is an error, and there are two distinct possibilities for dealing with errors: *error detection* and *error correction*. Error detection, like the use of checksums or CRCs, would tell the virus whether or not a change had occurred to it, and the virus could take action accordingly. On the other hand, error correction not only detects errors, but is able to repair a finite number of them. A robust virus would imply the use of error correction over error detection – this would guard against transmission errors and keep casual would-be virus writers from modifying the virus, and also be able to remove debugger breakpoint instructions.[117]

Single-stepping. Debuggers trace through code, instruction by instruction, using the single-stepping facilities available in many CPUs. After each instruction is executed, the CPU posts an interrupt which the debugger handles.

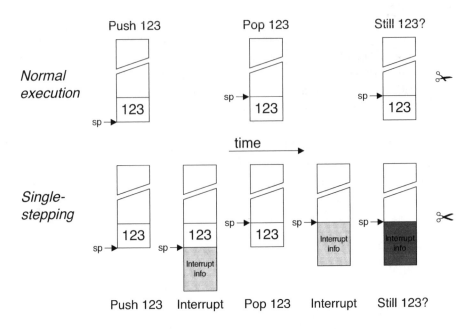

Figure 5.1. Checking for single-stepping

There are several ways to check for single-stepping:

- Push a value on the stack, pop it off, then check to see if it's still there.[7] As Figure 5.1 shows, an interrupt would dump information onto the stack, destroying the value that had been placed on there. Strictly speaking, *any* interrupt would cause this to happen, not just a single-stepping interrupt, but it is a conservative test from the virus' point of view.

- Handling interrupts is an expensive task. Sample the current time, and watch for the slowdown that would occur under single-stepping.[118]

- CPUs commonly have an instruction prefetch queue, where instructions are loaded prior to their execution for performance reasons. A virus can dynamically modify the *next* instruction immediately following the program counter; if the new instruction runs rather than the old one, then single-stepping may be enabled. Why? Because the instruction prefetch queue was flushed, which would occur on an interrupt.

The latter two methods are possible anti-emulation methods as well, because they would look for slow or incomplete emulators.

A general approach to anti-debugging is to look for changes to the addresses of interrupt handlers, and render the virus nonfunctional if the handler address is unexpected. One way to accomplish this is to include the addresses of the

```
main: e8 05 00 00 00 31 c0 8b 1d 42 58 c3 00
```

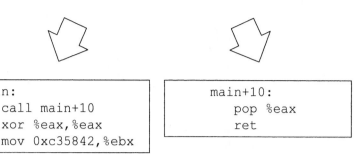

```
main:
    call main+10
    xor %eax,%eax
    mov 0xc35842,%ebx
```
False disassembly

```
main+10:
    pop %eax
    ret
```
True disassembly

Figure 5.2. False disassembly

breakpoint and single-stepping interrupt handlers as part of the virus' decryption key.[119]

And, if all else fails, ask. Windows has an API function called IsDebugger-Present which returns the calling process' debugging status. Elkern.C is one piece of malware that uses this technique.[120] The means of asking need not be direct, either. A request under Linux to trace a process more than once fails, and if a debugger has traced the virus' process already, an attempt by the virus to trace itself will fail.[121]

5.4.2 Anti-Disassembly

Any of the code obfuscation techniques used by polymorphic and metamorphic viruses are anti-disassembly techniques, but only in a weak sense. There are two goals for strong anti-disassembly:

1 Disassembly should not be easily automated; the valuable time of an expert human should be required to make sense of the code.

2 The full code should not be available until such time as the code actually runs.

To make automation difficult, a virus' code can make use of problems which are computationally very hard to solve. It turns out that the simple trick of mixing code and data is one such problem: precise separation of the two is known to be unsolvable.[122] In general, a virus may be structured so that separating code and data is also impossible – this can be done by using instructions as data values and vice versa.

A careful mix of code and data may even throw off human analysis temporarily. The x86 assembly code in Figure 5.2 starts with a subroutine call that

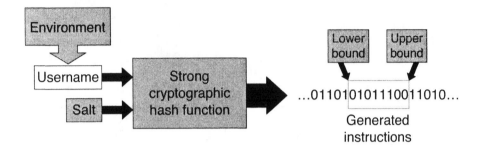

Figure 5.3. Anti-disassembly using strong cryptographic hash functions

never returns: when run, the called code pops the saved return address off the stack and returns, so the net effect of this code is the same as a single `return` instruction. However, some bytes have been placed after the call, causing a false disassembly to occur when `main` is disassembled.[8]

The second anti-disassembly goal, not having the full code available until run time, can be met in several ways:

- Code can be dynamically generated when the virus runs, much like a just-in-time (JIT) compiler.

- Existing code can modify itself as the virus runs.[9] Self-modifying code is a rarity now in typical, compiler-generated programs, and this behavior would act as a red flag for anti-virus heuristics.

- A more complex dynamic code generation scheme could draw on the execution environment for its instructions, much like the environmental key generation described in Section 3.2.7. An environmental parameter, like a username, is combined with a constant "salt" K which is chosen by the virus writer, and fed into a strong cryptographic hash function. Resulting bytes from the hash function are extracted and used as instructions. The value of K is selected to yield a desired instruction sequence when this is done. Direct analysis of this scheme is very difficult, because the viral code is not available to be analyzed and, even if an educated guess can be made about it, the strong cryptographic hash ensures that the exact value of the environmental parameter cannot be determined even when K is known. This scheme is illustrated in Figure 5.3, where the information in the shaded boxes indicates the information available to an analyst.[123]

- Keep the code in encrypted form, and decrypt parts of it only when needed.[10] Figure 5.4 shows how this can be done by inserting a breakpoint into the code immediately before an encrypted instruction, and supplying interrupt handlers for breakpoint and single-stepping interrupts.[124]

```
instruction
breakpoint
encrypted instruction
instruction
instruction
```

```
def breakpoint_handler():          def singlestep_handler():
    decrypt next instruction           re-encrypt last instruction
    enable single-stepping             disable single-stepping
    return from interrupt              return from interrupt
```

Figure 5.4. On-demand code decryption

Another suggestion is to use separate threads of execution, one to decrypt code ahead of the virus' program counter, the other to re-encrypt behind the virus' program counter.[125] This would intentionally be a delicately-tuned system, so that any variance (like that introduced by a debugger or emulator) would cause a crash, making it an anti-debugging technique too.

Anti-disassembly techniques are not solely for irritating human anti-virus researchers. They can also be seen as a defense against anti-virus software using static heuristics.

5.5 Tunneling

Anti-virus software may monitor calls to the operating system's API to watch for suspicious activity. A *tunneling* virus is one that traces through the code for API functions the virus uses, to ensure that execution will end up at the "right" place, i.e., the virus isn't being monitored. If the virus does detect monitoring, tunneling allows the monitoring to be bypassed.[126] An interesting symmetry is that the defensive technique in this case is exactly the same as the offensive technique: tracing through the API code.

The code "tracing" necessary for tunneling can be implemented by viruses in several ways,[127] all of which resemble anti-virus techniques. A static analysis method would scan through the code, looking for control flow changes. Dynamic methods would single-step through the code being traced, or use full-blown emulation.

Tunneling can only be done when the code in question can be read, obviously. For operating systems without strong memory protection between user processes and the operating system, like MS-DOS, tunneling is an effective technique. Many operating systems do distinguish between user space and kernel space, though, a barrier which is crossed by a trap-based operating system API. In other words, the kernel's code cannot be read by user processes. Surprisingly, tunneling can still be useful, because most high-level programming languages don't call the operating system directly, but call small library stubs that do the dirty work – these stubs can be tunneled into.

Anti-virus software can dodge this issue if it installs itself into the operating system kernel. (This is also a desirable goal for viruses, because a virus in the kernel would control the machine completely.)

5.6   Integrity Checker Attacks

In terms of anti-anti-virus techniques, integrity checkers warrant some careful handling, because they are able to catch *any* file change at all, not just suspicious code.[128]

Stealth viruses have a big advantage against integrity checkers. A stealth virus can hide file changes completely, so the checker never sees them. Companion viruses are effective against integrity checkers for the same reason, because no changes to the infected file are ever seen.

Stealth viruses can also infect when a file is read, so the act of computing a checksum by an integrity checker will itself infect a file. In that case, the viral code would be included in the checksum without any alarm being raised.

Similarly, a "slow" virus can infect only when a file was about to be legitimately changed anyway.[129] The infection doesn't need to be immediate, so long as any alert that the integrity checker pops up appears soon after the legitimate change; a user is likely to dismiss the alert as a false positive.

Finally, integrity checkers may have flaws that can be exploited. In one classic case, deleting the integrity checker's database of checksums caused the checker to faithfully recompute checksums for all files![11]

5.7   Avoidance

Those who admit to remembering the *Karate Kid* movies will know that the best way to avoid a punch is not to be there. The same principle applies to anti-anti-virus techniques. A virus can hide in places where anti-virus software doesn't look. If anti-virus software only checks the hard drive, infect USB keys and floppies; if anti-virus software doesn't examine all file types, infect those file types; if files with special names aren't checked, infect files with those names.[130] Unusual types of file archive formats may temporarily escape unpacking and scrutiny, too.[131] In general, avoidance is not particularly effective as a strategy, though.

Notes for Chapter 5

1 Retroviruses have also been called "anti-antivirus viruses." No, really [77].

2 This is an excerpt from Avkiller, which is actually a Trojan horse, but the name is irresistible in this context [185].

3 Although the Windows taskbar hides icons of "inactive" applications by default, so a vanishing anti-virus icon may not be noticed.

4 Windows and Unix systems, for example, both have multilevel feedback queues that operate this way [202, 294].

5 For example, VMware can be detected in a number of ways [233, 353].

6 Assuming a software-based debugger.

7 This, and the prefetch technique, are from Natvig [226]. He notes that the prefetch method's success depends upon how the CPU manages the prefetch queue.

8 Alas, this trick doesn't work as well for CPUs whose instructions need to be word-aligned in memory, but code and data can still be mixed.

9 Generally, self-modifying code can wreak havoc on static analysis tools [186].

10 grugq and scut [132] call this "running line code."

11 Proof of concept courtesy of the Peach virus [15].

100 See [149, 244], [77], and [242], respectively.

101 Molnár and Szappanos [210].

102 A student suggested this possibility, although no actual example of this technique has been found to date.

103 Analyses of Simile and Ganda can be found in Perriot et al. [249] and Molnár and Szappanos [210], respectively.

104 GriYo [131].

105 The issue of how long to emulate is mentioned in Nachenberg [217], also Szor [308].

106 See Nachenberg [217]. [314] mentions the problems of junk code and occasional replication.

107 These possibilities are from Veldman [332].

108 These first four are from Veldman [332].

109 See also Natvig [226].

110 Natvig [226] talks about library-related emulation problems.

111 Ször and Ferrie [314] point out the external resource problem.

112 See Krakowicz [172] for an early, pre-lowercase treatise on the subject.

113 Hasson [139] suggests this strategy when using anti-debugging for software protection.

114 Hasson [139] and CrackZ [81].

115 See Rosenberg [268] for more information on this and single-stepping.

116 Hasson [139].

117 Pless [254] talks about the error detection/correction distinction. The use of Hamming codes for error correction for the first two reasons is in Ferbrache [103]; RDA.Fighter uses them for anti-debugging [83].

118 CrackZ [81].

119 Stampf [302].

120 This suggestion was made by CrackZ [81]; the Elkern.C analysis is in [239].

121 Cesare [57].

122 Horspool and Marovac [146].

123 Aycock et al. [22].

124 Bontchev [46].

125 Stampf [302].

126 Bontchev [46]; Methyl [205].

127 Methyl [205].

128 This section is based on Bontchev [38].

129 Gryaznov [133].

130 The first two are from Bontchev [38], the last from Sowhat [297].

131 Hyppönen [149] notes this, along with a laundry list of anti-anti-virus techniques.

Chapter 6

WEAKNESSES EXPLOITED

Weaknesses are thin ice on the frozen lake of security, vulnerable points through which a system's security may be compromised. Thin ice doesn't always break, and not all weaknesses are exploitable. However, an examination of the devious and ingenious ways that security can be breached is enlightening.

Malware may exploit weaknesses to initially infiltrate a system, or to gain additional privileges on an already-compromised machine. The weaknesses may be exploited automatically by malware authors' creations, or manually by people directly targeting a system. In this chapter, the initiator of an exploit attempt will be generically called an "attacker."

Weaknesses fall into two broad categories, based on where the weakness lies. Technical weaknesses involve tricking the target computer, while human weaknesses involve tricking people.

6.1 Technical Weaknesses

Weaknesses in hardware are possible, but weaknesses in software are disturbingly common. After some background material, a number of frequent weaknesses are discussed, such as various kinds of buffer overflow (stack smashing, frame pointer overwriting, returns into libraries, heap overflows, and memory allocator attacks), integer overflows, and format string vulnerabilities. This is unfortunately not an exhaustive list of all possible weaknesses. At the end of this section, how weaknesses are found, and defenses to these weaknesses are examined. Where possible, weaknesses and defenses are presented in a language- and architecture-independent way.

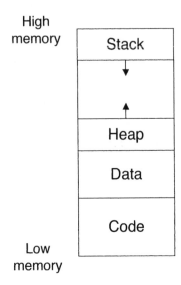

Figure 6.1. Conceptual memory layout

6.1.1   Background

Conceptually, a process' address space is divided into four "segments" as shown in Figure 6.1:[1]

- The program's code resides in the fixed-size code segment. This segment is usually read-only.

- Program data whose sizes are known at compile-time are in the fixed-size data segment.

- A "heap" segment follows the data segment and grows upwards; it also holds program data. The heap as used in this context has *nothing whatsoever* to do with a heap data structure, even though they share the name.

- A stack starts at high memory and grows downwards. In practice, the direction of stack growth depends on the architecture. Downwards growth will be assumed here for concreteness.

A variable in an imperative language, like C, C++, and Java, is allocated to a segment based on the variable's lifetime and the persistence of its data. A sample C program with different types of variable allocation is shown in Figure 6.2. Global variables have known sizes and persist throughout run-time, so they are placed into the data segment by a compiler. Space for dynamic allocation has to grow on demand; dynamic allocation is done from the heap segment. Finally, local variables don't persist beyond the return of a subroutine, and subroutine

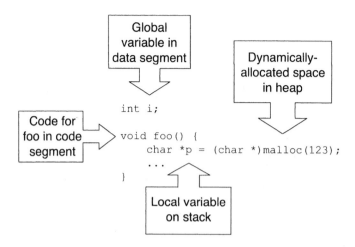

Figure 6.2. Sample segment allocation

calls within a program follow a stack discipline, so local variables are allocated space on the stack.

A subroutine gets a new copy of its local variables each time the subroutine is called. These are stored in the subroutine's *stack frame*, which can be thought of as a structure on the stack. When a subroutine is entered, space for the subroutine's stack frame is allocated on the stack; when a subroutine exits, its stack frame space is deallocated. The code to manage the stack frame is added automatically by a compiler.[2] Figure 6.3 shows how the stack frames change when code runs. Note that A is called a second time before the first call to A has returned, and consequently A has *two* stack frames on the stack at that point, one for each invocation.

More than local variables may be found in a stack frame. It serves as a repository for all manner of bookkeeping information, depending on the particular subroutine, including:

- Saved register values. Registers are a limited resource, and it is often the case that multiple subroutines will use the same registers. Calling conventions specify the protocol for saving, and thus preserving, register contents that are not supposed to be changed – this may be done by the calling subroutine (the *caller*), the called subroutine (the *callee*), or some combination of the two. If registers need to be saved, they will be saved into the stack frame.

- Temporary space. There may not be enough registers to hold all necessary values that a subroutine needs, and some values may be placed in temporary space in the stack frame.

```
def main(): ... A() ...
def A(): ... B() ...
def B(): ... C() ...
def C(): ... A() ...
```

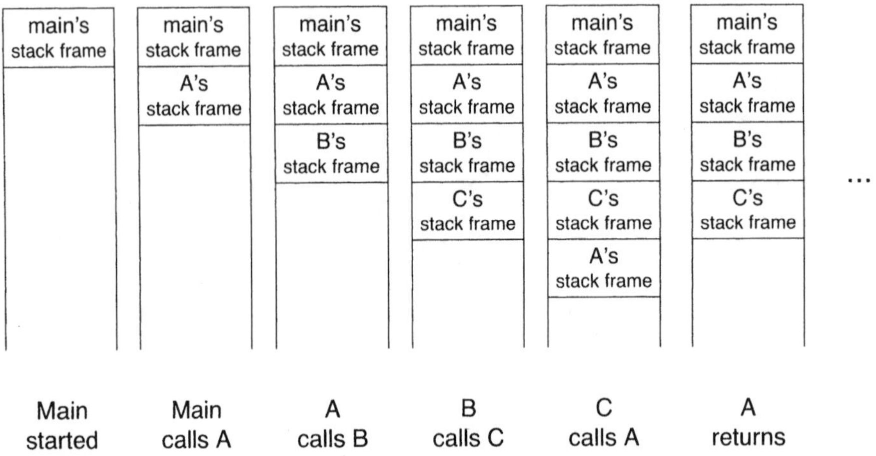

Main started	Main calls A	A calls B	B calls C	C calls A	A returns	
main's stack frame	main's stack frame	main's stack frame	main's stack frame	main's stack frame	main's stack frame	
	A's stack frame	A's stack frame	A's stack frame	A's stack frame	A's stack frame	
		B's stack frame	B's stack frame	B's stack frame	B's stack frame	...
			C's stack frame	C's stack frame	C's stack frame	
				A's stack frame		

Figure 6.3. Stack frame trace

- Input arguments to the subroutine. Arguments passed to the subroutine, if any.

- Output arguments from the subroutine. These are arguments that the subroutine passes to other subroutines that it calls.

- Return address. When the subroutine returns, this is the address at which execution resumes.

- Saved frame pointer. A register is usually reserved for use as a stack pointer, but the stack pointer may move about as arguments and other data are pushed onto the stack. A subroutine's *frame pointer* is a register that always points to a fixed position within the subroutine's stack frame, so that a subroutine can always locate its local variables with constant offsets. Because each newly-called subroutine will have its own stack frame, and thus its own frame pointer, the previous value of the frame pointer must be saved in the stack frame.

The inclusion of the last four as part of the stack frame proper is philosophical; some architectures include them, some don't. They will be assumed to be separate here in order to illustrate software weaknesses. For similar reasons, similar assumptions: arguments are passed on the stack, the return address and

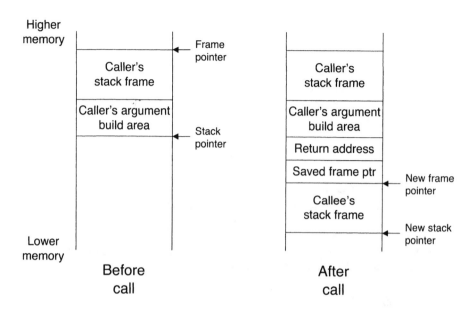

Figure 6.4. Before and after a subroutine call

saved frame pointer are on the stack. Variations of the weaknesses described here can often be found for situations where these assumptions aren't true.

Figure 6.4 shows the stack before and after a subroutine call. Prior to the call, the caller will have placed any arguments being passed into its argument build area. The call instruction will push the return address onto the stack and transfer execution to the callee.[3] The callee's code will begin by saving the old frame pointer onto the stack and creating a new stack frame.

6.1.2   Buffer Overflows

A *buffer overflow* is a weakness in code where the bounds of an array (often a buffer) can be exceeded. An attacker who is able to write into the buffer, directly or indirectly, will be able to write over other data in memory and cause the code to do something it wasn't supposed to. Generally, this means that an attacker could coerce a program into executing arbitrary code of the attacker's choice. Often the attacker's goal is to have this "arbitrary code" start a user shell, preferably with all the privileges of the subverted program – for this reason, the code the attacker tries to have run is generically referred to as *shellcode*.

One question immediately arises: why are these buffers' array bounds not checked? Some languages, like C, don't have automatic bounds checking. Sometimes, bounds-checking code *is* present, but has bugs. Other times, a buffer overflow is an indirect effect of another bug.

```
def main():
    fill_buffer()

def fill_buffer():
    character buffer[100]
    i = 0
    ch = input()
    while ch ≠ NEWLINE:
        buffer_i = ch
        ch = input()
        i = i + 1
```

Figure 6.5. Code awaiting a stack smash

Buffer overflows are not new. The general principle was known at least as far back as 1972,[100] and a buffer overflow was exploited by the Internet worm in 1988.

6.1.2.1 Stack Smashing

Stack smashing is a specific type of buffer overflow, where the buffer being overflowed is located in the stack.[101] In other words, the buffer is a local variable in the code, as in Figure 6.5. Here, no bounds checking is done on the input being read. As the stack-allocated buffer is filled from low to high memory, an attacker can continue writing, right over top of the return address on the stack. The attacker's input can be shellcode, followed by the address of the shellcode on the stack – when `fill_buffer` returns, it resumes execution where the attacker specified, and runs the shellcode. This is illustrated in Figure 6.6.

The main problem for the attacker is finding out the address of the buffer in the stack. Fortunately for the attacker, many operating systems situate a process' stack at the same memory location each time a program runs. To account for slight variance, an attacker can precede the shellcode with a sequence of "NOP" instructions that do nothing.[4] Because jumping anyplace into this NOP sequence will cause execution to slide into the shellcode, this is called a *NOP sled*.[102] The *exploit string*, the input sent by the attacker, is thus

NOP NOP NOP ... *shellcode new-return-address*

The space taken up by the NOP sled and the shellcode must be equal to the distance from the start of the buffer to the return address on the stack, otherwise the new return address won't be written to the correct spot on the stack. The saved frame pointer on the stack doesn't have to be preserved, either, because execution won't be returning to the caller anyway.

There are several other issues that arise for an attacker:

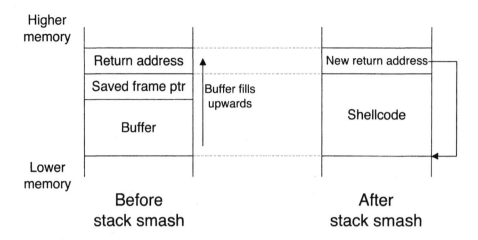

Figure 6.6. Stack smashing attack

- The length of the exploit string must be known, but the *exact* location on the stack may not be, due to the NOP sled. The addresses of strings in the shellcode cannot be hardcoded as a result – for example, shellcode may need a string containing the path to a user shell like /bin/sh. Some architectures allow addresses to be specified relative to the program counter's value, called *PC-relative addressing*. Other architectures, like the Intel x86, don't have PC-relative addressing, but do allow PC-relative subroutine calls. On the x86, a PC-relative jump from one part of the shellcode to another part of the shellcode will leave the caller's location on top of the stack. This location is the stack address of the shellcode.

- Depending on the code being attacked, some byte values can terminate the input before the buffer is overflowed. In Figure 6.5, for instance, a new-line character terminates the input. The exploit string cannot contain these input-terminating values. An attacker must rewrite their exploit string if necessary, to compute the forbidden values instead of containing them directly. For example, an ASCII NUL character (byte value 0) can be computed by XORing a value with itself.

- A buffer may be too small to hold the shellcode. One possible workaround is to write the shellcode *after* writing the new return address.

  Another possibility is to use the program's environment. Most operating systems allow *environment variables* to be set, which are variable names and values that are copied into a program's address space when it starts running. If an attacker controls the exploited program's environment, they can put their shellcode into an environment variable. Instead of making the

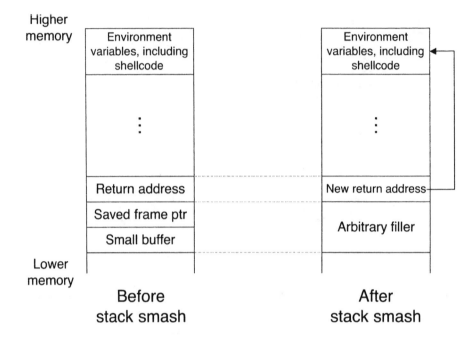

Figure 6.7. Environmentally-friendly stack smashing

new return address point to the overwritten buffer, the attacker points the new return address to the environment variable's memory location (Figure 6.7).[5]

6.1.2.2   Frame Pointer Overwriting

What if a buffer can be overrun by only one byte? Can an attack be staged? Under some circumstances, it can, except instead of overwriting the return address on the stack, the attack overwrites a byte of the saved frame pointer. This is a *frame pointer overwriting* attack.[103]

The success of this attack relies on two factors:

1 Some architectures demand that data be *aligned* in memory, meaning that the data must start at a specific byte boundary. For example, integers may be required to be aligned to a four-byte boundary, where the last two bits of the data's memory address are zero. When necessary, compilers will insert *padding* – unused bytes – to ensure that alignment constraints are met. There must be no padding on the stack between the buffer and the saved frame pointer for a frame pointer overwrite to work. Otherwise, writing one byte beyond the buffer would only alter a padding byte, not the saved frame pointer. Padding aside, no other data items can reside between the buffer and saved frame pointer, for similar reasons.

```
def main():
    fill_buffer()

def fill_buffer():
    character buffer[100]
    i = 0
    ch = input()
    while i <= 100 and ch ≠ NEWLINE:
        buffer_i = ch
        ch = input()
        i = i + 1
```

Figure 6.8. Code that goes just a little too far

2 The architecture must be little-endian. *Endianness* refers to the way an architecture stores data in memory. For example, consider the four-byte hexadecimal number aabbccdd. A *big-endian* machine would store the most significant byte first in memory; a *little-endian* machine like the Intel x86 would store the least significant byte first:

	X	X+1	X+2	X+3
Big-endian	aa	bb	cc	dd
Little-endian	dd	cc	bb	aa

On a big-endian machine, a frame pointer overwrite would change the most significant byte of the saved frame pointer; this would radically change where the saved frame pointer points in memory. However, on a little-endian machine, the overwrite changes the least significant byte, causing the saved frame pointer to only change slightly.

When the called subroutine returns, it restores the saved frame pointer from the stack; the caller's code will then use that frame pointer value. After a frame pointer attack, the caller will have a distorted view of where its stack frame is.

For example, the code in Figure 6.8 allows one byte to be written beyond the buffer, because it erroneously uses <= instead of <.[6] Figure 6.9 shows the stack layout before and after the attack. By overwriting the buffer and changing the saved frame pointer, the attacker can make the saved frame pointer point *inside* the buffer, something the attacker controls. The attacker can then forge a stack frame for the caller, convincing the caller's code to use fake stack frame values, and eventually return to a return address of the attacker's choice. The exploit string would be

NOP NOP NOP ... *shellcode fake-stack-frame*
fake-saved-frame-pointer shellcode-address
new-frame-pointer-byte

A saved frame pointer attack isn't straightforward to mount, but serves to demonstrate two things. First, an off-by-one error is enough to leave an exploitable weakness. Second, it demonstrates that just guarding the return address on the stack is insufficient as a defense.

6.1.2.3 Returns into Libraries

The success of basic stack smashing attacks relies on the shellcode they inject into the stack-allocated buffer. One suggested defense against these attacks is to make the stack's memory nonexecutable. In other words, the CPU would be unable to execute code in the stack, even if specifically directed to do so.

Unfortunately, this defense doesn't work. If an attacker can't run arbitrary code, they can still run other code. As it happens, there is a huge repository of interesting code already loaded into the address space of most processes: shared library code.[104] An attacker can overwrite a return address on the stack to point to a shared library routine to execute. For example, an attacker may call the system library routine, which runs an arbitrary command.

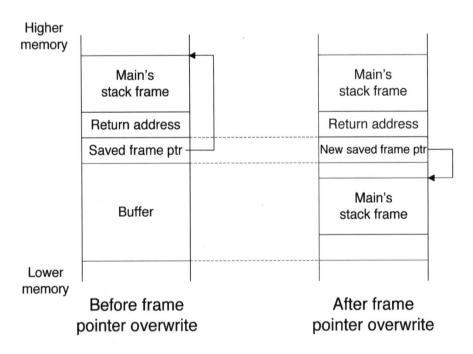

Figure 6.9. Frame pointer overwrite attack

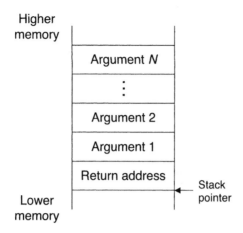

Figure 6.10. A normal function call with arguments

Arguments may be passed to library routines by the attacker by writing *beyond* the return address in the stack. Figure 6.10 shows the initial stack contents a subroutine would expect to see when called with arguments; Figure 6.11 shows a return-to-library attack which passes arguments. Notice the extra placeholder required, because the called library function expects a return address on the stack at that location.

This attack is often called a *return-to-libc* attack, because the C shared library is the usual target, but the attack's concept is generalizable to any shared library.

6.1.2.4 Heap Overflows

This next attack is somewhat of a misnomer. A *heap overflow* is a buffer overflow, where the buffer is located in the heap *or* the data segment.[105] The idea is not to overwrite the return address or the saved frame pointer, but to overwrite other variables that are adjacent to the buffer. These are more "portable" in a sense, because heap overflows don't rely on assumptions about stack layout, byte ordering, or calling conventions.

For example, the following global declarations would be allocated to the data segment:

```
character buffer[123]
function pointer p
```

Overflowing the buffer allows an attacker to change the value of the function pointer p, which is the address of a function to call. If the program performs a function call using p later, then it jumps to the address the attacker specified; again, this allows an attacker to run arbitrary code.

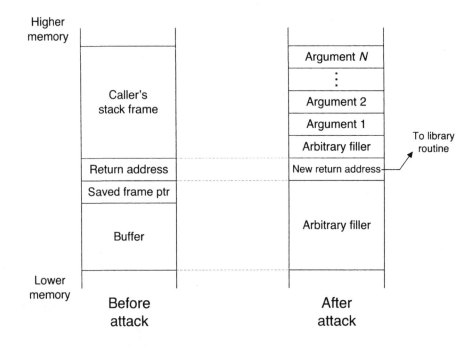

Figure 6.11. Return-to-library attack, with arguments

The range of possibilities for heap overflow attacks depends on the variables that can be overwritten, how the program uses those variables, and the imagination of the attacker.

6.1.2.5 Memory Allocator Attacks

One way heap overflows can be used is to attack the dynamic memory allocator. As previously mentioned, space is dynamically allocated from the heap. The allocator needs to maintain bookkeeping information for each block of memory that it oversees in the heap, allocated or unallocated. Allocators find space for this information by overallocating memory – when a program requests an X-byte block of memory, the allocator reserves extra space:

- Before the block, room for bookkeeping information.

- After the block, space may be needed to round the block size up. This may be done to avoid fragmenting the heap with remainder blocks that are too small to be useful, or to observe memory alignment constraints.

The key observation is that the bookkeeping information is stored in the heap, following an allocated block. Exploiting a heap overflow in one block allows the bookkeeping information for the following block to be overwritten, as shown in Figure 6.12.[106]

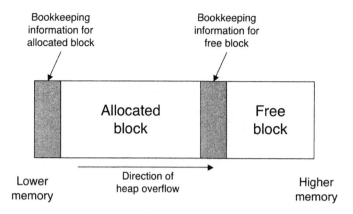

Figure 6.12. Overflowing the heap onto bookkeeping information

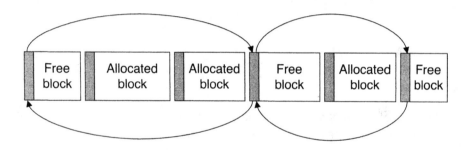

Figure 6.13. Dynamic memory allocator's free list

By itself, this isn't terribly interesting, but memory allocators tend to keep track of free, unallocated memory blocks in a data structure called a *free list*. As in Figure 6.13, the free list will be assumed here to be a doubly-linked list, so that blocks can be removed from the list easily. When an allocated block is freed, the allocator checks to see if the block immediately following it is also free; if so, the two can be merged to make one larger block of free memory. This is where the free list is used: the already-free block must be unlinked from the free list, in favor of the merged block.

A typical sequence for unlinking a block from a doubly-linked list is shown in Figure 6.14. The blocks on the list have been abstracted into uniform list nodes, each with two pointers as bookkeeping information, a "previous" pointer pointing to the previous list node, and a "next" pointer pointing to the next node. From the initial state, there are two steps to unlink a node B:

1 The next node, C, is found by following B's next pointer. C's previous pointer is set to the value of B's previous pointer.

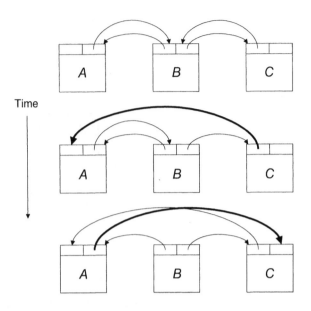

Figure 6.14. Normal free list unlinking

2 *B*'s previous pointer is followed to find the previous node, *A*. *A*'s next pointer is set to the value of *B*'s next pointer.

Now, say that an attacker exploits a heap overflow in the allocated block immediately before *B*, and overwrites *B*'s list pointers. *B*'s previous pointer is set to the address of the attacker's shellcode, and *B*'s next pointer is assigned the address of a code pointer that already exists in the program. For example, this code pointer may be a return address on the stack, or a function pointer in the data segment. The attacker then waits for the program to free the memory block it overflowed.

Figure 6.15 illustrates the result. The memory allocator finds the next adjacent block (*B*) free, and tries to merge it. When the allocator unlinks *B* from the list, it erroneously assumes that *B*'s two pointers point to free list nodes. Following the same two steps as above, the allocator overwrites the targeted code pointer with the shellcode's address in the first step. This was the primary goal of the exploit. The second step writes a pointer just past the start of the shellcode. This would normally render the shellcode unrunnable, but the shellcode can be made to start with a jump instruction, skipping over the part of the shellcode that is overwritten during unlinking.

After the allocator's unlinking is complete, the targeted code address points to the shellcode, and the shellcode is run whenever the program uses that overwritten code address.

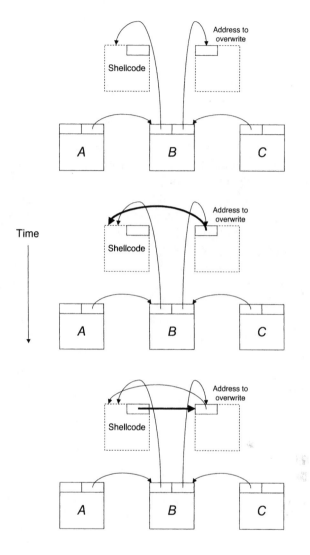

Figure 6.15. Attacked free list unlinking

6.1.3 Integer Overflows

In most programming languages, numbers do not have infinite precision. For instance, the range of integers may be limited to what can be encoded in 16 bits.[7] This leads to some interesting effects:[107]

- Integer overflows, where a value "wraps around." For example, 30000 + 30000 = -5536.

- Sign errors. Mixing signed and unsigned numbers can lead to unexpected results. The unsigned value 65432 is -104 when stored in a signed variable, for instance.

- Truncation errors, when a higher-precision value is stored in a variable with lower precision. For example, the 32-bit value 8675309 becomes 24557 in 16 bits.

Few languages check for these kinds of problems, because doing so would occasionally impose additional overhead, and more occasionally, the programmer actually intended for the effect to occur.

At this point in the chapter, it should come as little surprise that these effects can be exploited by an attacker – they are collectively called *integer overflow* attacks. Usually the attack isn't direct, but uses an integer overflow to cause other types of weaknesses, like buffer overflows.[108]

The code in Figure 6.16 has such a problem, and is derived from real code. All numbers are 16 bits long: n is the number of elements in an array to be read in; size is the size in bytes of each array element; totalsize is the total number of bytes required to hold the array. If an attacker's input results in n being 1234 and size being 56, their product is 69104, which doesn't fit in 16 bits – totalsize is set to 3568 instead. As a result of the integer overflow, only 3568 bytes of dynamic memory are allocated, yet the attacker can feed in 69104 bytes of input in the loop that follows, giving a heap overflow.

```
n = input_number()
size = input_number()
totalsize = n * size

buffer = allocate_memory(totalsize)

i = 0
buffer_pointer = buffer
while i < n:
    buffer_pointer_{0...size-1} = input_N_bytes(size)
    buffer_pointer = buffer_pointer + size
    i = i + 1
```

Figure 6.16. Code with an integer overflow problem

6.1.4   Format String Vulnerabilities

'Perhaps one of the most interesting errors that we discovered was a result of an unusual interaction of two parts of csh, along with a little careless programming. The following string will cause the VAX version of csh to crash

!o%8f

and the following string

!o%888888888f

will hang... most versions of csh.'   – Barton Miller et al.[109]

Format functions in C take as input a "format string" followed by zero or more arguments. The format string tells the function how to compose the arguments into an output string; depending on the format function, the output string may be written to a file, the standard output location, or a buffer in memory.[8] Format string problems, the cause of the errors in the above quote, were a curiosity in 1990 when those words were published. By 1999, format string problems were recognized as a security problem, and they were being actively exploited by 2000.[110]

The canonical example of a format function is `printf`:

```
char *s = "is page";
int n = 125;
printf("Hello, world!");
printf("This %s %d.", s, n);
```

The first call to `printf` prints `Hello, world!`; its format string doesn't contain any special directives telling `printf` to look for any additional arguments. The second call, on the other hand, does – `%s` says to interpret the next unread argument (`s`) as a pointer to a string, and `%d` treats the next unread argument (`n`) as an integer. The result is the output

This is page 125.

Saying "the next *unread* argument" implies that `printf` consumes the arguments as it formats the output string, and this is exactly what happens. Figure 6.17 shows the stack layout for a call to `printf`, assuming again that arguments are passed on the stack. As a format function reads its arguments, it effectively steps a pointer through the stack, where the pointer identifies the next argument to be read.

Format functions exhibit a touching faith in the correctness of the format string. A format function has no way of knowing how many arguments were *really* passed by its caller, which can be disastrous if an attacker is able to supply any part of a format string.[111] For example, if the program contains

printf(error);

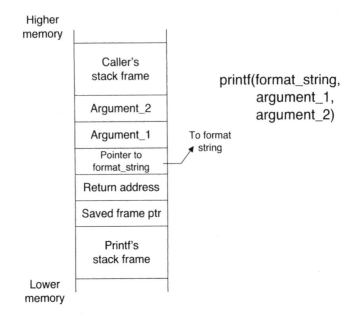

Figure 6.17. Stack layout for calling a format function

and an attacker manages to set the variable `error` to `"%s%s%s%s"`, then the program will almost certainly crash. `Printf`'s attacker-specified format string tells it to grab the next four items off the stack and treat each one as a pointer to a string. The problem is that the next four items on the stack *aren't* pointers to strings, so `printf` will make wild memory references in an effort to format its alleged strings.

As is, this attack can be used to print out the contents of a target program's stack: an attacker can craft a format string which walks up the stack, interpreting each stack item as a number and printing the result. Changing `error` to `"%d%d%d%d"` in the above example would be enough to print the stack contents. This is one possible way that addresses can be discovered for a later stack smashing attack.

Even more is possible if the attacker can control a format string located in the stack. The code in Figure 6.18 is a common scenario, where a buffer's contents are formatted for later output. The `snprintf` function is a format function with two additional arguments, a buffer and the buffer's length; `snprintf` writes its formatted output to this buffer. It also demonstrates that a format string vulnerability can be exploited indirectly, as the flaw here is in the call to `printf`, not `snprintf`.

With this code, the attacker's format string can be the ungainly construction

```
" \x78\x56\x34\x12 %d%d%d%d%d%d%d %n"
```

```
void print_error(char *s)
{
    char buffer[123];
    snprintf(buffer, sizeof(buffer),
            "Error: %s", s);
    printf(buffer);
}
```

Figure 6.18. Code with a format string vulnerability

The buffer, a local variable on the stack, contains `printf`'s format string after the call to `snprintf`. `Printf` is thus called with a format string that the attacker has supplied in part:

"Error: \x78\x56\x34\x12 %d%d%d%d%d%d%d %n"

There are four parts to this format string.

1 `Error:` is added by `snprintf`. It plays no part in this attack and can be ignored.

2 `\x78\x56\x34\x12` is the address 12345678 in little-endian format; in C strings, `\x` introduces a pair of hexadecimal digits.

3 `%d%d%d%d%d%d%d`, used as mentioned above to walk up the stack's contents.

4 `%n` is a format string directive. It tells `printf` to interpret the next unread argument as a pointer to an integer. `Printf` writes the number of bytes it's formatted so far into the pointed-to integer. Through this mechanism, the attacker has a way to have a value written to an arbitrary memory location.

The stack layout during an attack is given in Figure 6.19. The attacker's format string causes `printf` to walk up the stack, printing integers, until the next unread argument is the address the attacker encoded in the format string. (Remember that the buffer is in the stack, so the attacker's format string is there too.) The `%n` takes the attacker's address and writes a number at that address. The attacker can control the number written by adding junk characters to the format string, changing the number of bytes `printf` formats, and consequently the number written for `%n`.

Like other attacks, if an attacker can make a single specified value change, then the possibility of running shellcode exists.

6.1.5 Defenses

The underlying moral in studying these technical vulnerabilities is to never, ever, *ever* trust input to a program. Having bulletproof input routines and bug-

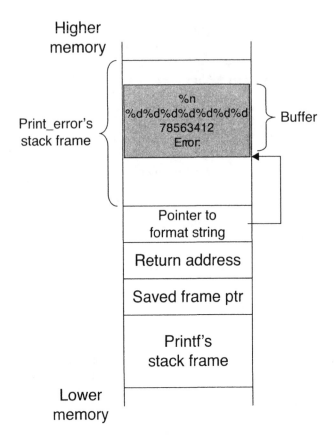

Figure 6.19. Format string attack in progress

free code is the best defense to technical vulnerabilities, but expecting this of all software is like asking Santa Claus for world peace – well intentioned, but unlikely to happen in the near future.

In the meantime, two types of defenses can be considered, ones that are specific to a type of vulnerability, and ones that are more general.

6.1.5.1 Vulnerability-Specific Defenses

Defenses can be directed to guarding against certain types of vulnerability. For example:

Format string vulnerabilities

- Source code auditing is a particularly effective defense, because the number of format functions is relatively small, and it is easy to search source code for calls to format functions.[112]

- Remove support for %n in format functions, or only allow constant format strings that an attacker can't change.[113] This defense would break existing code in addition to violating the C specification.

- If a format function knew how many arguments it had been called with, then it could avoid reading nonexistent arguments. Unfortunately, this information isn't available at run-time.

  A program's source code can be altered to supply this information. Calls to known format functions can be wrapped in macros that keep track of the number of arguments passed. Even this doesn't always work, because nonstandard format functions may be used, or standard format functions may be used in unusual ways. For example, the code may save a function pointer to `printf` and call it later, rather than calling `printf` directly.

Stack smashing

- As mentioned before, one defense against stack smashing is to mark the stack's memory as nonexecutable; the same idea can be extended to the data and heap segments. This is not a complete defense, since a return-to-library attack is still possible, but it does close one attack vector.

  Some programs legitimately need to have executable code in odd places in memory, like just-in-time compilers and nested C functions.[9] An alternative memory protection approach ensures that memory pages can be writable or executable, *but* not both at the same time. This provides the same protection, but with more flexibility for legitimate programs.[10]

- The control information in the stack, the return address and the saved frame pointer, can be guarded against inappropriate modification. This method prevents stack smashing attacks, and also catches some buggy programs. The way the control information is guarded is by using *canaries*.

  Miners used to use live canaries as a safety precaution. A buildup of toxic gases in a mine would kill a canary before a human, so canaries were taken down into mines as an early-warning system. Finding a metabolically-challenged canary meant that it was time for a coffee break on the surface.

  For stack smashing defense, a *canary* is a value which is strategically located in the stack frame, between the local variables and the control information (Figure 6.20). A canary can't withstand an attack – in theory – and if the canary is corrupted, then an attack may have occurred, so the program should issue an alert and exit immediately.[114]

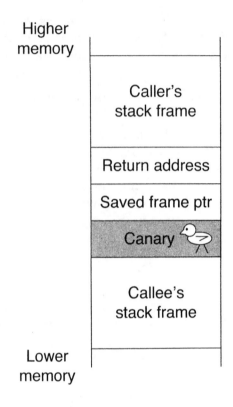

Figure 6.20. Canary placement

Support for canaries is provided by a language's compiler. Space for the canary must be added in each stack frame, code must be added at subroutine entry to initialize the canary, and code at subroutine exit must verify the canary's value for correctness. With all this code being added, overhead is a concern for canary-based defenses.

An attacker trying to compromise a program using canaries would have to overflow a buffer and overwrite control information as usual, *and* write the correct canary value so that the attack isn't discovered. There are three types of canary, distinguished by how they try and prevent an attacker from writing the correct canary value:

1 Terminator canaries. Assuming that the most common type of stack smashing involves input and strings, a terminator canary uses a constant canary value which is a combination of four bytes, line and string terminators all: carriage return, newline, NUL, and -1 for good measure. The hope is that an attacker, sending these bytes to overwrite the canary correctly, would unwittingly end their input before the exploit succeeds.

2 Random canaries. The canary value can also be changed to prevent an attacker from succeeding; the theory is that an attacker must know the canary value in order to construct an exploit string. A random canary is a secret canary value that is changed randomly each time a program runs.[11] The random canary value for a program is stored in a global location, and is copied from this global location to a stack frame upon subroutine entry. The global location may possibly be situated in a read-only memory page to avoid being altered by an attacker. However, note that the presence of a format string vulnerability can be used by an attacker to find out the secret canary value.

3 Random XOR canaries. This is a random canary, with some or all of the control information XORed in with the canary for each stack frame. Any successful attack must set the canary appropriately – not an impossible task, but not an easy one either.

Canaries can be extended to guard against some heap overflows as well, by situating a canary in the bookkeeping information of each dynamically-allocated block.[115] A general problem with canaries of any sort is that they only provide a perimeter guard for a memory area, and a program can still be attacked by overflowing a buffer onto other, unguarded variables within the guarded memory area.[116] A partial remedy is to alter the memory layout of variables, so that buffers are situated as close to a canary as possible, with no non-buffer variables in between.[117]

Generally, defenses to specific vulnerabilities that rely on the availability of source code or compilers won't work. Source code is not always available, as in the cases of third-party libraries and legacy code. Even if source code is available, compilers may not be, or users may lack the expertise or time to make source code changes, recompile, and reinstall.

6.1.5.2 General Defenses

Since most of the technical vulnerabilities stem from the use of programming languages with weaknesses, like the lack of bounds checking, one general approach is to stop using those languages. No more C, no more C++. This suggestion ignores many realities: legacy code, programmer training, programmer and management biases towards certain programming languages, the cost and availability of tools and compilers, constraints from third-party libraries. In any case, even if use of "weak" programming languages was stopped, history has shown that existing applications in those languages would linger in active use for decades.

A related idea is not to change programming languages, but to repair problems with an existing language after the fact. For example, bounds checking could be added to C programs. Current approaches to bounds checking C code are dogged by problems: incomplete protection, breaking existing code. This is also an area where adding 'less than 26%' overhead is deemed to make a tool practical for use.[118]

A more feasible defense is to randomize the locations of as many addresses as possible. If the locations of the stack, shared libraries, program code, and heap-allocated memory change each time the program is run, then an attacker's task is made more difficult.[119] However, it also makes legitimate debugging more difficult, in terms of finding spurious bugs, if these locations change non-deterministically. There is also evidence that the amount of randomization that can be provided is insufficient to prevent attacks completely.[120] A brute-force attack on a well-chosen target is possible, albeit much slower than attacking a system without any randomization.

A program's code can also be monitored as it runs, akin to behavior blocking anti-virus techniques.[12] The monitoring system looks for potential attacks by watching for specific abnormal behaviors, like a function return jumping into a buffer, or a return instruction not returning to its call site. The tricky part is pausing the monitored program's execution at critical points so that checks may be performed, without introducing excessive overhead, without modifying the monitored program's code. A solution comes in the form of caching:

- The monitoring system maintains a cache of code chunks that have already been checked against the monitor's security policy.

- Cached code chunks run directly on the CPU, rather than using slow emulation, and a chunk returns control back to the monitor when it's done running.

- Each control transfer is checked – if the destination corresponds to an already-cached code chunk, then execution goes to the cached chunk. Otherwise, the destination code chunk is checked for security violations and copied into the code cache.

Code chunks in the cache can be optimized, mitigating some of the monitoring overhead.

6.1.6   Finding Weaknesses

How do attackers find technical weaknesses in the first place? They can find the vulnerabilities themselves:

- Source code can be studied for vulnerabilities, when attacking a system where the source is available.[13] Even when a system is closed-source, it may be derived in part from a system with available source code.

- Disassembly listings of programs and libraries can be manually searched, looking for opportunities. For example, an attacker could look for buffer-handling code or calls to format functions. While this may sounds daunting, it is never wise to underestimate the amount of free time an attacker will dedicate to a task like this.

- Instead of poring over disassembly listings, an attacker can reconstruct a facsimile of the target program's source code using tools for reverse engineering, like decompilers. This provides a slightly higher-level view onto the target code.

- Vulnerabilities can be discovered even without direct access to the target program or its source code. Treating the target program as a "black box" might be necessary if the target program is running on a remote machine for which the attacker doesn't have access.[14] For example, an attacker can look for buffer overflows by feeding a program inputs of various lengths until a suspicious condition is seen, like abruptly-terminated output. More information, such as the buffer's length, can be found through trial-and-error at that point by performing a binary search using different input lengths. Computers excel at repeating such mundane tasks, and finding the length of a buffer can be automated.[15]

  In general, any research on automated program-testing can be applied by an attacker. Such methods have a demonstrated ability to find long sequences of inputs which cause a program to misbehave.[16]

The other option an attacker has is to wait for someone else to find a vulnerability, or at least point the way:

- There are a number of *full disclosure* mailing lists. Advocates of full disclosure argue that the best way to force software vendors to fix a vulnerability is to release all its details, and possibly even code that exploits the vulnerabilities. (The extreme contrast to this is *security through obscurity*, which holds that hiding security-related details of a system means that attackers will *never* be able to figure them out. Again, underestimating an attacker is a bad strategy.) An exploit made available on a full-disclosure list can either be used directly, or might be used to indicate the direction of more serious problems in the targeted code.

- A vendor security patch is a wealth of information. Either the patch itself can be studied to see what vulnerability it fixed, or a system can be compared before and after applying a patch to see what changed.

  Tools are available to help with the comparison task. All but the most trivial alteration to the patched executables will result in a flurry of binary changes: branch instructions and their targets are moved; information about a program's symbols changes as code moves around; new code optimization opportunities are found and taken by the code's compiler. For this reason, tools performing a straight binary comparison will not yield much useful information to an attacker.[121]

Useful binary comparison tools must filter out nonessential differences in the binary code. This is related to the problem of producing small patches for binary executables. Any observed difference between two executables must be characterized as either a primary change, a direct result of the code being changed, or a secondary change, an artifact of a primary change.[122] For example, an inserted instruction would be a primary change; a branch offset moved to accommodate the insertion is a secondary change. Spotting secondary changes can be done several ways:

–   An architecture-dependent tool effectively disassembles the code to find instructions like branches which tend to exhibit secondary changes.[123]

–   An architecture-independent tool can guess at the same information by assuming that code movements are small, only affecting the least-significant bytes of addresses.[124]

Naturally an attacker would only be interested in learning about primary changes, after probable secondary changes have been identified.

Other binary comparison approaches build "before" and "after" graphs of the code, using information like the code's control flow. A heuristic attempt is made to find an isomorphism between the graphs; in other words, the graphs are "matched up" as well as possible. Any subgraph that can't be matched indicates a possible change in the corresponding code.[125]

The Holy Grail for an attacker is the *zero-day exploit*, an exploit for a vulnerability that is made the same day as the vulnerability is announced – hopefully the same day that a patch for the vulnerability is released. From an attacker's point of view, the faster an exploit appears, the fewer machines that will be patched to plug the hole. In practice, software vendors are not always fast or forthcoming,[17] and an exploit may be well-known long before a patch for the vulnerability manifests itself.

6.2   Human Weaknesses

Humans are the weakest link in the chain of security. Humans forget to apply critical security patches, they introduce exploitable bugs, they misconfigure software in vulnerable ways. There is even an entire genre of attacks based on tricking people, called *social engineering*.

Classic social engineering attacks tend to be labor-intensive, and don't scale well. Some classic ploys include:[126]

- Impersonation. An attacker can pretend to be someone else to extract information from a target. For example, a "helpless user" role may convince the target to divulge some useful information about system access; an "important user" role may demand information from the target.[127]

- Dumpster diving. Fishing through garbage for useful information. "Useful" is a broad term, and could include discarded computer hard drives and backups with valuable data, or company organization charts suitable for assuming identities. Identity theft is another use for such information.

- Shoulder surfing. Discovering someone's password by watching them over their shoulder as they enter it in.

These classic attacks have limited application to malware. Even impersonation, which doesn't require the attacker to have a physical presence, works much better on the phone or in person.[128]

Technology-based social engineering attacks useful for malware must be amenable to the automation of both information gathering and the use of gathered information. For example, usernames and passwords can be automatically used by malware to gain initial access to a system. They can be collected automatically with social engineering:

- Phony pop-up boxes, asking the user to re-enter their username and password.

- Fake email about winning contests, directing users to an attacker's web site. There, the user must create an account to register for their "prize" by providing a username and password. People tend to re-use usernames and passwords to reduce the amount they must remember, so there is a high probability that the information entered into the attacker's web site will yield some real authentication information.

  The same principle can be used to lure people to an attacker's website to foist drive-by downloads on them. The website can exploit bugs in a user's web browser to execute arbitrary code on their machine, using the technical weaknesses described earlier.

- *Phishing* attacks send email which tricks recipients into visiting the attacker's web site and entering information. For example, a phishing email might threaten to close a user's account unless they update their account information. The attacker's web site, meanwhile, is designed to look exactly like the legitimate web site normally visited to update account information. The user enters their username and password, and possibly some other personal information useful for identity theft or credit card fraud, thus giving all this information to the attacker. Malware can use phishing to harvest usernames and passwords.

```
If you receive an email titled "It Takes Guts to Say
'Jesus'" do NOT open it. It will erase everything on
your hard drive.

Forward this letter out to as many people as you can.
This is a new, very malicious virus and not many
people know about it. This information was announced
yesterday morning from IBM; please share it with
everyone that might access the internet. Once again,
pass this along to EVERYONE in your address book so
that this may be stopped.

AOL has said that this is a very dangerous virus and
that there is NO remedy for it at this time. Please
practice cautionary measures and forward this to all
your online friends ASAP.
```

Figure 6.21. "It Takes Guts to Say 'Jesus'" virus hoax

User education is the best defense against known and unknown social engineering attacks of this kind. Establishing security policies, and teaching users what information has value, gives users guidelines as to the handling of sensitive information like their usernames and passwords.[129]

Social engineering may also be used by malware to spread, by tricking people into propagating the malware along. And, one special form of "malware" that involves no code uses social engineering extensively: virus hoaxes.

6.2.1   Virus Hoaxes

'This virus works on the honor system. Please forward this message to everyone you know, then delete all the files on your hard disk.'   – Anonymous[18]

A *virus hoax* is essentially the same as a chain letter, but contains "information" about some fictitious piece of malware. A virus hoax doesn't do damage itself, but consumes resources – human and computer – as the hoax gets propagated. Some hoaxes may do damage *through* humans, advising a user to make modifications to their system which could damage it, or render it vulnerable to a later attack.

There are three parts to a typical hoax email:[130]

1 The hook. This is something that grabs the hoax recipient's attention.

2 The threat. Some dire warning about damage to the recipient's computer caused by the alleged virus, which may be enhanced with confusing "technobabble" to make the hoax sound more convincing.

3 The request. An action for the recipient to perform. This will usually include forwarding the hoax to others, but may also include modifying the system.

Some examples are given in Figures 6.21 and 6.22.[19] Figure 6.21 is a classic virus hoax, whose only goal is to propagate. The virus hoax in Figure 6.22 is

```
I found the little bear in my machine because of that I am sending this
message in order for you to find it in your machine.  The procedure is
very simple:

The objective of this e-mail is to warn all Hotmail users about a new
virus that is spreading by MSN Messenger.  The name of this virus is
jdbgmgr.exe and it is sent automatically by the Messenger and by the
address book too.  The virus is not detected by McAfee or Norton and it
stays quiet for 14 days before damaging the system.

The virus can be cleaned before it deletes the files from your system.
In order to eliminate it, it is just necessary to do the following
steps:
1. Go to Start, click "Search"
2.- In the "Files or Folders option" write the name jdbgmgr.exe
3.- Be sure that you are searching in the drive "C"
4.- Click "find now"
5.- If the virus is there (it has a little bear-like icon with the name
        of jdbgmgr.exe DO NOT OPEN IT FOR ANY REASON
6.- Right click and delete it (it will go to the Recycle bin)
7.- Go to the recycle bin and delete it or empty the recycle bin.

IF YOU FIND THE VIRUS IN ALL OF YOUR SYSTEMS SEND THIS MESSAGE TO ALL
OF YOUR CONTACTS LOCATED IN YOUR ADDRESS BOOK BEFORE IT CAN CAUSE ANY
DAMAGE.
```

Figure 6.22. "jdbgmgr.exe" virus hoax

slightly more devious, sending Windows users on a mission to find bear-shaped icons. As it turns out, this is the icon for a Java debugger utility which is legitimately found on Windows.

Why does a virus hoax work? It relies on some of the same persuasion factors as social engineering:[131]

- A good hook elicits a sense of excitement, in the same way that a committee meeting doesn't. Hooks may claim some authority, like IBM, as their information source; this is an attempt to exploit the recipient's trust in authority.

- The sense of excitement is enhanced by the hoax's threat. Overloading the recipient with technical-sounding details, in combination with excitement, creates an enhanced emotional state that detracts from critical thinking. Consequently, this means that the hoax may be subjected to less scrutiny and skepticism than it might otherwise receive.

- The request, especially the request to forward the hoax, may be complied with simply because the hoax was persuasive enough. There may be other factors involved, though. A recipient may want to feel important, may want to ingratiate themselves to other users, or may genuinely want to warn others. A hidden agenda may be present, too – a recipient may pass the hoax around, perceiving the purported threat as a way to justify an increase in the computer security budget.

Virus hoaxes seem to be on the decline, possibly because they are extremely vulnerable to spam filtering. Even in the absence of technical solutions, education is effective. Users can be taught to verify a suspected virus hoax against anti-virus vendors' databases before sending it along; if the mail is a hoax, the chances are excellent that others have received and reported the hoax already.

Notes for Chapter 6

1 This is based on a simplified Unix memory model, with a few exceptions: the code segment is called the text segment, and what is lumped together here as the data segment is really a combination of the Unix data and bss segments.

2 Again, this is a simplification. An optimizing compiler may place some or all of a subroutine's stack frame into registers if possible, to avoid costly memory references. Some architectures, like the SPARC, are specifically designed to facilitate this.

3 Assumptions, assumptions, assumptions. RISC architectures tend not to push the return address, but dump it into a register so that it can be saved only if necessary.

4 An alternative is to replicate the new return address several times at the end, especially when the exact distance from the buffer to the return address on the stack isn't known.

5 On some systems, the stack location isn't consistent across executions of a program, but the environment variable location is, so the environment variable trick provides an alternative attack vector.

6 This assumes that array indexing starts from zero.

7 16-bit numbers are used in this section for clarity, but the same idea works for numbers with any finite precision.

8 This is a simplified explanation, and doesn't take into account format functions for input, various obscure format functions, and format functions that take an opaquely-typed variable argument list rather than the arguments themselves.

9 The latter being a peculiarity of the "gcc" dialect of C, the implementation of which is described in Breuel [48].

10 OpenBSD allows this with their "W^X" scheme [85].

11 For multithreaded programs, each thread has its own stack. The random canary could thus be changed on a per-thread basis, with the canary's correct value placed in thread-local storage instead of a global location.

12 Kiriansky et al. [164] call this "program shepherding," and build their system on top of HP's Dynamo dynamic optimization system [25]. Renert [261] does largely the same thing, code cache and all (albeit permitting more general security policies), but neglects to mention the highly-related Dynamo work.

13 This includes, but is not restricted to, open-source systems. "Available" doesn't necessarily imply "freely," "easily," or "widely."

14 Yet.

15 This technique of finding "blind" buffer overflows is described in [84, 194].

16 For example, Chan et al. [60] apply an evolutionary learning algorithm to testing the game AI in Electronic Arts' FIFA-99 game.

17 To be fair – at least on the vendor speed issue – patches must be thoroughly tested, and the same vulnerability may exist in several of a vendor's products [224].

18 This is one of many variants of the "honor system virus" circulating. No traces of this particular one seem evident before May 2000, right after the release of the (non-hoax) ILOVEYOU email worm. An honor system virus was posted to Usenet around this time, but it's unclear if it is the original source or merely another derivative [181].

19 There are many different versions of these hoaxes floating around; the ones given here are edited to include the essential features of each.

100 Anderson [12].

101 This section is based on Aleph One [8].

102 Erickson [100].

103 The description of this attack is based on klog [167].

104 This section is based on [231, 292].

105 This section is based on Conover [78].

106 The description of this vulnerability is based on Solar Designer [293] and an anonymous author [18].

107 This categorization is due to Howard [147].

108 blexim [36], who also provides the XDR code from which Figure 6.16 was derived.

109 Miller et al. [209, page 39].

110 Cowan et al. [80].

111 This format string vulnerability discussion is based on scut [284].

112 Koziol et al. [171].

113 The defenses against format string vulnerabilities are from Cowan et al. [80].

114 This ornithological discussion is based on Wagle and Cowan [339].

115 Robertson et al. [266].

116 Bulba and Kil3r [51].

117 Etoh [102].

118 Astonishingly, this claim is made in Ruwase and Lam [272, page 159].

119 A number of systems do this now: see Drepper [93] and de Raadt [85]. This type of randomization is one way to avoid software monocultures; see Just and Cornwall [157] for a discussion of other techniques.

120 Shacham et al. [285]. A related attack on instruction set randomization can be found in Sovarel et al. [296].

121 Hunt and McIlroy [148] describe the early Unix `diff` utility.

122 We follow the terminology from Baker et al. [24].

123 Baker et al. [24].

124 Percival [246].

125 Flake [110] and Sabin [273].

126 Granger [128].

127 Also in Allen [10].

128 Harl [136].

129 Granger [129].

130 CIAC [72].

131 Based on Gordon et al. [126], Gragg [127], and Granger [128].

Chapter 7

WORMS

The general structure of a worm is:

```
def worm():
    propagate()
    if trigger() is true:
        payload()
```

At this level of abstraction, there is no distinction between a worm and a virus. (For comparison, the virus pseudocode is on page 27.) The real difference is in how they propagate. Propagating by infecting other code is the domain of a virus; actively searching for vulnerable machines across a network makes a worm. A worm can either be said to *infest* or *infect* its victims; the latter term will be used here. A single copy of a worm will be called a worm *instance*, where it's necessary to avoid ambiguity.

In some cases, worms are classified by the primary method they use for transport. A worm using instant messaging (IM) to spread is called an *IM worm*, and a worm using email is an *email worm*. For example, many email worms arrive as an email attachment, which the user is tricked into running. When run, the worm harvests email addresses off the machine and mails itself to those addresses.

Tricking users into doing something is social engineering, and this is one mechanism that worms use to infect machines. Another mechanism that worms exploit for infection are technical weaknesses. A user doesn't have to be tricked into running an email attachment, if just viewing the email allows the worm's code to execute via a buffer overrun. A user doesn't have to be involved at all, if the worm spreads using buffer overruns between long-running network server processes on different machines.

A worm can also exploit existing, legitimate transactions. For example, consider a worm able to watch and modify network communications, especially one located on a network server machine. The worm can wait for legitimate transfers of executable files – file transfers, network filesystem use – and either substitute itself in place of the requested executable file, or insert itself into the requested file in a virus-like fashion.[100]

Most of the details about worms have already been covered in earlier chapters, like technical weaknesses and human weaknesses. Worms can also employ the same techniques that viruses do in order to try and conceal themselves; worms can use encryption, and can be oligomorphic, polymorphic, or metamorphic. This chapter therefore only examines the propagation which makes worms distinct from viruses, beginning with a look at two historically important worms.

7.1   Worm History

The origins of the term "worm" were mentioned in Section 2.1.5, along with some examples of early worms. This section examines two of these in more depth: the Xerox worm and the Internet worm.

7.1.1   Xerox PARC, c. 1982

'All worm behavior ceased. Unfortunately the embarrassing results were left for all to see: 100 dead machines scattered around the building.'   – John Shoch and Jon Hupp[101]

The worm used in the Xerox PARC experiments of the early 1980s wasn't *intentionally* malicious, despite the above quote. It was intended as a framework for distributed computation, to make use of otherwise unused CPU time. A user would write a program to run in parallel, on many different machines – this program would sit atop the worm mechanism, and the worm would manage the mechanics of making the program run on different machines.

It would be highly unusual to see a worm now that places an artificial limit on its own propagation, but that was exactly what the Xerox worm did. The Xerox worm was composed of multiple *segments*, by way of analogy to real biological worms; at most one worm segment could run on any one machine. A bounded, finite number of segments were started, and all segments kept in contact with one another. If the worm lost contact with a segment (for example, someone rebooted the machine that the segment was running on), then the other segments sought another machine upon which to run a segment.

Safety mechanisms were built in to the worm. This was done in part to assuage user concerns about having such a beast running on their computer; segments were not allowed to perform disk accesses, for example. Keeping segments in contact had a safety benefit, too, in that the entire worm could be shut down with a single command. And was, in the case from which the above quote was taken. The worm had gone out of control through an odd set of circumstances, and had to be stopped.

One of the key insights the researchers at Xerox PARC made from their worm experiments was that managing worm growth and stability are hard problems.

7.1.2   The Internet Worm, November 1988

'We are currently under attack from an Internet VIRUS. It has hit UC Berkeley, UC San Diego, Lawrence Livermore, Stanford, and NASA Ames.'   – Peter Yee[102]

Whether people called it a worm or a virus, the Internet worm was a major wake-up call for Internet security.[1] It worked in three stages:

Stage 1 The first stage was for the worm to get a shell on the remote machine being targeted. The worm would use one of three methods to acquire a shell, mostly relying on security holes of mythic proportion:

1   Users read and send email using mail programs which are generically called *mail user agents*. The actual gory details of transmitting and delivering mail across the network are handled by daemons called *mail transport agents*. Mail user agents send mail by passing it off to a mail transport agent, which in turn can talk to mail transport agents on different machines, to send the mail along its merry way.

   Sendmail was a widely-used mail transport agent at the time of the Internet worm. An example of sending mail, by talking to the sendmail daemon, is in Figure 7.1. Simple commands are used to identify the connecting machine, specify the mail's sender and receiver, send the mail, and complete the connection.

   Older versions of sendmail also supported a "debug" command, which allowed a remote user to specify a *program* as the email's recipient, without any authentication. The Internet worm trivially exploited this to start a shell on the remote machine.

2   The finger program was a user program which could be used to discover information about another Unix user; indeed, it was once common to sit in a terminal room and finger people. A sample output is shown in Figure 7.2.

   This example gets its information from the local machine only, but using an @ sign in the command line

```
finger aycock@cpsc.ucalgary.ca
```

   would cause information to be requested about the user from the specified machine. Finger would make a network connection to the *finger daemon* on the remote machine and send a query about the user.

```
220 mail.cpsc.ucalgary.ca ESMTP Sendmail
helo mymachine
250 mail.cpsc.ucalgary.ca Hello mymachine, pleased to meet you
mail from: elvis
250 2.1.0 elvis... Sender ok
rcpt to: aycock
250 2.1.5 aycock... Recipient ok
data
354 Enter mail, end with "." on a line by itself
From: elvis
To: aycock
Subject: the present you sent

Thank you, thank you very much.

Sincerely,

The King
.
250 2.0.0 hAQHNJxY002201 Message accepted for delivery
quit
221 2.0.0 mail.cpsc.ucalgary.ca closing connection
```

Figure 7.1. A conversation with sendmail

```
% finger aycock
Login: aycock                              Name: John Aycock
Directory: /home/aycock                     Shell: /bin/sh
On since Wed Nov 26 09:38 (MST) on pts/2 from server1
No mail.
No plan.
```

Figure 7.2. Finger output

The finger daemon read input from the network connection using C's gets function, which does no bounds checking on what it reads in. The Internet worm would exploit this by performing a stack smashing attack against the finger daemon to get a shell.

3 Several utility programs used to permit a user to run commands on a remote machine. The Internet worm tried two of these in an effort to get a remote shell: rexec and rsh.

Rexec required a password to log in to the remote machine. The worm's third stage would guess at passwords, trying obvious ones like the username, and mounting a dictionary attack too. A *dictionary attack* is where an attacker has a dictionary of commonly-used words, which are tried one by one as potential passwords. The worm's third stage carried a list of 432 words that it used for this purpose.

Rsh could be even more accommodating for getting a remote shell. It had a facility where users coming from specified "trusted" hosts didn't even have to supply a password.

Stage 2 Once a shell was obtained on the remote machine, the worm would send commands to create, compile, and run a small C program on the machine being infected. This program was portable across the prevalent Unix architectures of the time, and had another technical advantage. Because it was sent in source form, it was immune to damage from communication channels which only passed through seven bits out of eight, which would have destroyed a binary executable file.

The compiled program was a "grappling hook" which was used to pull the worm's Stage 3 executable files onto the machine being infected.[103] When run, the grappling hook would make a network connection *back* to the infecting machine (whose worm instance was expecting the incoming connection). This connection was used to transfer several Stage 3 executables, one for each architecture that the worm could infect. These executables would be tried until one succeeded in running.

Stage 3 At this point, the worm was fully established on the infected machine, and would begin trying to propagate itself to other machines.

Some rudimentary stealth measures were deployed. The worm named itself "sh" to appear as a user shell, and modified its command-line arguments; both these would make the running worm process look unremarkable to a casual observer. Previous remnants, like temporary files used for compiling the grappling hook, were removed. Finally, the worm prevented "core dump" files from being created – a Unix system will create core dump files for processes incurring fatal errors, or upon receipt of an explicit user request to do so. This latter step prevented easy capture of worm samples for analysis.

New target machines were selected using information from the infected machine. Information from network interfaces, network routing tables, and various files containing names of other computers were all used to locate new machines to try and infect.

The Internet worm carried no destructive payload. Worm damage was collateral, as each worm instance simply used lots and lots of machine and network resources.

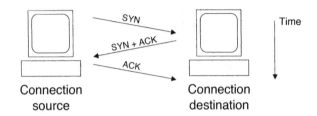

Figure 7.3. TCP connection establishment

7.2 Propagation

Humans are slow, compared to computers and computer networks. Worms thus have the potential to spread very, very quickly, because humans don't have to be involved in the process of worm propagation.[104]

At the extreme end of the scale are *fast burners*, worms that propagate as fast as they possibly can. Some of these worms have special names, reflecting their speed. A *Warhol worm* infects its vulnerable population in less than 15 minutes; this name comes from artist Andy Warhol's famous quote 'In the future everyone will be famous for fifteen minutes.' A *flash worm* goes one better, and infects the vulnerable population in a matter of seconds.

How can a worm propagate this quickly? With a combination of these methods:

- Shorten the initial startup time. Recalling the worm growth curve in Figure 1.2 (page 5), this shifts the growth curve to the left.

- Minimize contention between instances of the worm. This includes avoiding general contention in network traffic, as well as avoiding pointless attempts to re-infect the same machine.

- Increase the rate at which potential target machines are probed, by scanning them in parallel. This is a tradeoff, because such network activity can result in network traffic contention.

- Attack using low-overhead network protocols. The less back-and-forth that a network protocol requires, the faster a worm using that protocol can spread. The Slammer worm, for example, used the User Datagram Protocol (UDP) to infect SQL database servers using a buffer overflow.[105] UDP is a lightweight, connectionless protocol: there is no overhead involved to set up a logical network connection between two computers trying to communicate. From Slammer's point of view, this meant one network packet, one new victim.

  In contrast, worms using a connection-based network protocol like the Transmission Control Protocol (TCP) have several packets' worth of overhead to establish a connection, before any exploit can even be started.[106]

Figure 7.3 shows two computers establishing a connection using TCP. Each computer must send one SYN packet to the other, and acknowledge the other's SYN packet with an ACK. (One ACK is "piggybacked" on a SYN packet, so only three packets are exchanged in practice.) All this network traffic occurs *before* a worm is able to talk to and exploit a server, making TCP-based worms much slower in comparison to UDP-based worms.

At the other end of the speed scale are *surreptitious worms* that deliberately propagate slowly to avoid notice. Such a worm might hide in normal network traffic, like the network traffic for file-sharing. Slow propagation might be used to build up a zombie army for a massive DDoS attack, or for any other purpose for which a botnet might be used.

In the remainder of this section, the initial spread of a worm is considered, as are ways that a worm finds new victim machines to infect.

7.2.1   Initial Seeding

Worms need to be injected into a network somehow. The way that a worm is initially released is called *seeding*. A single network entry point would be relatively easy to trace back to the worm author, and start the worm's growth curve at its lowest point. An effective seeding method should be as anonymous and untraceable as possible, and distribute many instances of the worm into the network.

Three possibilities have been suggested:

- Wireless networks. There are many, many wireless networks connected to the Internet with little or no security enabled.[107] Using wireless networks for seeding satisfies the anonymity criterion, although physical proximity to the wireless access point by the worm writer is required, making this option not entirely risk-free. Barring a co-ordinated release, however, this method of seeding doesn't scale well to injecting large worm populations. A co-ordinated release is risky, too, as many people will know about the worm and its creator.

- Spam. Seeding a worm by spamming the worm out to people can satisfy both effectiveness criteria: anonymity and volume. Spamming can be used to seed worms even when the worm doesn't normally propagate through email.

- Botnets. Botnets may be used in several ways for seeding and, like spamming, meet both effectiveness criteria. Botnets may be used to send the worm's seeding spam, and they may be also used to release the worm directly in a highly-distributed way.

Access to common network services can be had in a hard-to-trace way, so this list is far from complete.

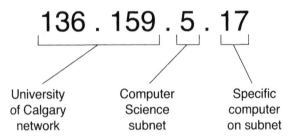

Figure 7.4.   IP address partitioning

7.2.2   Finding Targets

On the Internet, a machine is identified in two ways: by a domain name and an Internet Protocol (IP) address. Domain names are a convenience for humans; they are human-readable and are quietly mapped into IP addresses. IP addresses, which are just numbers, are used internally for the real business of networking, like routing Internet traffic from place to place.

IP addresses come in two flavors, distinguished by a version number: the most prevalent kind now are version 4 addresses (*IPv4*), but support for version 6 addresses (*IPv6*) is increasing. IPv4 addresses are shorter, only 32 bits compared to IPv6's 128 bits, and the same principles apply to both in terms of worm propagation; this book will use IPv4 addresses for conciseness.

The bits of an IP address are partitioned to facilitate routing packets to the correct machine. Part of the address describes the network, part identifies the computer (host) within that network. IP addresses are categorized based on their size:

Network Class	Network Bits	Host Bits
Class A	8	24
Class B	16	16
Class C	24	8

For example, Figure 7.4 breaks down the IP address for the web server at the University of Calgary's Department of Computer Science. The University of Calgary has a class B address, 136.159; its host part is further subdivided, to identify a subnet, 5, and the exact host on that subnet, 17.

Why is this relevant to worms? A worm has to identify a potential target machine. For worm propagation, it is substantially easier for a worm to guess at an IP address and find a target than it is for a worm to guess correctly at a domain name.

A worm looking for machines to infect is said to *scan* for targets; this is different from the use of "scan" to describe anti-virus activity. There are five basic strategies that a worm can use to scan:

Random scanning A worm may pick a target by randomly choosing a value to use as an IP address. This was done, for example, by Code Red I. Choosing an IP address randomly can select a target literally anywhere in the world.

Localized scanning Random scanning is good for widespread distribution, but it's a hit-and-miss approach for worms exploiting technical vulnerabilities to spread. It is much likelier that computers on the same network, in the same administrative domain, are going to be maintained in a similar fashion. For example, if one Windows machine on a network has an unpatched buffer overflow, the chances are good that another Windows machine on the same network is going to be unpatched too.

Localized scanning tries to take advantage of this. Target machines are again chosen randomly, but with a bias towards local machines; a "local machine" is heuristically selected by taking advantage of the IP address partitioning described above. For example, Code Red II picked target IP addresses in this way:[108]

Probability	Target Selection
1/8	All four bytes randomly chosen
3/8	Only last two bytes randomly chosen
4/8	Last three bytes randomly chosen

Hit-list scanning Prior to worm release, a "hit-list" can be compiled which contains the IP addresses of some machines known to be vulnerable to a technical flaw the worm plans to exploit. Compiling such a list is a possible application for a previously-released surreptitious worm, or a botnet. The list need not be 100% accurate, since it will only be used as a starting point, and doesn't need to contain a large number of IP addresses – 50,000 or less are enough.

After its release, the worm starts by targeting the machines named in the hit-list. Each time the worm successfully propagates, it divides the remainder of the list in half, sending half along with the new worm instance. Once the list is exhausted, the worm can fall back onto other scanning strategies.

Hit-list scanning is useful for two reasons:

1 Avoiding contention. The hit-list keeps multiple instances of a worm from targeting the same machines.

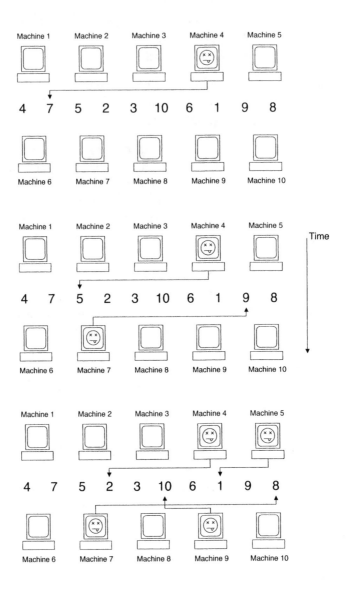

Figure 7.5. Permutation scanning

2 Speeding up initial spread. By providing a list of known targets, slow propagation by trial-and-error is avoided, and the worm's growth curve shifts to the left as a result.

A variation on the hit-list scheme precompiles a list of *all* vulnerable machines on the Internet, and sends it along with the worm in compressed form.

Permutation scanning If a worm is able to tell whether or not a target candidate is already infected, then other means of contention avoidance can be used. *Permutation scanning* is where instances of a worm share a common permutation of the IP address space, a pseudo-random sequence over all 2^{32} possible IP address values. Each new instance is given a position in the sequence at which to start infecting, and the worm continues to work through the sequence from there. Figure 7.5 has an example for a ten-value permutation.

If a machine is encountered which is already infected, then the worm picks a new spot in the sequence randomly. This gives the worm a simple mechanism for distributed coordination without any communication overhead between worm instances. (Interestingly, peer-to-peer networks for file sharing share the same need for low-overhead distributed coordination.[109])

This coordination mechanism can be used by the worm to heuristically detect saturation, too. If a worm instance continually finds already-infected machines, despite randomly resituating itself in the permutation sequence, then it can serve as an indicator that most of the vulnerable machines have been infected. More generally, a worm can mathematically model its own growth curve, to estimate how close it is to the saturation point.[110] The saturation point can signal the opportune time to release a payload, because there is little more to do in terms of spreading, and countermeasures to the worm are doubtlessly being deployed already.

Topological scanning Information on infected machines can be used to select new targets, instead of using a random search. This is called *topological scanning*, because the worm follows the topology of the information it finds.

The topology followed may or may not coincide with the physical network topology. A worm may follow information about a machine's network interfaces to new target hosts, but other types of information can result in propagation along *social* networks. Email worms can mail themselves to email addresses they mine off an infected machine, and IM worms can send themselves to people in a victim's "buddy list."[111]

Topological scanning is particularly useful for propagation in large, sparse address spaces. The Internet worm, for example, used topological scanning due to the relatively small number of machines in the IP address space of 1988. In contrast, random scanning would waste a lot of effort locating targets in such an address space.

Passive Scanning A surreptitious worm can wait for topological information to come to it. A *passive scanning* worm can eavesdrop, or *sniff*, network traffic to gather information about:[112]

- Valid IP addresses. The worm can gather the addresses of potential targets in a way that dodges some of the worm countermeasures in the next chapter.

- Operating system and services. A worm can benefit from knowing a target machine's operating system type, operating system version, network services, and network service versions.[2] Worms able to exploit multiple technical weaknesses can pick a suitable infection vector, and other worms can rule out unsuitable targets.

- Network traffic patterns. A slow worm can limit its network activity to times when there is normally legitimate network activity. The other network activity can act as cover traffic for the worm's operation.

In some cases targets have already been identified for other reasons, and a worm need only extract the information. For example, the Santy worm exploited a flaw in web software, and used Google to search for targets.[113]

Putting all the pieces together – virus-like concealment, exploitation of technical and human weaknesses, hijacking legitimate transactions, extremely rapid spreading – worms are a very potent type of malware. Equally potent defensive measures are needed.

Notes for Chapter 7

1 It wasn't just Yee that referred to it as a virus. Of the two primary sources used for this section, one calls it a virus, one a worm, both argue their case: Eichin and Rochlis [97] and Spafford [298].

2 This is called *passive fingerprinting* [301].

100 Nazario et al. [230].

101 Shoch and Hupp [287, page 176]. This section on the Xerox worm was based on this source too.

102 Yee [350].

103 The term "grappling hook" is from Eichin and Rochlis [97].

104 This section is based on Staniford et al. [304].

105 Ször and Perriot [315].

106 McKusick et al. [202].

107 Stampf [302] mentions the worm potential in wireless forms of communication.

108 CERT [55].

109 Wiley [346].

110 Vogt [337]. Ma et al. [190] analyze self-stopping worms in great detail.

111 Hindocha and Chien [142].

112 Nazario et al. [230].

113 Hypponen [150].

Chapter 8

DEWORMING

Work on handling worms, from a defender's point of view, can be classified three ways: defense, worm capture and containment, and automatic counter-measures. This chapter follows that organization.

Most of the techniques described here can be illustrated on a network like the one in Figure 8.1. An internal network is connected to the Internet through some

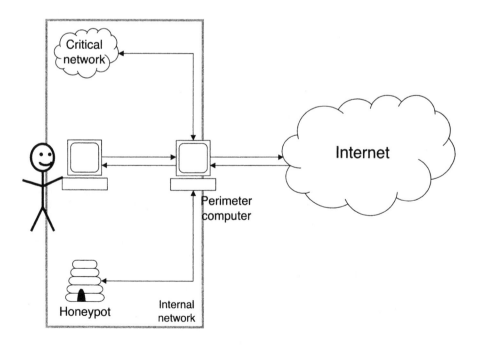

Figure 8.1. An example network

computer at the network's perimeter. The nature of this perimeter computer has been left deliberately vague; it can be a dedicated network router or a general-purpose computer, which may be performing a variety of defensive tasks in addition to shuffling network packets back and forth. The internal network has a critical subnet, a set of machines which special pains must be taken to protect. There is the user and their computer, which is a host on the network. Finally, a computer acting as a "honeypot" may be present, whose role will be described in Section 8.2.1.

First, defense.

8.1 Defense

How can worms be kept out in the first place? Looking at the path from the Internet to the user in Figure 8.1, defensive measures can be taken at any point along that path.

8.1.1 User

User education can't be forgotten. Education is especially useful to prevent the propagation of email worms that require an attachment to be run by a human. Users can also be thought of as finely-attenuated sensors which detect the most insignificant slowdowns in network speed, a fact to which any network administrator can attest. Network traffic from worms that is otherwise hidden may be detected by users.

8.1.2 Host

The next line of defense is the user's computer; defenses deployed here are called *host-based* defenses. Some of the best defenses against worms are the most mundane: applying patches, limiting the amount of available services on a machine. From there, defenses specific to likely attack vectors are the next step, followed by anti-virus software being used on the host to look for worms.

8.1.2.1 Patching

Many intrusions by malware are completely preventable. A lot of worms do not exploit previously-unknown vulnerabilities, but use known vulnerabilities for which a patch is available. Illustrated in Figure 8.2, the rate of patching is an exponential decay curve which never reaches zero.[100] In other words, many machines remain vulnerable for a long period of time after a patch is available, and some machines are never patched. The situation is even worse: the overall patching rate does not change dramatically even when a widely-publicized worm is circulating, exploiting the vulnerability.[1] Studies of a number of security vulnerabilities for which patches are available have shown similar, discouraging results.[101]

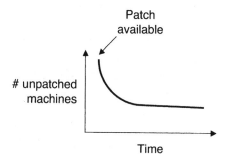

Figure 8.2. Rate of patching over time

There may be a variety of excellent reasons for the laxity of patching.[102] Qualified personnel may not be available to apply a patch, or may not have time. People may not know about the patch. Bureaucratic issues may preclude proper maintenance, or policy matters may prevail – for example, some companies require updates to be tested before distributing them. This policy may be seen to be a prudent precaution, because applying some patches (especially hastily-prepared ones made in response to a vulnerability) may break more software than it fixes.

New commodity operating systems (e.g., Windows, MacOS) have automated update systems which notify a user that updates are available, and lead them through the process of downloading and installing the updates. Not everyone runs the newest version of an operating system, and policy may trump the use of automated updates, but in the long term, automated update systems will probably have a positive impact on security.

8.1.2.2   Limiting Available Services

The reasoning for limiting available services comes from two premises:

1 Worms exploit technical weaknesses, like buffer overflows, in network servers. (Here, a server refers to the program that supplies a particular service.)

2 Technical weaknesses are likely to evenly manifest themselves throughout network server code.

Based on these premises, the conclusion can be drawn that the more network servers a machine runs, the likelier it is that some technical weakness is exposed that a worm can exploit. The corollary is that the fewer network servers a machine runs, the more secure it is.

While the soundness of this logic may be debated, the general idea of reducing potential attack vectors to defend against worms is a good one. There are pragmatic aspects to limiting network servers, too, in that it also limits the amount of software to patch.

The hard part is determining which servers to shut down. This can involve much trial-and-error even for experts, turning off one server after another to see if it affects the machine's operation. Some effects may only be apparent after an extended period of time, if a server is shut down that only sees occasional use.

8.1.2.3 Countermeasures against Specific Weaknesses

Besides trying to reduce the number of running servers that might contain weaknesses, countermeasures can be used to guard against specific kinds of technical weakness that are exploited by worms. A number of these were presented in Section 6.1.5, such as:

- Canaries to detect buffer overflows

- Randomizing memory locations to make finding memory addresses harder

- Code monitoring to watch for unusual behavior

Countermeasures to specific technical weaknesses are certainly an important part of worm defense. However, such countermeasures are based on assumptions about how worms are likely to break into a system. They are of little use against any new types of technical vulnerability that do not happen to be guarded against, and they do not catch worms that use social engineering to spread.

8.1.2.4 Anti-Virus Software

Anti-virus software can and does look for worms, but there are three major problems that hamper anti-virus software's effectiveness:

1 To function properly, anti-virus software detecting known worms needs an up-to-date virus database, but virus database updates cannot be prepared and deployed fast enough to counter rapidly-spreading worms.

2 Some powerful anti-virus techniques are unusable: integrity checking and emulation certify a program as malware-free at the start of the program's execution. These techniques are useless against a worm that injects its code into a running program which has already been declared clean.

3 A worm need not reside someplace that anti-virus software can analyze. Many anti-virus techniques are geared to catch malware that writes itself somewhere in a computer's filesystem; a worm that exploits a buffer overflow in a long-running network server can remain in memory only, undetected.

This suggests that anti-virus software is no panacea for worm defense. The last problem, detecting in-memory threats, can at least be addressed.

8.1.2.5 Memory Scanning

Searching for in-memory threats is called *memory scanning*. Once, memory scanning was an easy task for anti-virus software: the amount of physical memory on machines was small, and any program could read from any part of the memory. Now, two features have made their way into almost all operating systems, both of which complicate memory scanning:

Memory protection. Hardware protection prevents one process from accessing another process' memory unless they have both explicitly agreed to share memory. This memory protection greatly increases system stability, because it limits the effect of a misbehaving process – malicious or otherwise. The drawback from the anti-virus point of view is that memory protection prevents a memory scanner from directly looking at other processes' memory.

Virtual memory. The operating system and hardware can conspire to provide *virtual memory* to processes. With virtual memory, each process thinks it has an enormous amount of memory to use, more memory than is physically available. The virtual memory contents are stored on disk, and the physical memory acts as a cache for the virtual memory. The operating system, with hardware support, traps virtual memory references that refer to virtual memory pages which are not currently present in physical memory. The operating system arranges for the absent memory pages to be loaded from disk to physical memory, possibly evicting some physical memory contents to make room.

Disks are orders of magnitude slower than physical memory. If a process were to randomly access its virtual memory, it would slow to a crawl waiting for memory pages to be loaded from disk. Fortunately, that rarely happens. Most programs naturally exhibit a high degree of *locality of reference*, meaning that they tend to reference only a small set of memory areas at any given time.[2] As a program's execution continues, the set of memory areas referenced changes to a *different* small set of memory areas, and so on. The memory pages currently required by a process are called its *working set*, and the operating system ideally keeps all processes' working sets in physical memory to minimize slow disk activity.

Virtual memory is a huge convenience for programmers, because it reduces the need to work around physical memory restrictions. The net effect of virtual memory for anti-virus software is that a memory scanner doesn't have everything immediately accessible that it needs to scan.

An operating system can have memory protection without having virtual memory; virtual memory *can* be supported without having strong memory protection between processes, but this is not normally done. The remainder of this section only considers operating systems with both memory protection and virtual memory, because it is the hardest case to handle.

There are several different ways that memory scanning can be implemented in such operating systems:[103]

- As an ordinary user process, anti-virus software can scan memory by using operating system facilities intended for debugging. Debuggers need to examine (and modify) the memory of a process being debugged, and operating systems have an API to support debuggers.[104] Anti-virus software can use this API, pretending to be a debugger, to examine and scan processes' memory. This avoids memory protection issues.

  Care must be taken when scanning the memory of a process. Attempting to scan all the virtual memory that a process uses will force the operating system to bring in memory pages from disk, an incredibly slow operation in comparison to accessing physical memory. The victim process being scanned would have its working set of memory pages decimated until the operating system slowly recovers them. If possible, querying the operating system to determine what memory pages are already present in memory, and only scanning those pages, reduces unpleasantness with a process' virtual memory. The alternative is grim: one memory scanner increased the resident memory usage of a poor process being scanned by over 2000%.

  Memory scanning can further be limited, beyond restricting it to in-memory pages. Ideally, assuming that the anti-virus software already examined a process' executable code in the filesystem before it ran, the only thing that requires rescanning is memory that has been changed. Extracting this information from the operating system is not always possible, however.

  Not all processes can be debugged by a user process, for security reasons. For example, processes belonging to another user or privileged system processes will not permit just any user process to attach a debugger to them. The anti-virus software must run with escalated privileges to allow it to "debug" all other processes.

- Some of the problems with the memory scanning implementation above can be avoided if the anti-virus software runs as part of the operating system kernel. Kernel-based anti-virus software will have permission to access all processes' memory, avoiding access problems.

  A memory scanner can be integrated more deeply into the kernel for even better effect. Tying a memory scanner into the operating system's virtual memory manager would still avoid permission problems, plus give the memory scanner access to information about modified and in-memory pages.

Once a worm or other malware is discovered in memory, memory disinfection can be done by terminating the offending process completely. Riskier options are to terminate suspect threads within the infected process, or to patch the code in the infected process as it runs. Operating systems share memory pages between processes when possible, as for shared library code or read-only program code segments, and consequently many processes may be affected by an infection – the best memory disinfection may be a reboot. Disinfection may be an ultimately futile operation anyway, because if the infection vector was a technical weakness, then a worm can re-exploit the machine right away.

Any of the above implementations of memory scanning leave another window of opportunity for worms, because the scanning is not done continuously. Rescanning memory continuously, for each memory write, would involve a prohibitive amount of overhead except perhaps for interpreted languages that already proudly sport prohibitive overhead.

Philosophically, it is not clear that memory scanning by anti-virus software is a good idea. Memory scanning necessarily weakens the memory protection between unrelated code, in this case the anti-virus software and the process' code being examined. Strong memory protection was implemented in operating systems for good reason, and circumventing it may only introduce new attack vectors. Anti-virus software that doesn't scan memory, in combination with other defenses, may be a wiser choice.

8.1.3 Perimeter

The first line of defense for a network is at its perimeter. The computer at the perimeter forming the defense may be a general-purpose computer, or a special-purpose computer like a router. In either case, there are several functions the perimeter computer may serve to block incoming worms. Two functions, firewalls and intrusion detection systems, are presented in their "pure" form below; in practice, the perimeter computer may perform both of these functions and more.

8.1.3.1 Firewalls

A *firewall* is software which filters incoming network traffic to a network; if the software runs on a computer dedicated to this task, then that computer is also referred to as a firewall.[3] Firewall software can be run on a perimeter computer, a host computer, or both.

Each network packet in the traffic has two basic parts, header and data. This is analogous to sending a letter: the envelope has the addresses of the letter's sender and receiver, and the letter's contents are sealed inside the envelope. A packet's header has the sender and receiver information, and its data contains the packet contents that are meant for the recipient. Basic firewalls filter network packets based on header information:[4]

- The source IP address, or the computer that the packet purportedly comes from.

- The source port. Each computer has a fixed number of virtual "ports" for communication; the combination of an IP address and port identifies a communications endpoint.

- The IP address of the computer where the packet is destined.

- The destination port. The network servers providing services usually reside at well-known port numbers, so that a computer trying to contact a service knows where to direct its request.

- The protocol type. Filtering on the protocol type results in a very coarse-grained discrimination between different traffic types: connection-based (TCP), connectionless (UDP), and low-level control messages (ICMP).

A firewall will have a set of rules which describe the policy it should implement – in other words, which packets it should pass through, and which packets it should drop. A firewall *could* look at a packet's data too, called *deep packet inspection*, but the format and semantics of the data depend on exactly where the packet is going. Making sense of the packet data would require the firewall to understand the language of every network service, and doing so would both slow and complicate a firewall, just like opening and reading a letter is slower and more complicated than glancing at its envelope.

As a worm defense, a firewall provides a similar function to limiting available network services. A firewall prevents a worm from communicating with, and possibly exploiting, vulnerable network servers. It only defends against *outside* attacks, so any worm that makes it past the firewall (e.g., an email worm that a user runs on their computer behind the firewall) can operate with impunity.

8.1.3.2   Intrusion Detection Systems

An *intrusion detection system* analyzes incoming network traffic, performing deep packet inspection to watch for packets or sequences of packets that signal attacks.[105] Like firewalls, intrusion detection systems can run on the perimeter computer or a host computer. Like criminals, intrusion detection systems go by a wide variety of names:

- Intrusion detection systems (IDS).

- Host intrusion detection systems (HIDS), for host-based IDS.

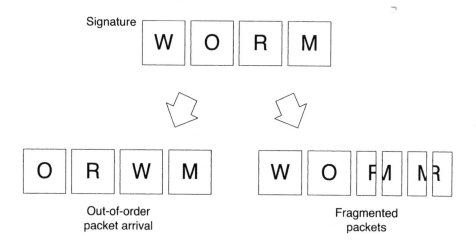

Figure 8.3. Signatures in network traffic

- Network intrusion detection systems (NIDS), for network-based IDS. These need not only be at the network perimeter. IDS (and firewalls) may also be deployed internally to a network, to add extra worm protection for critical internal subnets.[106]

- Intrusion prevention systems (IPS).[5] "Prevention" implies that an attack is thwarted rather than just noticed. Although there are no commonly agreed-upon definitions, an IPS would imply a system that filters traffic like a firewall, but that is able to do deep packet inspection like an IDS.[107] In contrast, an IDS doesn't filter traffic, only watches it and raises an alarm if suspicious activity is found.

For worms, an intrusion detection system can either look for the signatures of known worms, or for generic signatures of technical weakness exploits like a NOP sled.[6] Exactly the same algorithms can be used for IDS as for signature matching in anti-virus software, along with which come the same signature updating issues.[7]

IDS signature matching is not completely straightforward, because of the properties of network traffic. A signature may not be obvious in the stream of input packets (Figure 8.3):

- Packets containing a signature may arrive out of order.

- A packet may be *fragmented*, broken into smaller pieces which may be sent out of sequence.

Network traffic can be deliberately crafted to present an IDS with these non-obvious signatures. The host machine receiving the packets will reassemble

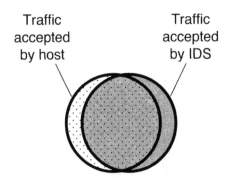

Figure 8.4. Traffic accepted by an IDS and a host

the fragments and reorder the packets. The IDS *should* reconstruct the correct packet stream also, but in practice may not do so correctly or may reconstruct it differently than the receiving host. In either case, the result is exploitable. One solution is *traffic normalization,* which ensures that network traffic is in a canonical, unambiguous form for the IDS and other hosts by reordering and reassembling packets if necessary.[108] Even so, a worm may defy easy signature-based detection by being encrypted, polymorphic, or metamorphic.

Other avenues of attack are possible against an IDS. With the exception of a host-based IDS, an IDS runs on a separate machine which may have different behavior than the hosts it protects. Figure 8.4 shows the results: an IDS may accept traffic that a host will reject; a host may accept traffic that an IDS will reject. An IDS may also see traffic that never reaches a host. For example, each IP packet has a "time-to-live" counter (TTL) that is decremented once for every time the packet is sent from machine to machine during its delivery; when the counter reaches zero, the packet is discarded. Figure 8.5 shows an attack exploiting the TTL counter. The traffic has been constructed so that the IDS receives extra packets that prevent it from seeing the attack signature, yet the extra packets expire due to a low TTL value before reaching the targeted host.[109]

The fact that an IDS can detect but not block attacks is exploitable too. In the simplest case, a fast-spreading worm attacks and executes its payload before an IDS alarm is responded to. But an IDS is a so-called *fail-open* system, meaning that it leaves the network accessible in the event that the IDS fails. A more advanced attack would first overload the IDS with a denial of service, then perform the worm infection while the IDS is struggling and unable to raise an alarm.

Finally, an IDS is a real-time system.[8] It must be able to keep up with the maximum rate of network traffic. Powerful, accurate, but high-overhead de-

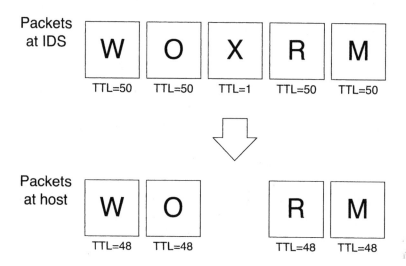

Figure 8.5. TTL attack on an IDS

tection techniques are not suitable for use in an IDS. Taken together, all these drawbacks make an IDS yet another partial worm defense.

8.2   Capture and Containment

If defense is about keeping a worm *out*, then capture and containment is about keeping a worm *in*. This may seem like a counterintuitive thing to do, but if a worm has breached the primary defenses, then limiting the worm's spread may be the best remaining option. It has even been suggested that it is naïve to assume that all machines can remain clean during a worm attack, and that some machines may have to be sacrificed to ensure the survival of the majority.[110]

Worm containment can limit internal spread within a network. This reduces the amount of worm infections to clean up, and also has wider repercussions. Containing a worm and preventing it from spreading to other people's networks is arguably part of being a good Internet neighbor, but more practically, reasonable containment measures may limit legal liability. Two containment measures are presented in this section, reverse firewalls and throttling.

Worm capture can be done for a variety of reasons. Capturing a worm can provide an early warning of worm activity. It can also slow and limit a worm's spread, depending on the type of worm and worm capture. Honeypots are one method of worm capture.

8.2.1   Honeypots

Honeypots are computers that are meant to be compromised, computers which may be either real or emulated. Early documented examples were intended to bait and study human attackers,[9] but honeypots can be used equally well to capture worms.[10]

There are three questions related to honeypots:

1 How is a honeypot built? A honeypot should be constructed so that a worm is presented with an environment complete enough to infect. In addition, a honeypot should ideally be impossible for a worm to break out of, and a honeypot should be easy to restore to a pristine state. Emulators are often considered for honeypot systems, because they meet all these criteria.

   The major problem with using emulators for honeypots is also a problem when using emulators for anti-virus software: it may be possible for a worm to detect that it is in an emulator.[111] For example, a worm can look for device names provided by common emulators.

2 How is a worm drawn to a honeypot? A honeypot should be located in an otherwise-unused place in the network, and not be used for any other purpose except as a honeypot. The reasoning is that a honeypot should have no reason to receive legitimate traffic – *all* traffic to a honeypot is suspicious.[112] A honeypot doesn't generate network traffic by itself, the downside being that a passive scanning worm will be able to avoid the honeypot.

   One honeypot with one IP address in an large network stands little chance of being targeted by a worm scanning randomly or quasi-randomly. A large range of consecutive addresses can be routed to a single honeypot to supply a larger worm target.[113]

   Other mechanisms can be used to lure the discriminating worm. A honeypot can provide a fake shared network directory containing goat files, for worms that spread using such shared directories – the goat files and shared directory can be periodically checked for changes that may signify worm activity. Email worms can be directed to a honeypot by salting mailing lists with fake email addresses residing on the honeypot.

3 What can a honeypot do with a worm? It can capture samples of worms, and be used to gauge the overall amount and type of worm activity. A honeypot is one way to get an early warning of worms; more ways will be seen in Section 8.3.

   Honeypots can deliberately respond slowly, to try and slow down a worm's spread. This type of honeypot system is called a *tarpit*.[114] A worm that scans for infectible machines in parallel will not be susceptible to a tarpit, however.[115]

Certain types of worms can be severely impacted by honeypot capture. A hit-list worm passes half its targets along to each newly-infected machine, so hitting a honeypot cuts the worm's spread from that point by half.[116]

It is questionable whether or not honeypots are as useful against worms as other means of defense. Early warning of a spreading worm is useful, but there are other ways to receive a warning, and worm capture is not generally useful to anyone except specialists.

8.2.2   Reverse Firewalls

A *reverse firewall* filters outgoing traffic from a network, unlike a normal firewall which filters incoming traffic. In practice, filtering in both directions would probably be handled by the same software or device.

As with firewalls, the key to an effective reverse firewall is its policy: what outbound connections should be permitted? The principle is that a worm's connections to infect other machines will not conform to the reverse firewall policy, and the worm's spread is thus blocked. The decision is based on the same packet header information as was used for a firewall, including source and destination IP addresses and ports. For example, policy may dictate that no machine in the critical network of Figure 8.1 may have an outgoing Internet connection, or that a user's computer may only connect to outside machines on port 80, the usual port for a web server.

A host-based reverse firewall can implement a finer-grained policy by restricting Internet access on a per-application basis. Only certain specified applications are allowed to open network connections, and then only connections in keeping with the reverse firewall's outbound traffic policy. A worm, as a newly-installed executable unknown to the reverse firewall, could not open network connections to spread. In theory. Still, worm activity is possible in the presence of a host-based reverse firewall:

- A worm can use alternative methods to spread when faced with a reverse firewall, such as placing itself in shared network directories. As a result, no worm code is run on the host being monitored by the reverse firewall.

- Legitimate code that is already approved to access the Internet can be subverted by a worm. A worm can simply fake user input to an existing mail program to spread via email, for instance. A worm could exhibit viral behavior, too, infecting an existing "approved" executable by indirect means, like a web browser plug-in, or more direct means that a virus would normally use. To guard against the latter case, a host-based reverse firewall can use integrity checking to watch for changes to approved executables.

- Social engineering may be employed by a worm. A host-based reverse firewall may prompt the user with the name of the program attempting to open a network connection, for the user to permit or deny the operation. This would typically happen under two circumstances:

  1 The program has never opened a network connection before. This would be the case for a worm, newly-installed software, or old, installed software that has never been used.

  2 The program was approved to use the network before, but has changed; a software upgrade may have occurred, or the program's code may have been infected.

A surreptitious worm could patiently wait until a user installs or upgrades software, then open a network connection. The user is likely to assume the reverse firewall's prompt is related to the legitimate software modification and permit the worm's connection. The worm may also give its executable an important-sounding name, which the reverse firewall will dutifully report in the user prompt, intimidating the user into allowing the worm's operation for fear that their computer won't work properly.

Legitimate applications may farm out Internet operations to a separate program. Legitimate user prompts from a reverse firewall can request network access approval for software with radically-different names than the application that the user ran. Users will likely approve any user prompts made shortly after they initiate an action in an application, and a worm can exploit this to sneakily receive a user's approval for its network operations.

The underlying problem with a reverse firewall is that it tries to block unauthorized activity by watching network connection activity, an action performed by worms *and* legitimate software. False positives are guaranteed, which open the possibility of circumventing the reverse firewall.

8.2.3 Throttling

A reverse firewall can be improved upon by taking context into account. Instead of watching for single connections being opened, the *overall* rate of new connections can be monitored. A system that limits the rate of outgoing connections that a given machine is allowed to make is called a *throttle*.[117]

A throttle doesn't attempt to distinguish between worms and legitimate software, nor does it try to prevent worms from entering. It only considers outbound connections, and throttles the rate at which *all* programs make them. As a throttle only slows down the connection rate, as opposed to dropping connections, no harm is done even if there are false positives – everything still works, just more slowly.

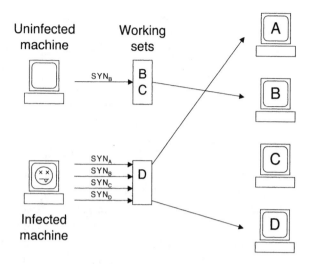

Figure 8.6. Network traffic throttling

The throttling process can be refined with more context. Most connections are established to machines that were recently connected to; this is similar to the locality of reference exploited by virtual memory. For example, a web browser may initially connect to a web site to download a web page, followed by subsequent connections to retrieve images for the page, followed by requests for linked web pages at the site. A working set of recently-connected machines can be kept for a throttled host. Connections to machines in the working set proceed without delay, as do new connections which fit into the fixed-length working set. Other connections are delayed by a second, not long enough to cause grief, but effective for slowing down fast-moving worms. Extreme worm-like behavior can be caught with the context provided by the throttling delay. Too many outstanding new connections can cause a machine to be locked out from the network.[11]

TCP connections are started by the connecting machine sending a SYN packet, and a throttle can use these SYN packets as an indicator of new connections. In Figure 8.6, a pair of machines are throttled with a working set of size two. The uninfected machine's new connection to machine B passes through immediately, because B was connected to recently, and is therefore present in the working set. The infected machine has its connection to machine A go through, because there is one free spot in the working set; machine D is in the working set, and that connection goes through as well. The other two connections the infected machine makes are delayed. With adaptations, the throttle concept can be extended beyond TCP to UDP, as well as higher-level applications like email and instant messaging.[118]

Throttles are designed around heuristics characterizing "normal" network usage. Like other heuristic systems, throttles can be evaded by avoiding behavior that the heuristics look for.[119] For example, a worm can slow its rate of spreading down, avoiding the lockout threshold; the number of infection attempts each worm instance makes can be constrained to the throttle's working set size to avoid delays. Because throttles are not widely used at present, a worm's best strategy may be to ignore the possibility of throttles altogether, as they will not significantly impact the overall worm spread.

One criticism leveled at throttles is that they may slow down some programs, like mail transport agents, that can legitimately have a high connection rate.[120] Different throttling mechanisms which address this criticism can be devised by using additional context information. Worms poking randomly for victims on the network will have a higher probability of failure than legitimate programs – either there is no machine at the address the worm generates, or the machine there doesn't supply a suitably-exploitable service.[121] A throttle can take the success of connection attempts into account.

A *credit-based* throttle assigns a number of credits to each host it monitors, akin to a bank account. Only hosts with a positive account balance are allowed to make outbound connections; a zero balance will result in a host's outgoing connections being delayed or blocked completely. A host starts with a small initial balance, and its account is debited for each connection attempt the host makes, and credited for each of the connection attempts that succeed. Host account balances are reexamined every second for fairness: too-high balances are pared back, and hosts with persistent zero balances are credited.[12]

Unfortunately, a credit-based throttle doesn't fare well against worms that violate its assumptions about worm scanning. A worm using hit-list, topological, or passive scanning would naturally tend to make successful connections, for instance. Special attacks can be crafted, too. A worm need only mix its random scans with connections to hosts (infected or otherwise) that are known to respond, to avoid being throttled.

In computer science, sometimes solving the general problem is easier than solving a more specific problem. Instead of trying to discern worm traffic from legitimate traffic, or watching individual hosts' new connections, a general problem can be considered: how can network load be fairly balanced? Allocating bandwidth such that high-bandwidth applications (fast-spreading worms, DDoS attacks, file transfers, streaming media) do not starve low-bandwidth applications (web browsing, terminal sessions) may effectively throttle the speed and network impact of worm spread.[122]

8.3   Automatic Countermeasures

The losses from worm attacks can be reduced in other ways besides slowing worm propagation. Especially for fast-spreading worms, automatic countermeasures are the only possible defense that can react quickly enough. There are two problems to solve:

1 How to detect worm activity. Activity detection serves as the trigger for automatic countermeasures.

2 What countermeasures to take. The reaction must be appropriate to the threat, keeping in mind that worm detection may produce false positives. Severing the Internet connection every time someone in Marketing gets overzealous surfing the web will not be tolerated for long.

Several methods to detect worm activity have been seen already. Worm capture using honeypots is one method; detecting a sudden spike in excessive throttling is another. Trying to capture various facets of worm behavior leads to other methods, for example:

- A worm may exploit a vulnerability in one particular network server, located at a well-known port. A worm activity monitor can watch for a lot of incoming *and* outgoing traffic destined to one port. This can be qualified by the number of distinct IP address destinations, on the premise that legitimate traffic between two machines may involve heavy use of the same port, but worms will try to fan out to many different machines.[123]

- Most network applications refer to other machines using human-readable domain names, which are mapped into IP addresses with queries to the *domain name system* (DNS). Worms, on the other hand, mostly scan using IP addresses directly. Worm activity may thus be characterized by correlating DNS queries with connection attempts – connections not preceded by DNS requests may signify worms.[124] Unfortunately, this registers false positives for some legitimate applications, so a Draconian reaction based on this classifier is not the best idea.

What reaction should be taken to worm activity? Some examples of automatic countermeasures are below.[125]

- Affected machines can be cut off from the network to prevent further worm spread. A more aggressive approach may be taken to guard critical networks, which may be automatically isolated to try and prevent a worm from getting inside them.

- Targeted network servers can be automatically shut down.

- Filtering rules can be inserted automatically into firewalls to block the hosts from which worm activity is originating.[13] Or, a filter can drop packets addressed to the port of a targeted network server,[126] which is less resource-intensive as the number of worm-infected machines increases.

Automatic countermeasures must be deployed judiciously, because an attacker can also use them, deliberately triggering the countermeasures to perform a DoS attack.[127] This danger can be mitigated by providing automatic countermeasure systems with a *whitelist*, a list of systems which are not allowed to be blocked.[128]

Notes for Chapter 8

1 Strictly speaking, the worm release causes another, smaller, exponential patching decay curve [262].

2 This is especially true of code, somewhat less so for data, although some data structures and algorithms play more nicely with virtual memory than others. Stacks, for example, exhibit a high degree of locality when they are accessed with "push" and "pop" operations.

3 The firewalls described here would be classed as "packet-filtering" firewalls. Cheswick and Bellovin, for example, distinguish between several different kinds of firewall [68].

4 The header information here is based on the information available for the widely-used IP protocol suite.

5 The acronyms NIPS and HIPS have tragically failed to materialize.

6 Although as with viruses, a worm may try to disguise this feature, possibly by using junk code instead of a NOP sled [253].

7 This describes only signature-based IDS. Another type, anomaly-based IDS, watches for traffic abnormalities rather than any specific feature [20]. Watching for abnormalities that may signify worm activity is examined in Section 8.3.

8 A soft real-time system, that is.

9 For example, Cheswick's famous observations of "Berferd" [67]. There do not seem to be any publicly-documented examples prior to 1990 [301]. It is interesting that a 1980 report specifically excluded a threat scenario which corresponds to a honeypot: 'Penetrator Not Authorized Use of Computer' but 'Penetrator Authorized to Use Data/Program Resource' [11, page 7].

10 Foulkes and Morris [115] and Overton [236]. A "virus trap" patent application in the mid-1990s arguably suggests this use of honeypots, but there the trap is used to execute programs before they are transferred to a protected machine [281].

11 The original work used a working set of length five, and a lockout threshold of 100 [325].

12 Suggested values are an initial balance of ten credits, a debit of one for initiated connections, and a credit of two for successful connections. Hosts over their initial balance have a third of their credits clawed back each second, and hosts are given one credit after having a zero balance for four seconds [276].

13 One vendor calls this *shunning* [73].

100 This section is based on Rescorla [262] except where otherwise noted. For simplicity, applying workarounds and upgrading to new, fixed software versions are also considered "patching" here because they all have the same net effect: fixing the vulnerability.

101 Arbaugh et al. [19], Moore et al. [212], and Provos and Honeyman [255].

102 Arbaugh et al. [19] and Provos and Honeyman [255].

103 These, and the disinfection options, are based on Ször [310].

104 Rosenberg [268].

105 This section is based on Ptacek and Newsham [256] unless otherwise noted.

106 Foulkes and Morris [115].

107 Desai [88].

108 Handley et al. [135].

109 Paxson [243].

110 Ford and Thompson [114].

111 Holz and Raynal [145] and Krawetz [173].

112 Oudot [234].

113 Foulkes and Morris [115] describe this, and the "other mechanisms" below. Overton [236] also talks about luring worms with fake shared network resources.

114 Oudot and Holz [235].

115 Oudot [234].

116 Nazario [229].

117 This section is based on Twycross and Williamson [325] except where otherwise noted.

118 See Twycross and Williamson [325] (UDP), Williamson [347] (email), and Williamson et al. [348] (instant messaging).

119 These suggestions are from Staniford et al. [303].

120 This, the credit-based throttle, and attacks on the credit-based throttle, are from Schechter et al. [276].

121 Chen and Ranka [62].

122 Matrawy et al. [197].

123 Chen and Heidemann [63].

124 Whyte et al. [345].

125 Foulkes and Morris [115] and Oudot [234].

126 Chen and Heidemann [63].

127 Jung et al. [156] and Ptacek and Newsham [256].

128 Jung et al. [156] and Whyte et al. [345].

Chapter 9

"APPLICATIONS"

Malware can arguably be used in many areas, for better or worse. This chapter briefly looks at a number of "applications" for malicious software, for want of a better word. The applications are roughly grouped in order of increasing gravity: good (benevolent malware), annoying (spam), illegal (access-for-sale worms and cryptovirology), and martial (information warfare and cyberterrorism).

9.1 Benevolent Malware

"Benevolent malicious software" is obviously a contradiction in terms. Normally specific types of malware would be named – a benevolent virus, a benevolent worm. The generic term *benevolent malware* will be used to describe software which would otherwise be classified as malware, yet is intended to have a "good" effect.[100]

Real attempts at benevolent malware have been made.[1] For example:

- Den Zuk, a boot-sector infecting virus in 1988, did no damage itself but removed the Pakistani Brain and Ohio viruses from a system. Later variants had the nasty habit of reformatting disks.[101]

- In 2001, the Cheese worm circulated, trying to clean up after the Lion (1i0n) worm that had hit Linux systems. The problem was that Cheese's operation produced a lot of network traffic.[102]

- The Welchia worm tried to clean up Blaster-infected machines in 2003, even going so far as to automatically apply an official Microsoft patch for the bug that Blaster exploited.[103] Again, Welchia produced so much network traffic that the cure was worse than the disease.

These latter two can be thought of as "predator" worms. Such a predator worm could both destroy existing instances of its target worm, as well as immunize a machine against further incursions through a particular infection vector. Studies have been done simulating the effect that a well-constructed predator worm would have on its worm "prey." Simulations predict that, *if* a predator worm and immunization method are ready in advance, then a predator worm can significantly curtail the spread of a target worm.[104] However, a number of hurdles remain, legal, ethical, and technical.

Legally, a predator worm is violating the law by breaking into machines, despite its good intentions. It may be possible to unleash a predator worm in a private network, in which the predator worm's author has permission for their worm to operate, but there is a risk of the worm escaping from an open network.

Ethically, releasing a predator worm on the Internet at large affects machines whose owners haven't permitted such an activity, and past examples have inspired no confidence that a predator worm's impact would be beneficial in practice. Even if a predator worm's network activity were controlled, unexpected software interactions could be expected on machines that are infected. A worm's effect would have to be incredibly damaging to society, far more so than any seen to date, before a predator worm's actions could be seen to contribute to a universal good.

Technically, there are the issues of control, compatibility, and consumption of resources mentioned above. There is also the thorny issue of verification: what is a predator worm doing, and how can its behavior be verified? Has a predator worm been subverted by another malware writer, and how can antivirus software distinguish good worms from bad?[105]

Of all the possible applications for benevolent malware, including predator worms, there has been no "killer application," a problem for which benevolent malware is clearly the best solution. Everything doable by benevolent malware can also be accomplished by other, more controlled means.

One possible niche for benevolent malware is the area of mobile agents. A *mobile agent* is a program that transfers itself from one computer to another as it performs one or more tasks on behalf of a user.[106] For example, a user's mobile agent may propagate itself from one airline site to another, in search of cheap airfares. From the point of view of malware, mobile agents bear more than a passing resemblance to rabbits, and serious questions have been raised about mobile agent security.[107] As was the case for benevolent malware, mobile agents may be a solution in search of a problem: one analysis concluded that mobile agents had overall advantages, but 'With one rather narrow exception, there is nothing that can be done with mobile agents that cannot also be done with other means.'[108]

9.2   Spam

An infected computer may just be a means to an end. Malware can install open proxy servers, which can be used to relay spam.[2] It can also turn infected machines into zombies that can be used for a variety of purposes, like conducting DDoS attacks. In either case, the malware writer would use the infected computer later, with almost no chance of being caught.

A zombie network can be leveraged to send more effective spam: infected computers can be viewed as repositories of legitimate email corpora. Malware can mine information about a user's email-writing style and social network, then use that analysis to customize new spam messages being sent out, so that they appear to originate from the user.[109] For example, malware can use saved email to learn a user's typical habits for email capitalization, misspellings, and signatures. The malware can then automatically mimic those habits in spam sent to people the user normally emails; these people are also discovered through malware mining saved email.

9.3   Access-for-Sale Worms

Access-for-sale worms are the promise of scalable, targeted intrusion. A worm author creates a worm which compromises machines and installs a back door on them. Access to the back door is transferred by the worm author to a "cyberthief," who then uses the back door to break into the machine.[3]

Access to a machine's back door would be unique to a machine, and guarded by a cryptographic key. By transferring the key, a worm author grants back door access to that one machine. There is a fine granularity of control, because access is granted on a machine-by-machine basis.

Why would access to a single machine be of interest, when entire botnets can be had? Crime, particularly stealing information which may later be used for blackmail or identity theft. The value of such access increases in proportion to its exclusivity – in other words, a competitor must not be allowed to obtain and sell access too. Ironically, this means that a good access-for-sale worm must patch the vulnerabilities in a machine it compromises, to prevent a competing access-for-sale worm from doing the same thing.

There are two "business models" for access-for-sale worms:

1 Organized crime. A crime organization retains the services of a worm author and a group of cyberthieves, shown in Figure 9.1. The worm author creates and deploys an access-for-sale worm, and the back door keys are distributed to the cyberthieves. This keeps the "turf" divided amongst the cyberthieves, who then mine the compromised machines for information.[4] Due to the insular nature of organized crime, countermeasures that come between the worm author and cyberthieves are unlikely to work. Standard worm countermeasures are the only reliable defenses.

2 Disorganized crime. Here, the worm author sells a back door key to a cyberthief. Compromised machines must first be advertised to potential customers by the worm author: this may be as crude as posting a list on some

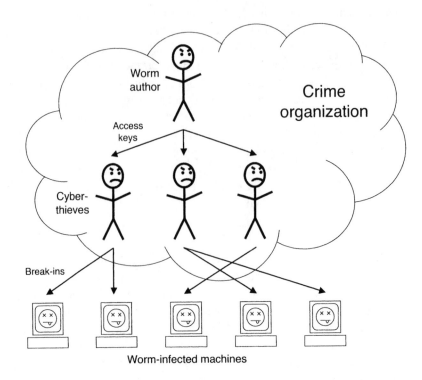

Figure 9.1. Organized crime and access-for-sale worms

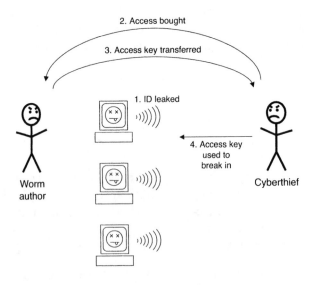

Figure 9.2. Disorganized crime and access-for-sale worms

underground website, or an infected machine may leak a unique identifier on some covert channel that a customer can detect.[5] The customer-cyberthief buys the back door access key for their chosen target machine from the worm author, which is used by the cyberthief to break in. The whole process is shown in Figure 9.2.

This model admits two additional defenses. First, the worm author's reputation can be attacked. The worm author and cyberthief probably don't know one another, so an access key sale is based on the seller's reputation and a certain amount of trust. One defense would make an infected machine continue to look infected, even after the machine has been cleaned, in the hopes of damaging the seller's reputation. Second, law enforcement authorities could set up honeypots and sell access as if the honeypots were access-for-sale machines. This would keep the doughnut budget in good stead, and might lead to the capture of some cyberthieves, or at least increase the cyberthieves' risk substantially.

The access-for-sale worm would require some verification mechanism to ensure that an access key did in fact come from the worm author. This mechanism can be constructed using *public-key cryptography*, where a message is strongly encrypted and decrypted using different keys: a *private key* known only to the message sender, and a *public key* known to everyone.[110]

The access-for-sale worm can carry the worm author's public key with it, and each compromised machine can be assigned a unique identifier (based on its network address, for example). When the worm author transfers an access key, they encrypt the machine's unique identifier with their private key; the worm can decrypt and verify the identifier using the public key. If a *symmetric* cryptographic scheme were used, where the same key is used for encryption *and* decryption, then capturing a worm sample would reveal the secret key, permitting access to all of the worm's back doors.

9.4 Cryptovirology

Using viruses and other malware for extortion is called *cryptovirology*.[111] After a virus has deployed its payload and been discovered, the effects of its payload should be devastating and irreversible for the victim, but reversible for the virus writer. The virus writer can then demand money to undo the damage.

For example, such a virus – a *cryptovirus* – could strongly encrypt the victim's data such that only the virus author can decrypt it.[6] The cryptovirus can employ public-key cryptography to avoid having to carry a capturable, secret decryption key with it to each new infection. The victim's data is encrypted using the virus writer's public key, and the virus writer can supply their private key to decrypt the data once a ransom is paid.

Even on fast computers, public-key encryption would be slow to encrypt large directories and filesystems. There are faster options for a cryptovirus:

- The cryptovirus can randomly generate a unique secret key for each infection. This secret key is used to strongly encrypt the victim's data using a faster, symmetric strong encryption algorithm. The cryptovirus then strongly encrypts the random secret key with the virus writer's public key and stores the result in a file. The victim transmits the file along with the ransom money; the virus writer is then able to recover the unique secret key without revealing their private key.

- Hardware mechanisms can be used. Some ATA hard drives have a rarely-used feature which allows their contents to be password-protected, rendering the contents unusable even if the computer is booted from different media. A cryptovirus can set this hard drive password if the feature is available.[112]

  This can be used in conjunction with the randomly-generated unique key scheme above, but the cryptovirus couldn't store the encrypted secret key file on the encrypted hard drive. If no other writable media is available, the cryptovirus could simply display the encrypted secret key on the screen for the victim to write down.

Both options avoid the virus writer needing a different public/private key pair for each new infection, lest a victim pay the ransom and publish the private decryption key for other victims as a public service.

There are only a few known instances of malware using encryption for extortion. The AIDS Trojan horse of 1989 was sent on floppy disks, mass-mailed worldwide via regular postal mail. It was an informational program relating to the (human) AIDS virus, released under a curious software license. The license gave it leave to render a computer inoperable unless the user paid for the software ($189 or $378, depending on the leasing option). It was true to its word: after approximately 90 reboots, the Trojan encrypted filenames using a simple substitution cipher.[113]

More recently, the PGPCoder Trojan encrypted files with specific filename extensions, roughly corresponding to likely user document types. A text file was left behind in each directory where files were encrypted, with instructions on how to buy the decryptor: a bargain at $200.[114]

9.5   Information Warfare

Information warfare is the use of computers to supplement or supplant conventional warfare. Computers can play a variety of roles in this regard, including acquiring information from an adversary's computers, planting information in their computers, and corrupting an adversary's data. Information warfare can also be applied in an isolating capacity, in an 'information embargo' that prevents an adversary from getting information in or out.[115] This section concentrates on malware-related information warfare only.

Computers are a great equalizer, and information warfare is a key weapon in *asymmetric* warfare, a form of warfare where an enemy possesses a decided advantage in one or more areas.[116] For example, the United States currently enjoys an advantage over many countries in terms of weaponry, and countries that cannot respond in kind have been proactively developing computer attack capabilities to counter this perceived threat.[7]

Laws, rules of engagement, and the level of conflict may constrain information operations. Legally, it is unclear whether information warfare constitutes warfare; this is an important point, as it governs what international law applies to information warfare. For example, civilian targets are usually off limits in conventional warfare, but information warfare may not be able to avoid substantial collateral damage to civilian computers and network infrastructure.[117] A conservative approach is that malware may never be used in peacetime, but may be deployed by intelligence agencies as the conflict level rises. In all-out war, both intelligence agencies and the military may use malware. Ultimately, information warfare of any kind may be limited if an adversary's communications infrastructure has been destroyed or otherwise disabled.[118]

It is interesting to think of malware-based information warfare as an electronic countermeasure.[119] An *electronic countermeasure*, or ECM, is any electronic means used to deny an enemy use of electronic technology, like radar jamming. Early jamming ECM was roughly analogous to a DoS attack, but current ECM systems heavily employ deception, making an enemy see false information.[8] A comparison of traditional ECM and malware is below.

Persistence

- Traditional ECM: The effect of the ECM only lasts as long as the transmission of the jamming signal or false information.
- Malware: The effect of malware lingers until the malware is stopped by the adversary. This longer persistence allows targets to be attacked in advance, with the malware lying dormant until needed.

Targeting

- Traditional ECM: Only direct targeting of an adversary's systems is possible.
- Malware: Both direct and indirect targeting is possible through connected, but weaker, points in an adversary's defenses.

  Malware can be a double-edged sword. Careful thought must be given to the design of malware for information warfare, so that it doesn't start targeting the computers of the *original* attacker and their allies.[120]

Deception

- Traditional ECM: Possible.

- Malware: Also possible. There are many possibilities for presenting false information to an adversary without them being aware of it.

Range of effects

- Traditional ECM: Because the targets are special-purpose devices with limited functionality, the range of effects that ECM can elicit from their targets is similarly limited.

- Malware: The targets are more general-purpose computers, and the malware's effects can be designed to fit the situation. For example:[121]

  - Logic bombs.
  - Denials of service at critical times.
  - Precision-guided attacks, to destroy a single machine or file.
  - Intelligence gathering, looking for specific, vital information. After the information is found, there is also the problem of smuggling it out. One possibility for worm-based intelligence gathering is to allow the information to propagate *with* the worm, in strongly-encrypted form, and intercept a copy of the worm later.[122]
  - A *forced quarantine* virus, which deliberately makes its presence known to an adversary. The adversary must isolate the affected machines, thus fragmenting and reducing the effectiveness of the adversary's computing infrastructure.

Reliability

- Traditional ECM: It is unknown until ECM is used whether or not it will work, a detriment to the planning of military operations.

- Malware: Depending on the setting, malware may be able to signal indicating that it is in place and ready for use. Whether or not it will actually work is still unknown, as with traditional ECM.

Continuity

- Traditional ECM: Must continually overcome the target, even if the target adapts to the attack using electronic counter-counter measures (ECCM).

- Malware: An adversary's defenses must only be overcome once, at their weakest point, unlike traditional ECM which attacks the strongest point.

The way that malware is inserted into an adversary's system may be more exotic in information warfare. Direct transmission is still an option, either by self-replication or by espionage. Indirect transmission is possible, too, such as passing malware through third parties like military contractors or other software vendors, who may be oblivious to the malware transmission. Malware may be present, but dormant, in systems sold by a country to its potential future enemies. Another indirect means of transmission is to deliberately leak details of a malware-infected system, and wait for an enemy to copy it.[123]

9.6 Cyberterrorism

'We do not use the term 'ice pick terrorism' to define bombings of ice-pick factories, nor would we use it to define terrorism carried out with ice picks. Thus we question the use of the term cyberterrorism to describe just any sort of threat or crime carried out with or against computers in general.'   – Sarah Gordon and Richard Ford[124]

The United Nations has been unable to agree on a definition of terrorism.[125] A definition of *cyber*terrorism that is universally agreed-upon is equally elusive. This lack of a standard cyberterrorism definition makes the classification of individual acts hard to pin down. Is malware that launches a DDoS attack against a government web site cyberterrorism? What about malware that simply carries a string with an anti-government slogan?

Terrorism has been compared to theater, in that terrorists want to maximize the emotional impact of their attacks. From the terrorists' point of view, an effective terrorist act is one that puts people in constant fear of their lives. Terrorist acts that merely irritate people are not effective.

By this token, cyberterrorist acts cannot be useful as terrorist tools unless their effect tangibly protrudes into the real world. Being unable to electronically access a bank account is inconvenient, but doesn't strike the fear of death into victims as would a cyberterrorist attack against nuclear facilities, the power grid, or hospitals. Luckily, no one is colossally stupid enough to connect such vital systems to the Internet.

In lieu of such attacks against critical systems, cyberterrorist acts might play the same role as malware does in information warfare. Cyberterrorism can be used as a complement to traditional, real-world physical attacks, to confuse an enemy by disrupting computer-based communications for rescue efforts, or by sowing disinformation during a terrorist attack. Prior to an attack, misleading intelligence traffic can be generated. Terrorists have unfortunately shown themselves to be very good at lateral thinking, and a cyberterrorist attack is likely to strike something unexpected and undefended.

Are stricter laws and standards needed for these new weapons, these Internet-connected computers?[126]

Notes for Chapter 9

1   The benevolent effect may be accidental in some unusual cases. A man surrendered himself to German police after receiving a (false) message from a variant of the Sober worm claiming that he was being investigated. When the police *did* investigate, they found child pornography on the man's computer [264].

2   For example, Sobig did this [188].

3   The eye-roll-inducing term "cyberthief" is due to Schechter and Smith [277], on whom this section is based. Arguably, the thieves aren't hackers/crackers, because the machine is pre-cracked for their safety and comfort.

4   This would presumably be "cyberturf."

5   A *covert channel* is a means of transmitting information which was never intended for that purpose. For example, information can be leaked from an infected machine in unused *or* used network packet bits [269]. The problem of trying to prevent information leaks via covert channels is referred to as the *confinement problem* [179].

6   Strictly speaking, the original cryptovirus definition *requires* the use of strong, public-key cryptography [352]. A more general view of cryptoviruses, without the public-key requirement, is taken here.

7   For example, countries possessing or developing offensive computer virus capabilities include Bulgaria [204], China [49, 71, 232], Cuba [204], North Korea [49], Russia [321], Singapore [49], and Taiwan [49].

8   Falsehoods are limited by law and convention. Falsely seeming to have a larger force than actually exists, or falsely appearing to be attacking elsewhere to draw off enemy troops are completely acceptable feints. Pretending to surrender in order to lure out and ambush enemy troops is called an act of *perfidy* and is prohibited [130].

100   Cohen [75] makes a case for benevolent viruses.

101   McAfee [199].

102   Barber [26].

103   Perriot and Knowles [250].

104   Predator worms and their effects are studied in Toyoizumi and Kara [323], and Gupta and DuVarney [134].

105   These issues are discussed at length by Bontchev [40].

106   White [344].

107   See, for example, Harrison et al. [138] and Jansen and Karygiannis [152].

108   Harrison et al. [138, page 17].

109 Aycock and Friess [23].

110 Schneier [279].

111 This section is based on Young and Yung [352].

112 Bögeholz [37] and Vidström [335].

113 Bates [29] and Ferbrache [103].

114 Panda Labs [240]. The $200 figure is from Panda Labs too [241].

115 The concept and term are from Kanuck [158, page 289].

116 O'Brien and Nusbaum [232].

117 Ellis [99] and Greenberg et al. [130].

118 This conservative approach and the point about communications infrastructure is from the Department of the Army [140].

119 The material on electronic countermeasures is based on Cramer and Pratt [82] unless otherwise noted.

120 From [16].

121 With the exception of intelligence gathering, these are also mentioned (occasionally using slightly different terminology) in Thomas [321].

122 Young and Yung [352].

123 These insertion possibilities are from [16, 82, 321].

124 Gordon and Ford [125, page 645], upon which this section is based.

125 Schaechter [275].

126 Ellis [99] examines the same suggestion in the context of information warfare.

Chapter 10

PEOPLE AND COMMUNITIES

10.1 Malware Authors

'... [virus writers] have a chronic lack of girlfriends, are usually socially inadequate and are drawn compulsively to write self-replicating codes.' – Jan Hruska, Sophos[100]

Very little is known about virus writers, much less malware authors in general. The reason for this is simple: very few of them are ever found.[1] Furthermore, the limited research that *has* been done does not support Hruska's quote above. The two big questions that the existing research begins to answer are who writes malware, and why do they do it?

10.1.1 Who?

Humans are a diverse lot, and there is always a danger when generalizing about any group of people. The work that has been done on virus writers has looked at four factors: age, sex, moral development, and technical skill.[101]

The age of virus writers is varied. There are the stereotypical young adolescents, but also college students and employed adult professionals. The explosive growth of malware has really only taken place since the mid-1980s, and it is possible that older virus writers will be seen as time goes on.

Virus writers are predominantly male, with only occasional exceptions.[2] Females are typically regarded as inferior in the virus community, so it wouldn't be a particularly welcoming environment for them. There is also a theory that gender differences in moral development may partially explain the lack of females.[102]

With respect to ethical and moral development, not all virus writers are the same, and some fall within "normal" ranges. There is also a general distaste for deliberately destructive code amongst the virus writers studied, and there is no one directly targeted by viruses – with the possible exception of anti-virus researchers! The lack of interest in destruction is borne out by the relatively small amount of malware which tries to do damage. The main reason that ethically-normal virus writers stop writing viruses is simply that they grow out of it.

Finally, there are the technical skills of virus writers, which are often derided by the anti-virus community. As with any software development, the barrier to entry is low for virus writing, and consequently a fair degree of bad programming is seen in virus writing as it is in any programming discipline. However, virus writers with real impact must have a variety of skills to field techniques like stealth and polymorphism, or employ lateral thinking to exploit new and unguarded attack vectors. Arguably the skill level of virus writers is a direct reflection of the increasing sophistication level of anti-virus defenses.[103]

10.1.2   Why?

Attributing the motivation to write malware to a single factor is a gross oversimplification. In fact, not all driving forces behind the creation of malware may even be conscious motivations.[104] Malware may be written for a variety of reasons, including:

Fascination with technology. Exploring technology underpins hacker culture, and the same ideas apply to creating malware. Creating malware, like writing any software, poses an intellectual challenge. In fact, since the anti-virus community acts as an opponent, writing malware may even have a greater draw from a game-playing point of view than other forms of software development.

Fame. Virus writers are known to form informal groups to exchange information and communicate with like-minded people.[3] As with any group, people may want to achieve fame within their community which would mean creating cleverly-written malware with impact. Having a creation appear on the "top ten" lists of malware that many anti-virus companies maintain for their customers' information can result in prestige for the creator.

Graffiti. Malware writing can serve as a form of expression in much the same way that graffiti does in the physical world. Arguably, this is a malicious act, but one not specifically targeted to any one person or group.

Revenge. Malware can be used to exact revenge for some real or imagined slight, by a disgruntled employee or ex-spouse, for instance.

Ideology. Ideological motivations are difficult to assess unless the malware writer is found, because what appears to be political or religious motivation may just be a red herring. Having said that, there have been some instances which suggest this underlying cause. One version of the Code Red worm attempted a DDoS on the White House web site, for instance.[4] The Cager Trojan horse[105] may have been religiously-motivated, because it tried to prevent infected machines from viewing adult web sites – an offender would be presented with a quote from the Qur'an in Arabic, English, and Persian, followed by advice in Persian on how to atone for looking at naughty pictures on the Internet.

Commercial sabotage. Malware can be hard to target accurately, but some attempts at sabotaging a single company have been seen. This may tie in to schemes for revenge, or possibly financial gain for a malware writer who hopes to take advantage of lower stock prices, for example.

Extortion. On occasion, malware has been used on a large scale to try and extort money from people.

Warfare and espionage. Malware can be used for military or intelligence purposes, or as a complement to traditional forms of warfare. Such malware can be employed by both established armies as well as terrorist groups.

Malware battles. A relatively recent development, malware writers can have their creations fight one another using the Internet as their battleground. This was seen in the Mydoom/Netsky/Bagle episode in 2004.[106]

Commercial gain. Malware skills may be leveraged in various ways by others, resulting in malware authors being paid for their wares. For example, use of worm-constructed botnets may be sold to spammers.

Again, humans are complicated, and their motivations may not be simple.

The graffiti motivation is an interesting one which deserves further research. There is a relatively large amount of research on graffiti artists, and the parallels to virus writers are compelling. Females are marginalized there too; it has been suggested that females express "graffiti urges" in different ways than males,[107] and also that the graffiti subculture is an inherently masculine one.[108] Graffiti writers have an adversarial relationship with the authorities trying to stop them, but the two groups also share a curious bond. Motivations for graffiti writers flow from the adversarial contest, but also a desire for fame within their subculture, and a love of the art. Equivalents to malware battles and commercial gain exist in the graffiti world too.

10.2   The Anti-Virus Community

Malware authors and people in the anti-virus community have one thing in common: there isn't a lot written about either. The anti-virus community is shaped by a number of external forces, including external perceptions of them as well as customer demands and legal minefields.

10.2.1 Perceptions

The most common perception about the anti-virus community is a conspiracy theory. Anti-virus companies have the most to gain by a steady stream of malware, so the argument goes, and anti-virus companies conveniently know how to defend against any new threats. There is no evidence whatsoever that supports this theory.

The evidence that *does* exist also doesn't support the conspiracy theory. If it were true, then anti-virus companies would want to boost revenue with the least amount of effort on their part – a rational plan. Any malware that wasn't noted by current or potential customers would therefore be wasted effort, and anti-virus researchers would work no more than was necessary.

There is lots and lots of malware that doesn't attract attention, though; not just variants but entire families of malware can go unnoticed by most anti-virus customers. Monitoring anti-virus updates and comparing that information to malware-related media stories is a good demonstration of this fact. The sheer volume of malware is inconsistent with the conspiracy theory, too, because far more effort is being expended by anti-virus researchers than would be necessary to sustain the industry.

Anti-virus researchers do benefit from staying ahead of malware writers, even if they don't produce the malware themselves. Researchers may monitor web sites frequented by malware writers for up-and-coming threats, especially so-called "virus exchange" or "vX" sites. Malware writers have also been known to send their latest creations directly to anti-virus companies, which tends to support the motivation of malware writing as an intellectual thrill rather than a destructive pursuit.[109]

10.2.2 Another Day in Paradise

A workday for an anti-virus researcher is long, to begin with. An 80-hour work week is not uncommon for researchers,[110] which can obviously exact a personal toll.

Samples of potential malware candidates can be captured by anti-virus companies' own defensive systems, like firewalls and honeypots. Malware samples may also be submitted by customers; this is the scenario depicted by the flowchart in Figure 10.1.[111] Conceptually, there are two databases kept: one with known malware, the other with known malware-free, or "clean" files. Any submission is first checked against both these databases, in order to avoid re-analyzing a submission and to respond to customers as quickly as possible.

If the submission is absent from both databases, then it must be analyzed. There is still no guarantee that the submission is malicious, so this is the next thing to determine; if the answer is negative, then the clean file database can be updated with the result. Otherwise, for replicating malware, a large number of

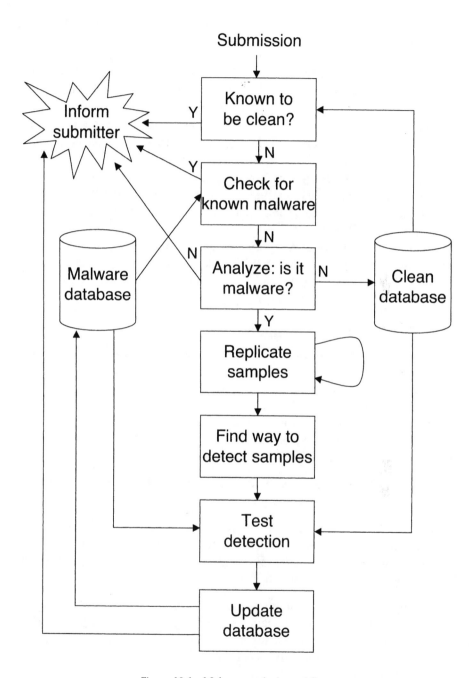

Figure 10.1. Malware analysis workflow

samples are produced to ensure that all manifestations of the malware variant are able to be detected. (Virus writers can try to derail this process by having their viruses mutate slowly.)[5]

Adding detection to the anti-virus software comes next. The result is verified against *both* databases, because detection of the new malware shouldn't interfere with existing detection, nor should it cause false positives. Testing will also try to catch problems on any of the platforms that the anti-virus software runs on. For this reason alone, anti-virus software is more challenging than malware writing, because malware doesn't have a customer base that complains if something goes wrong.

Finally, the malware database gets updated and the customer is notified. Most anti-virus companies have online "malware encyclopedias" which provide details about malware to the public, and these would also be updated at this time.

While a workday for an anti-virus researcher may be long, the workday for an anti-virus company may be endless. Anti-virus companies may maintain offices worldwide, strategically located in different time zones, so that around-the-clock security coverage can be given to their customers.[112]

10.2.3   Customer Demands

Anti-virus customers have certain expectations of their anti-virus software, which can be simply stated: 100% perfect detection of known and unknown threats, with no false positives. This is an impossible task, of course.

Complicating matters is that different customers may want different "threats" to be detected. Techniques used by anti-virus software may be applied more generally to locate many types of programs – this is called *gray area detection*.[113] Anti-virus software may be employed to look for:

Jokes and games. "Joke" executables and games may be completely harmless, yet having them may violate corporate IT policies.

Cracking tools. The legitimacy of programs like password crackers and port scanners may depend on context. System administrators can use these programs to check for vulnerabilities and weak passwords in their own systems, but other users possessing these may be cause for alarm.

Adware. Spyware is now largely recognized as a threat, but adware may also pose a risk of leaking information to another party. Some people see adware as performing a useful function, and it's not always obvious what programs have been installed quietly, and what programs have been deliberately installed by a user.

Remote administration tools. Again, RATs may provide a useful service, but their presence may also constitute a security breach or a policy violation.

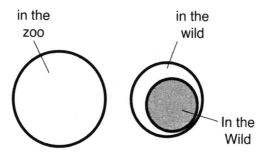

Figure 10.2. In the zoo vs. in the wild

Gray area detection is a delicate matter, because vendors of legitimate software may object to having their product negatively classified by anti-virus software, and there may be legal ramifications for doing so. Some anti-virus vendors attempt to forestall legal action, especially for spyware, through an appeals process which software producers can follow if they feel that their software has been misclassified.[114] More generally, the threat of legal action is possible for any false positive.

10.2.4 Engineering

Malware is often categorized based on where it's located.[115] Malware is said to be *in the wild* if it's actively spreading or otherwise functioning on anyone's computer. Malware not in the wild, which only exists in malware collections and anti-virus research labs, is *in the zoo*.[6] Accurately determining whether malware is actually in the wild requires omniscience in the general case, so an approximation is used. An organization called the WildList Organization[116] has a worldwide membership of anti-virus experts who verify malware occurrences and report their data, which is combined to form the WildList, a (presumably close) approximation of the malware in the wild at any given time. Malware on the WildList is confusingly referred to as being *In the Wild* (ItW). As Figure 10.2 shows, this means that malware can be in the wild but not In the Wild, but something In the Wild must be in the wild. Hopefully that clarifies things.[7]

An argument can be made, from an engineering point of view, that the only threats that need to be detected are those that are in the wild, since anything in the zoo cannot pose a direct threat. Anti-virus software could potentially be made smaller and faster by only detecting malware in the wild, whose numbers can be several orders of magnitude lower than the total number of threats.[117]

From a marketing point of view, however, this would be a bad idea. If company *A* advertises that they protect against 100,000 threats, and company *B*'s product only guards against 500 threats – even if they're really the only ones that are in the wild – then company *B* is at a competitive disadvantage.

Marketing is somewhat of a sore spot in the anti-virus community in any case. Product claims of detecting 100% of known and unknown threats are obviously silly, and misrepresentation is one possible legal concern.[118]

10.2.5   Open Questions

There are a number of interesting questions which (at least at this time) have no obvious answer.

- Anti-virus products are installed in computer systems in an ideal place to perform any number of tasks,[119] like gray area detection. Should anti-virus software...

  - ...supply a firewall? This is clearly in the realm of computer security, yet integrating firewall and anti-virus software may make both defenses vulnerable to attack by reducing the amount of software diversity.

  - ...provide content filtering? More gray area detection, content filtering would block objectionable content – or any content that might violate IT policy – from being received. Filtering might also watch outgoing content too, since sending offensive material (either intentionally, or through zombies) could damage a company's reputation.

  - ...perform spam detection? Anti-spam is a growing concern for anti-virus companies, although spam detection techniques have comparatively little overlap with malware detection techniques.

  - ...apply software patches? Where technical weaknesses are exploited by worms, for example, anti-virus disinfection may only be temporary if the vulnerability used as an infection vector is still present. The safest approach is probably not to apply relevant software patches, since doing so may accidentally break software, introducing more customer support and liability issues.

- Anti-virus researchers perform reverse engineering and decompilation legitimately as part of their jobs, and also routinely decipher "protection measures." It's unlikely that any malware author will take them to task for this, but researchers may also trace into legitimate code or need to understand undocumented software mechanisms. At what point does this run afoul of copyright laws?[120]

- Users of anti-virus software may occasionally be presented with quarantined files to assess. Are there situations in which looking at these files, or the data within them, violates privacy laws? This may be even riskier in the case of a false positive.

- For computer owners, use of anti-virus software is a widespread practice. Does this mean that computer owners are liable for negligence if they don't use anti-virus software?[121] Do anti-virus companies have a captive market?

Notes for Chapter 10

1 This raises the question of where virus writers are physically located. There was once a virus "scene" which shifted from country to country [123], but the Internet has largely made geographical location irrelevant.

2 Gigabyte was one example of a female virus writer [207].

3 Arguably, virus writers form a subculture distinguished by their interest in viruses.

4 This was Code Red version 2, and the DDoS attack was thwarted [211].

5 Bontchev [46] calls this "slow polymorphism."

6 The "zoo" label is often heard applied to viruses, as in "a zoo virus."

7 If this figure were drawn to scale, the In the Wild circle would be a barely-visible dot in comparison to the zoo circle.

100 As quoted in an interview with Reuters [263].

101 Unless otherwise noted, this section and the next are based on [121, 123].

102 Gordon [121] and Bissett and Shipton [35] both suggest this.

103 Suggested, for example, in Nachenberg [217].

104 Bisset and Shipton [35] speculate on unconscious motivations, and suggest some possible conscious motivations, as do Harley et al. [137].

105 Laguerta [177].

106 Covered in a number of places, such as Sherer [286].

107 Landy and Steele [180], and expanded upon by Abel and Buckley [1]. The latter also examines whether graffiti derives from a Freudian urge to smear feces, no doubt an excellent topic for dinner conversation.

108 Macdonald [191], which was used for the remainder of these comments on graffiti as well.

109 These assertions are made in Schmehl [278], and virus trading is mentioned in interviews with virus writers [120].

110 This figure is from Bontchev [41].

111 This section is based on Vibert [334] and (to a lesser degree) Schmehl [278].

112 Kirsner [165].

113 Gray area detection is discussed in Purisma [257].

114 For example, [52].

115 This section is based on Wells [343].

116 http://www.wildlist.org

117 An argument in favor of zoo virus detection is made in Ferrie and Perriot [104].

118 Gamertsfelder [116].

119 Purisma [257].

120 These latter three questions are raised and analyzed in Gamertsfelder [116].

121 This was mentioned at the EICAR 2004 conference during the presentation of Vasiu and Vasiu's "Taxonomy of Malware" paper. Opinions are varied: de Villiers concludes (after a lengthy analysis) that '... most cases of virus infection involve negligence' [86, page 169], but Owens [237] is skeptical about individuals being held liable for infections.

Chapter 11

WHAT SHOULD WE DO?

A book of this nature would not be complete without some kind of prediction about the future of malware. Such predictions share the distinguished quality of being invariably wrong, so this prediction will cover a wide range of scenarios.

> *Vicious cyberattacks will cause the Internet to melt down,* and *all malware-related problems will disappear within a year's time.*

In reality, there is no magic single solution to malware. (And, if there was, be assured that a bread-crumb trail of patents would cover every part of it.) Current and foreseeable defenses are but a house of cards. They are based on assumptions about "typical" malware behavior, and assumptions about malware writers which dramatically underestimate them. One violation of the assumptions and the house of cards comes tumbling down, defenders left scrambling to prop it up again.

What is clear is that no human intervention is possible in some attacks due to their speed. More automatic countermeasures are needed, not necessarily to stop malware completely – there is no such thing as absolute security, after all – but slowing malware down to a manageable rate would be valuable in itself.

As for malware detection, it is an undecidable problem. No perfect solution is possible, and the only way to tackle such a problem is with heuristics. Heuristics, rules of thumb, are fallible. In other words, a technical arms race rages on between attackers and defenders. Whether or not the race is winnable is immaterial now; the finish line is still far off. Many excellent defensive steps that can be taken are not very technical at all, though:

Plan B. Organizations, and to some extent individual computer users, must have a plan for disaster recovery. What happens *when* defenses fail and malware strikes? Can machines be rebuilt, data be restored?

Education. A broad view of education must be taken. Users must be educated to harden them to social engineering attacks, but education can't stop there. The next generation of computer scientists and computer programmers must be educated in depth about malware. Treating malware as a taboo subject is only security through obscurity.

Vendor pressure. It must be made clear to software vendors that security is a priority for their customers, a higher priority than more frilly features. Customers can also demand to know why software is riddled with technical weaknesses, which should make customers and vendors both ask some pointed questions of educators and software researchers.

Minimalism. Users must responsibly use features that are present, which in part comes through education. Enabled features like network servers provide more potential attack vectors than having all such features turned off.

At the extreme end of the minimalism scale, it can be argued that computers are *too* general-purpose. Malware affects computers because they are just another form of software for a computer to gleefully run. Special-purpose devices doing one thing, and only one thing, are one way to help avoid exploitable problems.

Software updating. Until less-vulnerable software can be produced, software updating will still be a necessity. Mechanisms and policies that facilitate updating are a good thing.

Layers of defense. If each defensive technique is only a partial solution, then deploy a variety of defenses. Defenses should ideally be chosen that are based on different underlying assumptions, so that the patchwork defensive quilt will hopefully still work even if some assumptions turn out to be false.

Avoiding monocultures. In biology, having all members of a species the same is a potentially fatal problem: one disease can wipe the species out. Yet that is exactly the fatal problem the majority of computers exhibit. This isn't necessarily to say that everyone should change operating systems and applications, although that is one coarse-grained way to avoid a monoculture. Monocultures can be avoided in part just by automatically injecting randomness into the data locations and code of programs.

Diversity can be achieved by separating functionality physically, too. For example, moving firewall functionality to a different physical device makes the overall defenses that much harder to completely overcome.

Will malware ever go away? Even if all technical vulnerabilities are fixed, there will still be human vulnerabilities. But the point is academic, because human nature virtually guarantees the large-scale availability of technical vulnerabilities for the foreseeable future. Suffice it to say that the computer security industry will continue to flourish, and security researchers will be employed for some time to come.

References

Many of these sources can be found on the Internet using a search engine, and underground sites tend to move around anyway, so URLs have been omitted except where there appears to be a meaningful single location for a document. The spelling and capitalization of author names/handles in the original sources has been preserved.

[1] E. L. Abel and B. E. Buckley. *The Handwriting on the Wall: Toward a Sociology and Psychology of Graffiti*. Greenwood Press, 1977.

[2] B. Acohido and J. Swartz. Going price for network of zombie PCs: $2,000–$3,000. USA Today, 8 September 2004.

[3] L. M. Adleman. An abstract theory of computer viruses. In *Advances in Cryptology – CRYPTO '88 (LNCS 403)*, pages 354–374, 1990.

[4] P.-M. Agapow. Computational brittleness and evolution in machine language. *Complexity International*, 3, 1996.

[5] A. V. Aho and M. J. Corasick. Efficient string matching: An aid to bibliographic search. *Communications of the ACM*, 18(6):333–340, 1975.

[6] A. V. Aho, M. Ganapathi, and S. W. K. Tjiang. Code generation using tree matching and dynamic programming. *Journal of the ACM*, 11(4):491–516, 1989.

[7] I. A. Al-Kadi. Origins of cryptology: the Arab contributions. *Cryptologia*, XVI(2):97–126, 1992.

[8] Aleph One. Smashing the stack for fun and profit. *Phrack*, 7(49), 1996.

[9] $\aleph_0$. Darwin. *Software – Practice and Experience*, 2:93–96, 1972.

[10] M. Allen. The use of 'social engineering' as a means of violating computer systems. SANS Information Security Reading Room, 13 August 2001.

[11] J. P. Anderson. Computer security threat monitoring and surveillance, 15 April 1980.

[12] J. P. Anderson. Computer security technology planning study: Volume II, October 1972. ESD-TR-73-51, Vol. II.

[13] Anonymous. Understanding encryption and polymorphism. Written by J. Wells?

[14] Anonymous. Double trouble. *Virus Bulletin*, page 5, April 1992.

[15] Anonymous. Peach virus targets Central Point. *Virus Bulletin*, pages 17–18, May 1992.

[16] Anonymous. Disabling technologies – a critical assessment. *Jane's International Defense Review*, 27(7), 1994.

[17] Anonymous. Winword.Concept. *Virus Bulletin*, page 3, October 1995.

[18] anonymous. Once upon a free().... *Phrack*, 0x0b(0x39), 2001.

[19] W. A. Arbaugh, W. L. Fithen, and J. McHugh. Windows of vulnerability: A case study analysis. *IEEE Computer*, 33(12):52–59, 2000.

[20] S. Axelsson. Aspects of the modelling and performance of intrusion detection. Licentiate thesis, Department of Computer Engineering, Chalmers University of Technology, 2000.

[21] J. Aycock and K. Barker. Creating a secure computer virus laboratory. In *13th Annual EICAR Conference*, 2004. 13pp.

[22] J. Aycock, R. deGraaf, and M. Jacobson, Jr. Anti-disassembly using cryptographic hash functions. Technical Report 2005-793-24, University of Calgary, Department of Computer Science, 2005.

[23] J. Aycock and N. Friess. Spam zombies from outer space. Technical Report 2006-808-01, University of Calgary, Department of Computer Science, 2006.

[24] B. S. Baker, U. Manber, and R. Muth. Compressing differences of executable code. In *ACM SIGPLAN Workshop of Compiler Support for System Software*, 1999.

[25] V. Bala, E. Duesterwald, and S. Banerjia. Dynamo: A transparent dynamic optimization system. In *Proceedings of the ACM SIGPLAN '00 Conference on Programming Language Design and Implementation (PLDI)*, pages 1–12, 2000.

[26] B. Barber. Cheese worm: Pros and cons of a "friendly" worm. SANS Information Security Reading Room, 2001.

[27] A. Bartolich. The ELF virus writing HOWTO, 15 February 2003.

[28] L. E. Bassham and W. T. Polk. Threat assessment of malicious code and human threats. Technical Report IR 4939, NIST, October 1992.

[29] J. Bates. Trojan horse: AIDS information introductory diskette version 2.0. *Virus Bulletin*, pages 3–6, January 1990.

[30] BBC News. Passwords revealed by sweet deal, 20 April 2004.

[31] BBC News. How to sell your self for a song, 24 March 2005.

[32] J. R. Bell. Threaded code. *Communications of the ACM*, 16(6):370–372, 1973.

[33] G. Benford. *Worlds Vast and Various*. EOS, 2000.

[34] J. L. Bentley. *Writing Efficient Programs*. Prentice-Hall, 1982.

[35] A. Bissett and G. Shipton. Some human dimensions of computer virus creation and infection. *International Journal of Human-Computer Studies*, 52:899–913, 2000.

[36] blexim. Basic integer overflows. *Phrack*, 0x0b(0x3c), 2002.

[37] H. Bögeholz. At your disservice: How ATA security functions jeopardize your data. c't 8/2005, S. 172: Hard Disk Security, 1 April 2005.

[38] V. Bontchev. Possible virus attacks against integrity programs and how to prevent them. In *Virus Bulletin Conference*, pages 131–141, 1992.

[39] V. Bontchev. Analysis and maintenance of a clean virus library. In *Virus Bulletin Conference*, pages 77–89, 1993.

[40] V. Bontchev. Are "good" computer viruses still a bad idea? In *Proceedings of the 3rd Annual EICAR Conference*, pages 25–47, 1994.

[41] V. Bontchev. Future trends in virus writing, 1994.

[42] V. Bontchev. Possible macro virus attacks and how to prevent them. *Computers & Security*, 15(7):595–626, 1996.

[43] V. Bontchev. Macro virus identification problems. *Computers & Security*, 17(1):69–89, 1998.

[44] V. Bontchev. Anti-virus spamming and the virus-naming mess: Part 2. *Virus Bulletin*, pages 13–15, July 2004.

[45] V. Bontchev. The real reason for the decline of the macro virus. *Virus Bulletin*, pages 14–15, January 2006.

[46] V. V. Bontchev. *Methodology of Computer Anti-Virus Research*. PhD thesis, University of Hamburg, 1998.

[47] Jordi Bosveld. Online malware scan. http://virusscan.jotti.org/.

[48] T. M. Breuel. Lexical closures for C++. In *USENIX C++ Conference Proceedings*, pages 293–304, 1988.

[49] D. Bristow. Asia: grasping information warfare? Jane's Intelligence Review, 1 December 2000.

[50] J. Brunner. *The Shockwave Rider*. Ballantine, 1975.

[51] Bulba and Kil3r. Bypassing StackGuard and StackShield. *Phrack*, 0xa(0x38), 2000.

[52] CA. eTrust PestPatrol vendor appeal process. CA Spyware Information Center, 25 April 2005. Version 1.1.

[53] CARO. A new virus naming convention, c. 1991.

[54] K. Carr. Sophos anti-virus detection: a technical overview, October 2002.

[55] CERT. Cert incident note IN-2001-09. http://www.cert.org/incident_notes/IN-2001-09.html, 6 August 2001.

[56] K. Cesare. Prosecuting computer virus authors: The need for an adequate and immediate international solution. *The Transnational Lawyer*, 14:135–170, 2001.

[57] S. Cesare. Linux anti-debugging techniques (fooling the debugger), 1999.

[58] S. Cesare. Unix viruses, Undated, post-October 1998.

[59] D. A. Chambers. Method and apparatus for detection of computer viruses. United States Patent #5,398,196, 14 March 1995.

[60] B. Chan, J. Denzinger, D. Gates, K. Loose, and J. Buchanan. Evolutionary behavior testing of commercial computer games. In *Proceedings of the 2004 IEEE Congress on Evolutionary Computation (CEC)*, pages 125–132, 2004.

[61] E. Y. Chen, J. T. Ro, M. M. Deng, and L. M. Chi. System, apparatus and method for the detection and removal of viruses in macros. United States Patent #5,951,698, 14 September 1999.

[62] S. Chen and S. Ranka. Detecting Internet worms at early stage. *IEEE Journal on Selected Areas in Communications*, 23(10):2003–2012, 2005.

[63] X. Chen and J. Heidemann. Detecting early worm propagation through packet matching. Technical Report ISI-TR-2004-585, University of Southern California, Information Sciences Institute, 2004.

[64] D. M. Chess. Virus verification and removal. *Virus Bulletin*, pages 7–11, November 1991.

[65] D. M. Chess, R. Ford, J. O. Kephart, and M. G. Swimmer. System and method for detecting and repairing document-infecting viruses using dynamic heuristics. United States Patent #6,711,583, 23 March 2004.

[66] D. M. Chess, J. O. Kephart, and G. B. Sorkin. Automatic analysis of a computer virus structure and means of attachment to its hosts. United States Patent #5,485,575, 16 January 1996.

[67] B. Cheswick. An evening with Berferd in which a cracker is lured, endured, and studied. In *Proceedings of the Winter USENIX Conference*, 1992.

[68] W. R. Cheswick and S. M. Bellovin. *Firewalls and Internet Security: Repelling the Wily Hacker*. Addison-Wesley, 1994.

[69] D. Chi. Detection and elimination of macro viruses. United States Patent #5,978,917, 2 November 1999.

[70] E. Chien and P. Ször. Blended attacks exploits, vulnerabilities and buffer-overflow techniques in computer viruses. In *Virus Bulletin Conference*, pages 72–106, 2002.

[71] Chosun Ilbo. N. Korea's hackers rival CIA, expert warns. Digital Chosunilbo (English Edition), 2 June 2005.

[72] CIAC. Information about hoaxes. http://hoaxbusters.ciac.org/HBHoaxInfo.html.

[73] Cisco Systems, Inc. Cisco threat defense system guide: How to provide effective worm mitigation, April 2004.

[74] F. Cohen. Computer viruses: Theory and experiments. *Computers & Security*, 6(1):22–35, 1987.

[75] F. B. Cohen. *A Short Course on Computer Viruses*. Wiley, second edition, 1994.

[76] C. Collberg, C. Thomborson, and D. Low. A taxonomy of obfuscating transformations. Technical Report 148, University of Auckland, Department of Computer Science, 1997.

[77] Computer Associates. Security advisor center glossary. http://www3.ca.com/securityadvisor/glossary.aspx, 2005.

[78] M. Conover and w00w00 Security Team. w00w00 on heap overflows, 1999.

[79] E. Cooke, F. Jahanian, and D. McPherson. The zombie roundup: Understanding, detecting, and disrupting botnets. In *USENIX SRUTI Workshop*, 2005.

[80] C. Cowan, M. Barringer, S. Beattie, and G. Kroah-Hartman. FormatGuard: Automatic protection from printf format string vulnerabilities. In *Proceedings of the 10th USENIX Security Symposium*, 2001.

[81] CrackZ. Anti-debugging & software protection advice, 25 April 2003.

[82] M. L. Cramer and S. R. Pratt. Computer virus countermeasures – a new type of electronic warfare. In L. J. Hoffman, editor, *Rogue Programs: Viruses, Worms, and Trojan Horses*, chapter 20, pages 246–260. Van Nostrand Reinhold, 1990.

[83] I. Daniloff. Fighting talk. *Virus Bulletin*, pages 10–12, December 1997.

[84] I. Dawson. Blind buffer overflows in ISAPI extensions. SecurityFocus, 25 January 2005.

[85] T. de Raadt. Exploit mitigation techniques. AUUG'2004 Annual Conference.

[86] M. de Villiers. Computer viruses and civil liability: A conceptual framework. *Tort Trial & Insurance Practice Law Journal*, 40:1:123–179, 2004.

[87] J. Dellinger. Re: Prize for most useful computer virus. *Risks Digest*, 12(30), 1991.

[88] N. Desai. Intrusion prevention systems: the next step in the evolution of IDS. SecurityFocus, 27 February 2003.

[89] t. detristan, t. ulenspiegel, yann_malcom, and m. s. von underduk. Polymorphic shellcode engine using spectrum analysis. *Phrack*, 0x0b(0x3d), 2003.

[90] R. B. K. Dewar. Indirect threaded code. *Communications of the ACM*, 18(6):330–331, 1975.

[91] A. K. Dewdney. In the game called Core War hostile programs engage in a battle of bits. *Scientific American*, 250(5):14–22, 1984.

[92] A. K. Dewdney. A Core War bestiary of viruses, worms and other threats to computer memories. *Scientific American*, 252(3):14–23, 1985.

[93] U. Drepper. Security enhancements in Red Hat Enterprise Linux (beside SELinux), 16 June 2004.

[94] P. Ducklin. Counting viruses. In *Virus Bulletin Conference*, pages 73–85, 1999.

[95] T. Duff. Experience with viruses on UNIX systems. *Computing Systems*, 2(2):155–171, 1989.

[96] EICAR. The anti-virus test file. http://www.eicar.org/anti_virus_test_file.htm, 1 May 2003.

[97] M. W. Eichin and J. A. Rochlis. With microscope and tweezers: An analysis of the Internet virus of November 1988. In *Proceedings of the 1989 IEEE Symposium on Security and Privacy*, pages 326–343, 1989.

[98] I. K. El Far, R. Ford, A. Ondi, and M. Pancholi. On the impact of short-term email message recall on the spread of malware. In *Proceedings of the 14th Annual EICAR Conference*, pages 175–189, 2005.

[99] B. W. Ellis. The international legal implications and limitations of information warfare: What are our options? USAWC Strategy Research Report, 10 April 2001.

[100] J. Erickson. *Hacking: The Art of Exploitation*. No Starch Press, 2003.

[101] F. Esponda, S. Forrest, and P. Helman. A formal framework for positive and negative detection schemes. *IEEE Transactions on Systems, Man, and Cybernetics*, 34(1):357–373, 2004.

[102] H. Etoh. Stack protection schemes: (propolice, StackGuard, XP SP2). PacSec/core04 Conference, 2004.

[103] D. Ferbrache. *A Pathology of Computer Viruses*. Springer-Verlag, 1992.

[104] P. Ferrie and F. Perriot. Detecting complex viruses. SecurityFocus, 6 December 2004.

[105] P. Ferrie and H. Shannon. It's Zell(d)ome the one you expect. *Virus Bulletin*, pages 7–11, May 2005.

[106] P. Ferrie and P. Ször. Zmist opportunities. *Virus Bulletin*, pages 6–7, March 2001.

[107] E. Filiol. Strong cryptography armoured computer viruses forbidding code analysis: The Bradley virus. In *Proceedings of the 14th Annual EICAR Conference*, pages 216–227, 2005.

[108] C. Fischer. TREMOR analysis (PC). *VIRUS-L Digest*, 6(88), 1993.

[109] N. FitzGerald. A virus by any other name – virus naming updated. *Virus Bulletin*, pages 7–9, January 2003.

[110] H. Flake. Structural comparison of executable objects. In *Workshop on Detection of Intrusions and Malware & Vulnerability Assessment (DIMVA)*, 2004.

[111] B. Flint and M. Hughes. Fast virus scanning using session stamping. United States Patent #6,735,700, 11 May 2004.

[112] E. Florio. Backdoor.Ryknos. Symantec Security Response, 22 November 2005.

[113] R. Ford and J. Michalske. Gatekeeper II: New approaches to generic virus prevention. In *Virus Bulletin Conference*, pages 45–50, 2004.

[114] R. Ford and H. H. Thompson. The future of proactive virus detection. In *13th Annual EICAR Conference*, 2004. 11pp.

[115] R. Foulkes and J. Morris. Fighting worms in a large corporate environment: A design for a network anti-worm solution. In *Virus Bulletin Conference*, pages 56–66, 2002.

[116] L. Gamertsfelder. Anti-virus technologies – filtering the legal issues. In *Virus Bulletin Conference*, pages 31–35, 2003.

[117] S. Garfink and M. Landesman. Lies, damn lies and computer virus costs. In *Virus Bulletin Conference*, pages 20–23, 2004.

[118] D. Gerrold. *When Harlie Was One*. Nelson Doubleday, 1972.

[119] P. Gillingwater. Re: Where did they come from ? (PC). comp.virus, 27 November 1989.

[120] S. Gordon. Faces behind the masks, 1994.

[121] S. Gordon. The generic virus writer. In *Virus Bulletin Conference*, 1994.

[122] S. Gordon. What a (Winword.)Concept. *Virus Bulletin*, pages 8–9, September 1995.

[123] S. Gordon. The generic virus writer II. In *Virus Bulletin Conference*, 1996.

[124] S. Gordon. Spyware 101: Exploring spyware and adware risk assessment. In *14th Annual EICAR Conference*, pages 204–215, 2005.

[125] S. Gordon and R. Ford. Cyberterrorism? *Computers & Security*, 21(7):636–647, 2002.

[126] S. Gordon, R. Ford, and J. Wells. Hoaxes & hypes. In *Virus Bulletin Conference*, 1997.

[127] D. Gragg. A multi-level defense against social engineering. SANS Information Security Reading Room, 2002.

[128] S. Granger. Social engineering fundamentals, part I: Hacker tactics. SecurityFocus, 18 December 2001.

[129] S. Granger. Social engineering fundamentals, part II: Combat strategies. SecurityFocus, 9 January 2002.

[130] L. T. Greenberg, S. E. Goodman, and K. J. Soo Hoo. *Information Warfare and International Law*. National Defense University Press, 1998.

[131] GriYo. EPO: Entry-point obscuring. *29A e-zine*, 4, c. 2000.

[132] grugq and scut. Armouring the ELF: Binary encryption on the UNIX platform. *Phrack*, 0x0b(0x3a), 2001.

[133] D. O. Gryaznov. Scanners of the year 2000: Heuristics. In *Virus Bulletin Conference*, pages 225–234, 1995.

[134] A. Gupta and D. C. DuVarney. Using predators to combat worms and viruses: A simulation-based study. In *20th Annual Computer Security Applications Conference*, 2004.

[135] M. Handley, V. Paxson, and C. Kreibich. Network intrusion detection: Evasion, traffic normalization, and end-to-end protocol semantics. In *Proceedings of the 10th USENIX Security Symposium*, 2001.

[136] Harl. People hacking: The psychology of social engineering. Access All Areas III, 1997.

[137] D. Harley, R. Slade, and U. E. Gattiker. *Viruses Revealed*. Osborne/McGraw-Hill, 2001.

[138] C. G. Harrison, D. M. Chess, and A. Kershenbaum. Mobile agents: Are they a good idea? IBM Research Report, 28 March 1995.

[139] R. Hasson. Anti-debugging tips. http://www.soft-analysts.com/debugging.php, 13 February 2003.

[140] Headquarters, Department of the Army. Information operations. Field manual No. 100-6, 27 August 1996. United States Army.

[141] H. J. Highland. A macro virus. *Computers & Security*, 8(3):178–188, 1989.

[142] N. Hindocha and E. Chien. Malicious threats and vulnerabilities in instant messaging. In *Virus Bulletin Conference*, pages 114–124, 2003.

[143] S. A. Hofmeyr, S. Forrest, and A. Somayaji. Intrusion detection using sequences of system calls. *Journal of Computer Security*, 6:151–180, 1998.

[144] G. Hoglund and J. Butler. *Rootkits: subverting the Windows kernel*. Addison-Wesley, 2006.

[145] T. Holz and F. Raynal. Defeating honeypots: System issues, part 1. SecurityFocus, 23 March 2005.

[146] R. N. Horspool and N. Marovac. An approach to the problem of detranslation of computer programs. *The Computer Journal*, 23(3):223–229, 1980.

[147] M. Howard. Reviewing code for integer manipulation vulnerabilities. MSDN Library, 28 April 2003.

[148] J. W. Hunt and M. D. McIlroy. An algorithm for differential file comparison. Technical Report 41, Bell Laboratories, Computer Science, 1976.

[149] M. Hyppönen. Retroviruses – how viruses fight back. In *Virus Bulletin Conference*, 1994.

[150] M. Hypponen. Santy. F-Secure Virus Descriptions, 21 December 2004.

[151] C. Itshak, N. Vitaly, and M. Taras. Virus detection system. Canadian Patent Application #2,460,607, 27 March 2003.

[152] W. Jansen and T. Karygiannis. Mobile agent security. NIST Special Publication 800-19, 1999.

[153] Japan Times. Bug in antivirus software hits LANs at JR East, some media, 24 April 2005.

[154] M. Jordan. Dealing with metamorphism. *Virus Bulletin*, pages 4–6, October 2002.

[155] R. Joshi, G. Nelson, and K. Randall. Denali: a goal-directed superoptimizer. In *Proceedings of the ACM SIGPLAN 2002 Conference on Programming language design and implementation*, pages 304–314, 2002.

[156] J. Jung, V. Paxson, A. W. Berger, and H. Balakrishnan. Fast portscan detection using sequential hypothesis testing. In *Proceedings of the 2004 IEEE Symposium on Security and Privacy*, pages 211–225, 2004.

[157] J. E. Just and M. Cornwall. Review and analysis of synthetic diversity for breaking monocultures. In *Proceedings of the 2004 ACM Workshop on Rapid Malcode*, pages 23–32, 2004.

[158] S. P. Kanuck. Information warfare: New challenges for public international law. *Harvard International Law Journal*, 37(1):272–292, 1996.

[159] E. Kaspersky. Dichotomy: Double trouble. *Virus Bulletin*, pages 8–9, December 1994.

[160] E. Kaspersky. RMNS – the perfect couple. *Virus Bulletin*, pages 8–9, May 1995.

[161] Kaspersky Lab. Virus.DOS.Whale, 2000. *Whale appeared c. 1990*.

[162] Kaspersky Lab. Virus.Win16.Apparition.a, 2000. *Apparition appeared c. 1998*.

[163] J. O. Kephart, A. G. G. Morin, G. B. Sorkin, and J. W. Wells. Efficient detection of computer viruses and other data traits. United States Patent #6,016,546, 18 January 2000.

[164] V. Kiriansky, D. Bruening, and S. Amarasinghe. Secure execution via program shepherding. In *Proceedings of the 11th USENIX Security Symposium*, 2002.

[165] S. Kirsner. Sweating in the hot zone. *Fast Company*, 99, October 2005.

[166] P. Klint. Interpretation techniques. *Software – Practice and Experience*, 11:963–973, 1981.

[167] klog. The frame pointer overwrite. *Phrack*, 9(55), 1999.

[168] D. E. Knuth. *The Art of Computer Programming, Volume 3: Sorting and Searching*. Addison-Wesley, second edition, 1998.

[169] C. W. Ko. Method and apparatus for detecting a macro computer virus using static analysis. United States Patent #6,697,950, 24 February 2004.

[170] V. Kouznetsov and A. Ushakov. System and method for efficiently managing computer virus definitions using a structured virus database. United States Patent #6,622,150, 16 September 2003.

[171] J. Koziol, D. Aitel, D. Litchfield, C. Anley, S. Eren, N. Mehta, and R. Hassell. *The Shellcoder's Handbook: Discovering and Exploiting Security Holes*. Wiley, 2004.

[172] Krakowicz. Krakowicz's kracking korner: The basics of kracking II, c. 1983.

[173] N. Krawetz. Anti-honeypot technology. *IEEE Security & Privacy*, pages 76–79, January/February 2004.

[174] S. Kumar and E. H. Spafford. A generic virus scanner in C++. In *Proceedings of the 8th Computer Security Applications Conference*, pages 210–219, 1992.

[175] C. J. Kuo, J. Koltchev, D.-C. Zheng, and J. Peter. Method of treating whitespace during virus detection. United States Patent #6,230,288, 8 May 2001.

[176] J. Kuo and D. Beck. The common malware enumeration (CME) initiative. *Virus Bulletin*, pages 14–15, September 2005.

[177] Z. M. Laguerta. TROJ_CAGER.A. Trend Micro Virus Encyclopedia, 6 September 2005.

[178] A. Lakhotia, A. Kapoor, and E. U. Kumar. Are metamorphic viruses really invincible? part 1. *Virus Bulletin*, pages 5–7, December 2004.

[179] B. W. Lampson. A note on the confinement problem. *Communications of the ACM*, 16(10):613–615, 1973.

[180] E. E. Landy and J. M. Steele. Graffiti as a function of building utilization. *Perceptual and Motor Skills*, 25:711–712, 1967.

[181] T. Laundrie. All we need is love. rec.humor.funny ILOVEYOU digest, joke attributed to M. Barker, 8 May 2000.

[182] A. J. Lee. Hunting the unicorn. *Virus Bulletin*, pages 13–16, May 2004.

[183] J. R. Levine. *Linkers and Loaders*. Morgan Kaufmann, 2000.

[184] J. Leyden. Americans are pants at password security. The Register, 6 May 2005.

[185] Y. Liu. Avkiller.Trojan. Symantec Security Response, 17 May 2002.

[186] R. W. Lo, K. N. Levitt, and R. A. Olsson. MCF: a malicious code filter. *Computers & Security*, 14(6):541–566, 1995.

[187] M. Ludwig. *The Giant Black Book of Computer Viruses*. American Eagle, second edition, 1998.

[188] LURHQ. Sobig.a and the spam you received today, 21 April 2003.

[189] J. Lyman. Name that worm – how computer viruses get their names. NewsFactor Technology News, 8 January 2002.

[190] J. Ma, G. M. Voelker, and S. Savage. Self-stopping worms. In *Proceedings of the 2005 ACM Workshop on Rapid Malcode*, pages 12–21, 2005.

[191] N. Macdonald. *The Graffiti Subculture: Youth, Masculinity and Identity in London and New York*. Palgrave, 2001.

[192] G. M. Mallén-Fullerton. The minimum size of virus identification signatures. In *Fifth International Computer Virus & Security Conference*, pages 813–817, 1992.

[193] O. Mann. Method for recovery of a computer program infected by a computer virus. United States Patent #5,408,642, 18 April 1995.

[194] Marc. Re: Blind remote buffer overflow. VULN-DEV List, 28 April 2000.

[195] A. Marinescu. Win32/CTX virus description. RAV AntiVirus, 15 November 1999 (detection date).

[196] H. Massalin. Superoptimizer: a look at the smallest program. In *Proceedings of the Second International Conference on Architectual Support for Programming Languages and Operating Systems*, pages 122–126, 1987.

[197] A. Matrawy, P. C. van Oorschot, and A. Somayaji. Mitigating network denial-of-service through diversity-based traffic management. In *Proceedings of the 3rd International Conference on Applied Cryptography and Network Security*, LNCS 3531, pages 104–121, 2005.

[198] McAfee Inc. ZeroHunt. Virus Information Library, 15 December 1990.

[199] McAfee Inc. Den Zuk. Virus Information Library, 1988.

[200] McAfee Inc. WM/Colors.D;M;P. Virus Information Library, 1997.

[201] M. D. McIlroy, R. Morris, and V. A. Vyssotsky. Letter to $\aleph_0$, c/o C. A. Lang, editor, *Software – Practice and Experience*. http://www.cs.dartmouth.edu/~doug/darwin.pdf, 29 June 1971.

[202] M. K. McKusick, K. Bostic, M. J. Karels, and J. S. Quarterman. *The Design and Implementation of the 4.4BSD Operating System*. Addison-Wesley, 1996.

[203] MessageLabs. *MessageLabs Intelligence Annual Email Security Report 2004*, 2004.

[204] E. Messmer. Threat of 'infowar' brings CIA warnings. Network World, 13 September 1999.

[205] Methyl. Tunneling with single step mode, Undated, post-1989.

[206] Z. Michalewicz and D. B. Fogel. *How to Solve It: Modern Heuristics*. Springer-Verlag, 2000.

[207] J. Middleton. Virus writers get behind Gigabyte. vnunet.com, 13 May 2002.

[208] MidNyte. An introduction to encryption, part I, April 1999.

[209] B. P. Miller, L. Fredriksen, and B. So. Study of the reliability of UNIX utilities. *Communications of the ACM*, 33(12):32–44, 1990.

[210] G. Molnár and G. Szappanos. Casualties of war: W32/Ganda. *Virus Bulletin*, pages 7–10, May 2003.

[211] D. Moore and C. Shannon. The spread of the code-red worm (crv2). CAIDA analysis, c. 2001.

[212] D. Moore, C. Shannon, and J. Brown. Code-Red: a case study on the spread and victims of an Internet worm. In *2nd Internet Measurement Workshop*, 2002.

[213] P. Morley. The biggie. *Virus Bulletin*, pages 10–11, November 1998.

[214] I. Muttik. Stripping down an AV engine. In *Virus Bulletin Conference*, pages 59–68, 2000.

[215] C. Nachenberg. Antivirus accelerator. United States Patent #6,021,510, 1 February 2000.

[216] C. Nachenberg. Behavior blocking: The next step in anti-virus protection. SecurityFocus, 19 March 2002.

[217] C. Nachenberg. Computer virus-antivirus coevolution. *Communications of the ACM*, 40(1):46–51, 1997.

[218] C. Nachenberg. Emulation repair system. United States Patent #6,067,410, 23 May 2000.

[219] C. S. Nachenberg. Data driven detection of viruses. United States Patent #6,851,057, 1 February 2005.

[220] C. S. Nachenberg. Dynamic heuristic method for detecting computer viruses using decryption exploration and evaluation phases. United States Patent #6,357,008, 12 March 2002.

[221] C. S. Nachenberg. Polymorphic virus detection module. United States Patent #5,826,013, 20 October 1998.

[222] C. S. Nachenberg. Histogram-based virus detection. Canadian Patent Application #2,403,676, 20 September 2001.

[223] C. S. Nachenberg. State-based cache for antivirus software. United States Patent #5,999,723, 7 December 1999.

[224] R. Naraine. Microsoft's security response center: How little patches are made. eWeek, 8 June 2005.

[225] K. Natvig. Sandbox technology inside AV scanners. In *Virus Bulletin Conference*, pages 475–488, 2001.

[226] K. Natvig. Sandbox II: The Internet. In *Virus Bulletin Conference*, pages 125–141, 2002.

[227] G. Navarro and M. Raffinot. *Flexible Pattern Matching in Strings*. Cambridge, 2002.

[228] G. Navarro and J. Tarhio. LZgrep: a Boyer-Moore string matching tool for Ziv-Lempel compressed text. *Software – Practice and Experience*, 35(12):1107–1130, 2005.

[229] J. Nazario. *Defense and Detection Strategies against Internet Worms*. Artech House, 2004.

[230] J. Nazario, J. Anderson, R. Wash, and C. Connelly. The future of Internet worms. In *Blackhat Briefings*, 2001.

[231] Nergal. The advanced return-into-lib(c) exploits: PaX case study. *Phrack*, 0x0b(0x3a), 2001.

[232] K. O'Brien and J. Nusbaum. Intelligence gathering on asymmetric threats – part one. Jane's Intelligence Review, 1 October 2000.

[233] H. O'Dea. Trapping worms in a virtual net. In *Virus Bulletin Conference*, pages 176–186, 2004.

[234] L. Oudot. Fighting Internet worms with honeypots. SecurityFocus, 23 October 2003.

[235] L. Oudot and T. Holz. Defeating honeypots: Network issues, part 1. SecurityFocus, 28 September 2004.

[236] M. Overton. Worm charming: Taking SMB-Lure to the next level. In *Virus Bulletin Conference*, 2003.

[237] R. C. Owens. Turning worms: Some thoughts on liabilities for spreading computer infections. *Canadian Journal of Law and Technology*, 3(1):33–47, 2004.

[238] M. C.-H. Pak, A. Ouchakov, K. N. Pham, D. O. Gryaznov, and V. Kouznetsov. System and method for executing computer virus definitions containing general purpose programming language extensions. United States Patent #6,718,469, 6 April 2004.

[239] Panda Software. Elkern.C. Virus Encyclopedia, 2005.

[240] Panda Software. PGPCoder.A. Virus Encyclopedia, 2005.

[241] Panda Software. A Trojan digitally encrypts files and asks for a ransom. Press release, 25 May 2005.

[242] paperghost. We're calm like a bomb: The antivirus virus. Vitalsecurity.org, 1 June 2005.

[243] V. Paxson. Bro: A system for detecting network intruders in real-time. In *Proceedings of the 7th USENIX Security Symposium*, 1998.

[244] J. Pearce. Antivirus virus on the loose. ZDNet Australia, 20 January 2003.

[245] T. J. Pennello. Very fast LR parsing. In *Proceedings of the SIGPLAN '86 Symposium on Compiler Construction*, pages 145–151, 1986.

[246] C. Percival. Naive differences of executable code, 2003.

[247] F. Perriot. Defeating polymorphism through code optimization. In *Virus Bulletin Conference*, pages 142–159, 2003.

[248] F. Perriot and P. Ferrie. Principles and practise of X-raying. In *Virus Bulletin Conference*, pages 51–66, 2004.

[249] F. Perriot, P. Ferrie, and P. Ször. Striking similarities. *Virus Bulletin*, pages 4–6, May 2002.

[250] F. Perriot and D. Knowles. W32.Welchia.Worm. Symantec Security Response, 28 July 2004.

[251] R. Perry. Extensions to CVDL, the CyberSoft virus description language. CyberSoft White Paper, 11 August 2001.

[252] R. Perry. CyberSoft CVDL tutorial. CyberSoft White Paper, 16 September 2001.

[253] phantasmal phantasmagoria. On polymorphic evasion. BugTraq, 2 October 2004.

[254] V. Pless. *Introduction to the Theory of Error-Correcting Codes*. Wiley, 1982.

[255] N. Provos and P. Honeyman. ScanSSH – scanning the Internet for SSH servers. In *Proceedings of the LISA 2001 15th Systems Administration Conference*, pages 25–30, 2001.

[256] T. H. Ptacek and T. N. Newsham. Insertion, evasion, and denial of service: Eluding network intrusion detection. Secure Networks, Inc., 1998.

[257] J. Purisma. To do or not to do: Anti-virus accessories. In *Virus Bulletin Conference*, pages 125–130, 2003.

[258] P. Radatti. Computer viruses in Unix networks, 1995.

[259] P. V. Radatti. The CyberSoft virus description language. CyberSoft White Paper, 1996.

[260] E. S. Raymond, ed. The jargon file, version 4.4.7, 2003.

[261] C. Renert. Proactive detection of code injection worms. In *Virus Bulletin Conference*, pages 147–158, 2004.

[262] E. Rescorla. Security holes... who cares? In *Proceedings of the 12th USENIX Security Symposium*, pages 75–90, 2003.

[263] Reuters. Looking into the mind of a virus writer. CNN.com, 19 March 2003.

[264] Reuters. Computer worm traps child porn offender in Germany. reuters.com, 20 December 2005.

[265] J. Riordan and B. Schneier. Environmental key generation towards clueless agents. In *Mobile Agents and Security (LNCS 1419)*, pages 15–24, 1998.

[266] W. Robertson, C. Kruegel, D. Mutz, and F. Valeur. Run-time detection of heap-based overflows. In *Proceedings of the 17th Large Installation Systems Administration Conference*, pages 51–59, 2003.

[267] E. C. Rosen. Vulnerabilities of network control protocols: An example. *ACM SIGCOMM Computer Communication Review*, 11(3):10–16, 1981.

[268] J. B. Rosenberg. *How Debuggers Work: Algorithms, Data Structures, and Architecture*. Wiley, 1996.

[269] C. H. Rowland. Covert channels in the TCP/IP protocol suite. *First Monday*, 2(5), 1997.

[270] RSA Security. Internet identity theft threatens to be the next crime wave to hit Britain. Press release, 20 April 2004.

[271] M. Russinovich. Sony, rootkits and digital rights management gone too far. Mark's SysInternals Blog, 31 October 2005.

[272] O. Ruwase and M. S. Lam. A practical dynamic buffer overflow detector. In *Proceedings of the Network and Distributed System Security (NDSS) Symposium*, pages 159–169, 2004.

[273] T. Sabin. Comparing binaries with graph isomorphisms. BindView white paper, 2004.

[274] A. Saita. Security no match for theater lovers. SearchSecurity.com, 24 March 2005.

[275] I. Schaechter. Definitions of terrorism. http://www.unodc.org/unodc/terrorism_defini-tions.html, 2000.

[276] S. E. Schechter, J. Jung, and A. W. Berger. Fast detection of scanning worm infections. In *Seventh International Symposium on Recent Advances in Intrusion Detection (RAID)*, LNCS 3224, pages 59–81, 2004.

[277] S. E. Schechter and M. D. Smith. Access for sale: A new class of worm. In *Proceedings of the 2003 ACM Workshop on Rapid Malcode*, pages 19–23, 2003.

[278] P. Schmehl. Past its prime: Is anti-virus scanning obsolete? SecurityFocus, 2002.

[279] B. Schneier. *Applied Cryptography*. Wiley, second edition, 1996.

[280] B. Schneier. Insurance and the computer industry. *Communications of the ACM*, 44(3):114–115, 2001.

[281] J. Schnurer and T. J. Klemmer. Computer virus trap. Canadian Patent Application #2,191,205, 7 December 1995.

[282] K. Schöldström. How to use live viruses as an education tool. In *Virus Bulletin Conference*, pages 251–261, 2002.

[283] M. G. Schultz, E. Eskin, E. Zadok, and S. J. Stolfo. Data mining methods for detection of new malicious executables. In *Proceedings of the 2001 IEEE Symposium on Security and Privacy*, pages 38–49, 2001.

[284] scut. Exploiting format string vulnerabilities, version 1.2, 1 September 2001.

[285] H. Shacham, M. Page, B. Pfaff, E.-J. Goh, N. Modadugu, and D. Boneh. On the effectiveness of address-space randomization. In *Proceedings of the 11th ACM Conference on Computer and Communications Security*, pages 298–307, 2004.

[286] L. Sherer. Keeping pace in a war of worms. *Virus Bulletin*, page 2, May 2004.

[287] J. F. Shoch and J. A. Hupp. The "worm" programs – early experience with a distributed computation. *Communications of the ACM*, 25(3):172–180, 1982.

[288] E. Skoudis and L. Zeltser. *Malware: Fighting Malicious Code*. Prentice Hall, 2004.

[289] R. Skrenta. Elk cloner. http://www.skrenta.com/cloner.

[290] F. Skulason. New Zealand – causing chaos worldwide. *Virus Bulletin*, pages 9–10, May 1990.

[291] F. Skulason. More about UVDs. comp.virus, 28 January 1990.

[292] Solar Designer. Getting around non-executable stack (and fix). Bugtraq, 10 August 1997.

[293] Solar Designer. JPEG COM marker processing vulnerability in Netscape browsers. OW-002-netscape-jpeg, revision 1, 25 July 2000.

[294] D. A. Solomon and M. E. Russinovich. *Inside Microsoft Windows 2000*. Microsoft Press, third edition, 2000.

[295] J. T. Soma, T. F. Muther, Jr., and H. M. L. Brissette. Transnational extradition for computer crimes: Are new treaties and laws needed? *Harvard Journal on Legislation*, 34:317–371, 1997.

[296] A. N. Sovarel, D. Evans, and N. Paul. Where's the FEEB? The effectiveness of instruction set randomization. In *Proceedings of the 14th USENIX Security Symposium*, pages 145–160, 2005.

[297] Sowhat. Multiple antivirus reserved device name handling vulnerability. BugTraq, 19 October 2004.

[298] E. H. Spafford. The Internet worm program: An analysis. Technical Report CSD-TR-823, Purdue University, Department of Computer Sciences, 1988.

[299] E. H. Spafford. Computer viruses as artificial life. *Journal of Artificial Life*, 1(3):249–265, 1994.

[300] Spammer-X. *Inside the SPAM Cartel*. Syngress, 2004.

[301] L. Spitzner. *Honeypots: Tracking Hackers*. Addison-Wesley, 2003.

[302] N. Stampf. Worms of the future: Trying to exorcise the worst. SecurityFocus, 2 October 2003.

[303] S. Staniford, D. Moore, V. Paxson, and N. Weaver. The top speed of flash worms. In *Proceedings of the 2004 ACM Workshop on Rapid Malcode*, pages 33–42, 2004.

[304] S. Staniford, V. Paxson, and N. Weaver. How to 0wn the Internet in your spare time. In *Proceedings of the 11th USENIX Security Symposium*, 2002.

[305] J. M. Stanton, K. R. Stam, P. Mastrangelo, and J. Jolton. Analysis of end user security behaviors. *Computers & Security*, 24(2):124–133, 2005.

[306] Symantec. Symantec norton protected recycle bin exposure. SYM06-002, 10 January 2006.

[307] Symantec. Understanding heuristics: Symantec's Bloodhound technology. Symantec White Paper Series, Volume XXXIV, 1997.

[308] P. Szor. Generic disinfection. In *Virus Bulletin Conference*, 1996.

[309] P. Szor. Win95.Memorial, 1997.

[310] P. Ször. Memory scanning under Windows NT. In *Virus Bulletin Conference*, pages 325–346, 1999.

[311] P. Szor. W95.Zperm.A, 2000.

[312] P. Szor. *The Art of Computer Virus Research and Defense*. Addison-Wesley, 2005.

[313] P. Szor. W2K.Stream. Symantec Security Response, 7 September 2000.

[314] P. Ször and P. Ferrie. Hunting for metamorphic. In *Virus Bulletin Conference*, pages 123–144, 2001.

[315] P. Ször and F. Perriot. Slamdunk. *Virus Bulletin*, pages 6–7, March 2003.

[316] J. Tarala. Virii generators: Understanding the threat. SANS Information Security Reading Room, 2002.

[317] R. F. Templeton. Method of managing computer virus infected files. United States Patent #6,401,210, 4 June 2002.

[318] G. Tesauro, J. O. Kephart, and G. B. Sorkin. Neural networks for computer virus recognition. *IEEE Expert*, 11(4):5–6, 1996.

[319] The Honeynet Project & Research Alliance. Know your enemy: Tracking botnets, 13 March 2005.

[320] The Mental Driller. Metamorphism in practice. *29A e-zine*, 6, March 2002.

[321] T. L. Thomas. Russian views on information-based warfare. *Airpower Journal*, pages 25–35, 1996.

[322] K. Thompson. Reflections on trusting trust. *Communications of the ACM*, 27(8):761–763, 1984.

[323] H. Toyoizumi and A. Kara. Predators: Good will mobile codes combat against computer viruses. In *Proceedings of the 2002 Workshop of New Security Paradigms*, pages 11–17, 2002.

[324] N. Tuck, T. Sherwood, B. Calder, and G. Varghese. Deterministic memory-efficient string matching algorithms for intrusion detection. In *IEEE INFOCOM 2004*, volume 4, pages 2628–2639, 2004.

[325] J. Twycross and M. M. Williamson. Implementing and testing a virus throttle. In *Proceedings of the 12th USENIX Security Symposium*, pages 285–294, 2003.

[326] United States Attorney's Office. Former computer network administrator at New Jersey high-tech firm sentenced to 41 months for unleashing $10 million computer 'time bomb'. News release, 26 February 2002.

[327] United States of America v. Roger Duronio, Indictment, United States District Court, District of New Jersey, 2002.

[328] United States v. Lloyd, 269 F.3d 228 (3rd Cir. 2001).

[329] United States v. Morris, 928 F.2d 504 (2nd Cir. 1991).

[330] United States of America v. Jeffrey Lee Parson, Plea agreement, United States District Court, Western District of Washington at Seattle, Case 2:03-cr-00379-mjp, 2004.

[331] Ferry van het Groenewoud. Info wanted on spy-ware. comp.sys.ibm.pc.hardware.networking (cross-posted), 5 November 1994.

[332] F. Veldman. Generic decryptors: Emulators of the future. IVPC Conference, 1998.

[333] VGrep. How is the vgrep database created?, 2005.

[334] R. Vibert. A day in the life of an anti-virus lab. SecurityFocus, 2000.

[335] A. Vidström. Computer forensics and the ATA interface. Technical Report FOI-R– 1638–SE, Swedish Defense Research Agency, Command and Control Systems, 2005.

[336] Virgil. *The Aeneid*. 19 BCE. Translation by J. Dryden, P. F. Collier & Son, 1909.

[337] T. Vogt. Simulating and optimising worm propagation algorithms. SecurityFocus, 29 September 2003.

[338] R. Vossen. Win95 source marketing. comp.programming, 16 October 1995.

[339] P. Wagle and C. Cowan. StackGuard: Simple stack smash protection for GCC. In *Proceedings of the GCC Developers Summit*, pages 243–255, 2003.

[340] J. Walker. The animal episode. Open letter to A. K. Dewdney, 1985.

[341] J. E. Walsh and E. H. A. Altberg. Method and apparatus for protecting data files on a computer from virus infection. United States Patent #5,956,481, 21 September 1999.

[342] M. Weber, M. Schmid, M. Schatz, and D. Geyer. A toolkit the detecting and analyzing malicious software. In *18th Annual Computer Security Applications Conference*, 2002.

[343] J. Wells. A radical new approach to virus scanning. CyberSoft White Paper, 1999.

[344] J. White. Mobile agents white paper. General Magic, 1996.

[345] D. Whyte, E. Kranakis, and P. C. van Oorschot. DNS-based detection of scanning worms in an enterprise network. In *Proceedings of the 12th Annual Network and Distributed System Security Symposium*, 2005.

[346] B. Wiley. Curious Yellow: The first coordinated worm design. http://blanu.net/curious_yellow.html.

[347] M. M. Williamson. Design, implementation and test of an email virus throttle. In *19th Annual Computer Security Applications Conference*, 2003.

[348] M. M. Williamson, A. Parry, and A. Byde. Virus throttling for instant messaging. In *Virus Bulletin Conference*, pages 38–44, 2004.

[349] S. Wu and U. Manber. A fast algorithm for multi-pattern searching. Technical Report 94-17, University of Arizona, Department of Computer Science, 1994.

[350] P. E. Yee. Internet VIRUS alert. comp.protocols.tcp-ip, 3 November 1988.

[351] T. Yetiser. Polymorphic viruses: Implementation, detection, and protection, 1993.

[352] A. Young and M. Yung. Cryptovirology: Extortion-based security threats and counter-measures. In *Proceedings of the 1996 IEEE Symposium on Security and Privacy*, pages 129–140, 1996.

[353] z0mbie. Vmware has you, 13 June 2002.

[354] D. Zenkin. Fighting against the invisible enemy. *Computers & Security*, 20(4):316–321, 2001.

Index